Maud and Pearl:

The Matriarch and the Odyssey

Pearl Allen Andree

1904 Allen Homestead

Maud and Pearl:

The Matriarch and the Odyssey

THE STORY OF MAUD ALLEN'S FAITH AND
ENDURANCE, RAISING HER YOUNGEST CHILD,
AND THE LOVING FAMILY THAT SHE GREW

Pearl Allen Andree

2024 Tranquility Press

Copyright 2024 Pearl Allen Andree

All rights reserved.
Other than brief quotations for review purposes, no portion of this book may be copied or distributed in any way or by any means without prior written permission.
Any use of this publication or any part thereof to train artificial intelligence technologies in any way without prior written consent of the author is expressly prohibited.

For information:
Tranquility Press, www.TranquilityPress.com
723 W University Ave #234, Georgetown TX 78626

The information contained herein was drawn from a variety of sources and is accurate to the best knowledge of the author. However, memory is affected by perspective and other individuals may remember things differently. Thus, although the author and publisher have made every effort to ensure that the information in this book is correct, they do not assume and hereby disclaim any liability to any party for any loss, damage, or disruption caused by any errors or omissions.

Cover art and interior sketches © 2024 Louis Daniel
Photo "Arrowhead and Quarter" © 2024 Amanda Coleman

"The Print of His Shoes" © 1993 Jerry Allen
Song lyrics from "Getting to Know You" © 1951 Rodgers and Hammerstein
All other songs included are in the public domain.

ISBN: 978-1-950481-47-7

Contents

Great-Grandparents	11
Stella Maud and Ezekiel's Family	13
Preface	15
Part I: The Allen Family	**19**
The Martha Bowling and George C. Affair	21
The Mother of My Mother	24
Stella Maud	27
Ezekiel	29
The Catesby Homestead	34
Maud: Dawn of a Family	38
Leo and Ira	40
The Chickasha Years	45
Twins Apart but Ties Forever	48
Leo's Life	53
Thoughts on My Dad Leo	59
Ornan	61
Allendale Oil Co.	65
Fort Worth Sequel: The Duncan Years	68
Ornan: Growing Up Early, a Long Life	71
The Saint and the Counselor	78
"What'd You Boys Do?!"	80
Letter to a Cousin Back Home	82
Zeke Jr.	88
We Were Broke, and I Mean Broke!	92
To Ellen From Pearl: A Birthday Note	99
Martha	101
Parents and Grandparents	104

Mom, Dad, the Farm, and the Relatives	107
Wartime, 1941 to 1945	109
Mama and the Windy Chicken Story and Mr. Killer the Rooster	115
Pete	117
The Print of His Shoes	119
Pete the Balladeer	121
Ballad of Zebra Dun	122
Red Wing	124
Pete and Dorothy	126
Wartime West of Oklahoma: Arizona and California	128
Settling the West: Peaks and Valleys	130
Pete, Dorothy, and the Little Grandsons	137
Motel and Tevye Meet on the Fiddler's Roof	139
Lanier	141
Years in Tolleson and Brentwood	143
A Memory of My Father, Pete Allen	153
Alma	154
Alma Remembered	164
Photo Section	**166**
The Great Depression Through A Young Pearl's Eyes and Ears	176
Pearl	178
Ruth Berry	180
Extended Family Relatives Remembered	182
You Can't Go Back	185
Discipline	188
Stover Elementary School	190
Race	192
Birthday Party	194
The Sugar Bowl	195
A Christmas Story	197
Do You Know Where Your Shoes Are?	199
The Porch on a Summer Afternoon	200
Relaxation and Drama	202
A Pet of My Own	203
The Ol' Fire and Wasp Story	207

A Class Just Below God	209
Cyclone	210
Sickness	212
Summer of 1936	214
Vignettes	216
The Encyclopedia	218
Cameo Shot Memories	220
Beginning Arizona	224
The Arrowhead and the Quarter	226
Union Grammar School	228
Moving to Tolleson	232
Divorce	236
Allen's Alley	238
Tolleson Union High School	241
The Cedar Chest	244
High School Years	247
Farewell to Dad	251
Finishing High School	252
College in Tempe	255
Homemade Butter	259
Jimmy Goggin	260
Marriage and a Humorous Man	268
Photo Section	**270**
Part II: Pearl's Life	**283**
Jimmy and Pearl	285
Hank's Thingamajig and Swooning Aunt Mandy	291
Back to Home, Work, Study, and So On	293
1948: On the Road to Parenthood	294
Mother's Daughter's Mothering	300
Early 1950s: The Goggin Military Family	303
And Now for My Next Magic Trick	311
Laredo AFB: What Will Kids Say and Do Next?	314
Stardust Melody	318
Letter to Mother Goggin	326
Screen Memories	327
Postscript	329
Beginning Life in Tempe	332

The Summer of 1956: Crisis	334
The Mulberry Tree	337
Meeting Bill Andree	339
Origins	344
The Coming of the Fonz	345
A Look Back at the Family Car	349
Building Polynesia in Tempe	351
The 1960s: The Blended Andree Family	353
Character	354
The Outcasts of Tempe Flat	356
Middle Child Syndrome	358
More 1960s, More Blending, More Growing Up	360
Grandma's Quilts: My Soul Is Fed by Needle and Thread	367
Forks in the Road: Finishing High School	370
Steel-drivin' Man	375
Photo Section	**378**
Australia	392
The Australian Years	396
The Church Potluck Legend: Grandma's Buns and Antiquitas	398
Letting Jesus In: Wedding In Buderim	400
Pearl's Christmas Story	402
Quilts, Faith, and the Tie that Binds	406
Perth	409
Ray's Choice	411
Mama's Moonlit Years	413
Bicentennial	416
Odysseus: Voyage Home	419
Why Am I a Member of the Church of Christ?	421
The Summer of 1977	423
August Sunset	425
Photo Section	**426**
Allen Family Tree	432
Acknowledgments	439
Red River Valley	443

Great-grandparents

ISAAC Heaton Hall, "Ike," was born in Lancaster, Dallas County, Texas in 1848, the same year that his family came from Pennsylvania in covered wagons. He was the second child of Peter and Susannah Hall, who had a total of eight sons and one daughter. The family moved to Parker County. Ike was 28 when he received permission to marry Amanda. He took his family to homestead in Indian Territory in the first Oklahoma land rush of 1889, near Noble. In August 1901, he won land in the federal lottery and moved near Marlow. After decades of farming, he and Amanda moved into Marlow, where he died in 1929.

Amanda Augusta Campbell Hall, "Mandy," was born in Neosho, Missouri in 1861, near the Mason-Dixon line, and some of her earliest memories were of her mother's conversations with Civil War soldiers and raiding guerrilla fighters. Her parents, John and Rachel, moved to farm land near Weatherford, Texas, where she met Ike. She was the second-oldest of six brothers and three sisters. She and Ike each came from families of nine children, and they themselves had nine children, eight of whom survived childhood.

George McIntyre C.'s family traced its ancestry to Cnut, King of both England and Denmark in the eleventh century. His great-grandfather fought in the American Revolutionary War, and for services rendered received a land grant in what became Grayson County in western Virginia. George was born in 1859. After the Civil War, while he was still a child, the family moved west to Laurel County, Kentucky. He was the seventh of ten children. His father was a farmer and a teacher.

Maud and Pearl

Martha Bowling came from an even larger family, which was complicated. Her father, Preston Bowling, had married a very young Elizabeth Owens, age 15 at the time. Martha was born in 1861, the oldest of six children, five of whom survived childhood. Her father passed away in the late 1870s. Elizabeth began a relationship with Hiram Johnson, who already had seventeen children by two wives. They later married, and the combined family had 22 children. It's quite possible that Martha, while in her late teens and becoming emotionally close to George C., was at the same time beset by her father's loss and an awareness of her mother's relationship with Mr. Johnson.

Robert Allen was a very young man, only 19, from neighboring Clay County, Kentucky, when he met and fell in love with the older Martha Bowling, an unmarried young lady with three children in Laurel County. Women who were widowed or otherwise on their own with children were somewhat vulnerable in those days, but Martha realized that Robert's affection was genuine. Because he was underage, his father gave written permission to the county clerk for him to marry Martha. Informally but lastingly, Robert gave Ezekiel, Mary, and Bernice his last name. The couple and their growing family migrated to Arkansas.

Stella Maud & Ezekiel's Family

See the full Allen family tree in the back of this book.

Isaac Heaton Hall married Amanda Augusta Campbell, 1877

- Effie
- Gertie (d. in infancy)
- **Stella Maud**
- Ernest
- Emma
- Dona
- John
- Eula
- Herman

Martha Bowling and George McIntyre C.

- **Ezekiel**
- Mary Angeline
- Bernice

Martha Bowling married Robert Allen, 1886
- Emory
- Norris Jerry "Neri"
- Bertha

Maud and Pearl

In 1902, **Stella Maud Hall** married **Ezekiel Allen**.
They had nine children.

- Effie Bernice, b. 1903, d. 1904 (in infancy)
- Isaac Leo, name changed to Wilfred Leo, b. 1904, d. 1983
- Ira Eugene, b. 1905, d. 1927 (in accident)
- Ornan Robert, b. 1907, d. 2004
- Ezekiel Jr., b. 1909, d. 1987
- Martha Amanda, b. 1911, d. 1981
- Huber Ernest "Pete," b. 1913, d. 2006
- Alma Mae, b. 1916, d. 1973
- **Iralene Pearl,** b. 1927
  married James Daniel "Jimmy" Goggin, 1945
  married William H. "Bill" Andree, 1957

Preface

I WANTED to write about my mother, Stella Maud Allen, and how her spirituality influenced her when raising a family. She had a scriptural answer for almost every problem. If it wasn't scriptural, it was a wise proverb to quote.

When I began to write about Mama and me, I became aware that, in a certain way, it was troubling to do so, because I began to recall and realize how much she had sacrificed to make me healthy. I spent much time alone with Mom in my early years. The time she and I spent together made me wonder sometimes if she had memorized the whole Bible. There is no doubt that her guiding light was God and His Son, Jesus Christ. I admired all my older siblings, and I knew they had been influenced by that same guidance.

From the time of my first memories, neither I nor Mama ever existed out of poverty, in my case for the first two decades of my life and for Mama much longer. Wanting my mama was primal for me, because Mama covered me and warded off fear, winter harshness, and lack and more lack. When I was ill again with bronchitis, she nursed me. Part of me has always wanted to title this book *I Want My Mama!*

Another apt title for all of this story would be *Mama Said*. Mama almost always spoke softly but evenly and definitely. She was the biblical lamppost who molded and steeled the guideposts of my life as well as my older brothers' and sisters'. When something was spoken humorously, she ignited the laughter in the room with her hearty, infectious laugh. She could easily laugh at

Maud and Pearl

herself. Throughout this story, so often remembered as wisely if not sincerely spoken, is what Mama said.

Mama raised eight children by faith in God's help, and I chose to write a chapter for each, except for the two oldest sons.

My five brothers, including what I had learned about my brother Ira, who died before I was born, were the finest Christian men that I have known. I relied on my brothers many times in life. My brother Zeke, whom my son Ray called "Grandpa," took me to my first "father-daughter" banquet. My brother Ornan gave me away when I married Jimmy. Pete and Dorothy were who I went to when I lost Jimmy.

My sisters and sisters-in-law have also always been my role models. My two sisters and I may have encountered more pitfalls along the way than my brothers in trying to live our Christian lives, but we always knew what Mama wanted us to be.

Her life spanned 94 years, from an era of covered wagons to one of space travel. For her entire life, she was poor in possessions but rich in heart and priceless in terms of caring for others and giving of herself.

From the loss of her oldest child in infancy and life in a sod house on one of the last frontiers to living through times of feast and famine and the Great Depression and an unwanted divorce, Mama was truly a pioneer among women. Really, among everyone.

As it was for Mama, life for me became a travel across several crossroads. I was born the same year that Charles Lindbergh made the first transatlantic flight, 1927. I wasn't born in a log cabin, but whatever I was born in is no longer there. When Mama and I moved, Arizona provided opportunities for me for improved health, higher education, and financial stability.

In 1943, I began Arizona State Teachers College in Tempe in pre-engineering. I met and married Jimmy Goggin, an Air Force fighter pilot, and life was action-packed, having children and beginning our family, which was tragically stopped. After ups and downs in widowhood, I remarried to Bill Andree, a newspaper advertiser turned self-made architect and builder, and had a second family. I became skilled and knowledgeable in

Pearl Allen Andree

apartment management and real estate. Within the family, Bill and I became known as Mr. Spend It and Mrs. Hold It, although those roles flip-flopped at times. Forty years after leaving, I returned to Arizona State University, and completed a bachelor's degree in drama and theater. Then, I became a professional storyteller, which included pro bono nursing home work and paid storytelling in school rooms. Even before that, though, I had begun having the natural urge to interview, tape, and write down my siblings' stories, the Allen family history.

In my own life, I experienced a lot of stories to tell. I had a very good life, but sometimes I reached a place on the road where there were a lot of rocks. I was always aware that when there are rocks in the road, you remove them, and I tried to do that. Said another way, when the hard and harder decisions came along, I thought them over, made my choices practically, and then went on. Through the difficulties of my marriages and the time between them, I remained open to each new day—on the sunny side, upright, and with my compass pointed north.

I was always the "tag-along" kid among my siblings, but because of Mama's living example and overarching spiritual leadership, when we Allens got together, the joys of our closeness and gladness to be together were wonderful! Mama was there with her mythical large baked buns, fried chicken, and carrot cake. Of course, despite babies crying, kids crawling under our legs, and older kids huddled up clandestinely, we had lively discussions amongst our Democrat and Republican selves about politics, current events, and, yes, religion. Despite the intensity and the back-and-forth, love was always in the air. And even later, Mama was still there in spirit.

That's how the decades rolled by...

Part I: The Allen Family

The Early Family, 1902–1927
The 20-Acre Farm, 1929–1936
Pearl Growing Up, Tolleson 1937–1945

The Martha Bowling and George C. Affair

THEY met in Laurel County, Kentucky. Martha Bowling was one of a very large family from the marriage of Preston Bowling and the widow Elizabeth Owens. George C.'s family had moved to the area from across the border in Grayson County, Virginia when he was a young child. They courted, fell in love, and she became pregnant. There is no confirmed evidence that they married.

George wanted to go west, seek work, build a future, return to Kentucky to get Martha, and then return west again. He wanted to go to Oregon, and he did. While working there, at first on sheep ranches in central Oregon, he became known by the nickname "Mack" (his middle name was McIntyre).

An accurate history is fogged by the passage of time. He may have headed west as early as 1879. After he went west, Martha gave birth to their son, Ezekiel, on April 29, 1880. George moved to Prineville, Oregon and started in business in the early 1880s. He returned to see Martha and their son, but he told her he needed to return to Oregon to work and earn more money in order for them to marry. She became pregnant yet again with Mary Angeline, who was born December 30, 1882. George went back and forth one more time, and Martha gave birth to their third child, a daughter she named Bernice.

As far as we know, George C. never returned to Kentucky. He became successful in several businesses in and around Prineville as the years went by: land and ranch holdings, a mercantile store, and banking. His greatest success was his visionary start-up of a

Maud and Pearl

stagecoach business since the area was not served by the railroads. As motor cars became dependable, he incorporated them into his fleet. He married in the early 1890s, a woman named Effie T., and together they had four daughters. Widowed late in life, he remarried briefly, without additional children, and died in the early years of the Great Depression.

What kind of man was George C.? Even if he returned to Kentucky, whether or not secretly, to visit Martha and the children, he didn't send financial support despite his business success. To Allen family members' knowledge, he never spoke to Martha again. He seemed to have decided to leave her and their children behind in his past and chose to live with that for the rest of his life. He lived in a time when geographical escape to the unpopulated West was achievable because of the limits of transportation and communication over huge distances in America. Did he change his plans and the lives of others because he got caught up in his business affairs or another love? His destiny was to remain a distant and mysterious enigma to his and Martha's progeny.

At some point, Martha Bowling came to realize that George was gone for good. Did word get back to his family in Kentucky that he had changed his intentions, and by some means, she came to learn this? Had his broken promises become too many? Did she lose hope and feel rejected?

Fortunately for her, as a young, attractive, deserted, and unmarried woman with three children, her life changed for the better. She met Robert Allen, who fell very much in love with her. He asked her to marry him and offered to raise her children as his own. They married in 1886. After moving southwest from Kentucky and settling in Little Rock, Robert and Martha had two sons, Emory and Norris Jerry, or "Neri," and a daughter, Bertha, who sadly died in late childhood. For many years, they operated a dairy, adding the service of home delivery.

Little is known about Robert. It is known that he had little education and could not write his name, so he signed documents with an "X," but he was always hard working. It is known that he had a loving and compassionate character toward Martha and her

Pearl Allen Andree

and their children, and he parentally recognized and responded to their needs.

In a symbolic way, the Martha Bowling and George C. affair exemplified America's westward expansion: greener and more fertile valleys ahead, unrequited loves left behind, heartbreak and loss along the trails. But, of course, what happened was very personal. In family photos, George certainly looks like an Allen. His last name became the Allen riddle: the name is not the name that will remain. He fathered seven children, only one of whom (Ezekiel, no middle name) was a son but whose last name was never C. but always Allen due to Robert's love and kindness. George C.'s destiny, however, was to help create the Allen family.

The Mother of My Mother

In her later years, my maternal grandmother, Amanda Augusta Hall, often described her life in a brief monologue, and this is what I remember that she said, in her words.

~~~

I was born at the beginning of the Civil War on March 10, 1861. Some people call it Civil, but I never saw anything 'civil' about it as it was an awful thing.

We lived just south of the Mason-Dixon line, where a lot of terrible things took place. My father was a Confederate soldier. He was gone into service.

Many times, the bushwhackers came into our home asking if soldiers had been there and would not believe my Ma. After looking the place over for men, they would ask for what food we had on the place. One time Ma was asked to bring out her meal. The bushwhackers were just about to take all she had when she asked if they wouldn't leave some for the children and pay her for the rest. They told her she would be paid over the left eye. However, they left her with a full bag of flour.

During the war, Ma cooked for the soldiers who came by. One day the biscuits looked so good I slipped one. Ma said, "Mandy, that's for the soldiers."

One soldier answered, "You let her have a biscuit." At that time, I was very young, but I remember many things that took place.

Pearl Allen Andree

After the war Pa thought it was too dangerous living on the Line, so we started in a covered wagon to Texas. People we met on the way would say, 'Yes, and the wild Indians will get your children.' They didn't get any of Pa's children, but our friend Mr. Davis's son was taken and buckled on his horse and taken to an Indian camp. He couldn't eat the raw meat that was given to him, so the Indians cooked it for him over a fire. Later, the government patrol found the boy and gave him back to his father.

Pa settled about 18 miles northeast of Weatherford, Texas, and that's the place I met Ike, who had been boarding with us while working our crops. Pa paid for the labor by giving him a few acres of wheat. One day Ike waited till Pa got a big armload of wood and then said, "I thought I'd wait till you got a load of wood on your shoulder then ask for your girl."

Pa wasn't a Christian at that time so he said, "The devil you will."

Anyway, Ike and I married when I was only 16. We settled down between Reno and Springtown, Texas and began raising our family. He came from a large family of eight boys and one girl. His father, Peter, had been a chaplain during the Civil War. There were some preachers and singers in the family so we began to study the Bible, and before I was seventeen, I was baptized and a member of the Church of Christ.

We were living near Veal Station when little Gertie, our second child, died. We buried her at Day Bird (or Union Grove) by the side of my brother Luther and sister Ada Pierce's three children. Five of our children were born in Texas: Effie, little Gertie, Maud, Ernest, and Emma. Then we moved to Oklahoma between Noble and Norman, then called Indian Territory. Afterward, four more children, Dona, John, Eula, and Herman, were added to the family, making the number of children nine.

During 1901, Ike made a run to file on a farm twelve miles northwest of Marlow, and that's where we lived for a number of years. We sent our children to Burns Community School just over the line of Grady in Comanche County.

As time went on, the children began to marry off, so we moved to Marlow and lived for a few years on Second and Payne

Maud and Pearl

until we bought a block of land with a good peach orchard at 711 West McNeese. That's where Ike passed away, leaving me this little home all covered with the blossoms of spring, and that's where I want to live until I die.

~~~

The above story, often repeated, was written down by her daughter Eula on the occasion of Grandma Hall's death at the age of 90 in 1951. She said many times, "Ike was the only man I loved." Grandma had hardening of the arteries in her later years, which was why she repeated the "story of my life" over and over until distracted from it. She was called Aunt Mandy by many in the community around her. My mother, Stella Maud Hall, was Ike and Amanda's third child.

Stella Maud

MAUD was five years old when the Hall family forded the Red River from Texas to Oklahoma with other families in covered wagons for the Cherokee Run in 1889. It must have been frightening, as she said to her sister Effie, "I'm going to close my eyes so I don't see myself drown." A little boy in another family did drown.

The first home they had in the new territory was a dugout. It was a space dug into a hill, big enough to make two rooms. Ike had a partition of sorts to define the rooms. He and Mandy used the back room for their bedroom, including the baby. The "front room" was where the other three children slept on pallets. They had managed to acquire a puppy, which also occupied this space. Ike had not yet put a door over the entrance.

One night the puppy started barking ferociously enough to awaken everyone, including Ike. He came out of his room carrying his shotgun to find a panther entering their home. He fired the gun out the doorway and the panther turned and fled. He followed outside and yelled a howl like a panther, a yell Maud remembered all her life and enjoyed telling how a puppy saved their lives. Ike put a door over that entrance the next day.

After moving to the Marlow farm in 1901, Burns School became an integral part of the lives of the Hall children. Maud loved school and later in life instilled this love for learning in all her children. She only finished fifth grade, but she never stopped studying and learning. She was older and was needed to help in the home and care for younger siblings, but her sisters were able to become teachers. The community's social life centered round the

Maud and Pearl

school. Instead of Friday night football, the surrounding schools had competitive spelling bees, entered into by the adults as well as students.

Years later, Maud's older sister Effie had married Jim Wilkinson, and they had a son named Hall who attended the school. Dona, another sister of Maud and Effie, was teaching Hall's class, and one of the other students was Wiley Post. One time when the spelling team from Duncan came to compete, Hall spelled them down. Wiley overheard the Duncan boys plotting to beat up Hall. He confronted them and dared them to fight, saying, "Hall does my spelling and I do his fighting, so come on."

Maud's other siblings were Ernest, Emma, John, Eula, and Herman. Emma never married and taught until retirement age. Dona and Eula also became teachers. The three girls went to Normal School for certification after graduating from eighth grade.

It was at one of these social evenings that Maud met Zeke. Ezekiel Allen had just come into the area looking for farm work. Sometimes he was called Zeke and sometimes EZ. His formal schooling had been cut short, so when he was asked to spell *soup*, he answered, "S, double o, p. Soup." Everyone laughed, so each time it was his turn to spell, they repeated that word.

The next day, he asked who the girl was with the beautiful hair. Maud's hair was brown with a slight red tint and the length was below her waist. When she wore it in braids, there were little natural curls along the nape of her neck.

The chemistry must have been mutual, as Maud told her girlfriends, "This one is mine." She was eighteen and a half by the time they married—almost "on the shelf" in that culture.

Ezekiel

When EZ first met Maud at the spelling bee social, he'd traveled to the area looking for farm work. Was he a traveling man like his real father? Was he going to be a wanderlust? Maud became very attracted to him, but what kind of person was he, really, and what did he aspire to do in life?

Some answers never surfaced. Ezekiel was born in Kentucky to Martha Bowling and George C., who had promised to marry her when he returned from a trip to Oregon. He'd seen his biological father as a toddler. Martha later married Robert Allen, who raised him and his sister Mary. He grew up in a blended farm family, and his parents were responsible and worked. Although he left home young, for the rest of his life he was close to his adoptive father, Robert; his mother, Martha; and sister, Mary; and his younger half brothers, Emory and "Neri," including visits and stays and jobs together. He lacked formal schooling, but he had the confidence to seek employment and support himself. He was handsome and knew it.

He left home in Arkansas at age 14, and oral tradition was that he crisscrossed the country from St. Louis to San Francisco twice, a lot of that on a bicycle. After several years, he came to Marlow, found farm work, and met Maud at that spelling bee social. His son Pete clearly recalled him saying later in life that once he had gotten to Oregon and met his father, but left disappointed that his father did not want much of a relationship with him.

Zeke and Maud courted briefly, were mutually attracted, and began marriage with zest. Over the years, he farmed well despite his era's hardships, but not enthusiastically. Perhaps his

Maud and Pearl

early independent life had programmed him to be wayfaring and to have a roaming eye for entrepreneurship that would lead to wealth. His aspirations molded his behavior as his life matured and his family grew around him.

Zeke had not gone beyond the fifth grade in school and knew men who had even less formal schooling yet attained high levels in their careers. His philosophy developed into the thought that a person didn't need much education—that if one had "what it takes," he or she could attain their goals and be productive citizens. Zeke always promoted himself as a self-made man.

Like his biological father, he believed he could be successful at whatever he decided to do. As time went by, he repeatedly took leave from farming to look for success elsewhere, usually in the oil prospecting and producing industries. Throughout the years, he'd succeed for a while but then falter or fail. For example, in Pete's little-boy memory (in 1919 he was five turning six), the family lived in a 13th-floor penthouse atop one of Ft. Worth's tallest buildings; but his memory was probably of visiting the Allendale Oil Co.'s office because the family actually lived on St. Louis Ave. in Fort Worth. But in early 1920, they moved back to the Hall farm in Oklahoma, then on to the Duncan rental.

So, times of feast and material gains were followed by famine and poverty, and times of working steadily at home were followed by lengthy absences. Of course, this also affected Maud and Zeke's children, and sometimes the bad times were more so for them. Men like him were striking it rich all around him at frequent intervals. Why should he waste his energy farming? From farming, he became a self-styled geologist and oil wildcatter, but not so much after Ira was tragically killed in an oil rig accident in 1927. At that time, his increased sense of responsibility led him to buy the Allen family plot in the Marlow cemetery.

When the Great Depression started, Zeke began to farm Leo's 20-acre farm west of town. Later, from the mid-1930s on, he farmed less and dabbled in real estate, and he returned to buying and selling mineral rights, more often with Native peoples.

His biological father had married, had children, and built successful mercantile and transportation (early coach routes and

Pearl Allen Andree

later toll roads across rugged terrain that previously hindered travel, from which he received income) businesses in Oregon, as mentioned before. However, EZ's attempts to establish a relationship with his biological father never worked out and were repeated disappointments. Ornan remembered that Zeke refused to talk about George C. Once Zeke told the story that he had written to George in Oregon and asked for help, probably financial, about something. After a long time, he received a negative reply. After that, Zeke never tried to communicate again.

Zeke was winsome, personable, and even somewhat charismatic. There was an undercurrent that he may have been too much so with women. He sang and played musical instruments well, including the fiddle and harmonica, and he knew how to create good times. He was known to do good deeds for others quietly. He had a sense of humor and a jolly laugh. Because of the family migrations, he didn't see his grandchildren, the Allen cousins, very much. But Martha's daughter, Margaret (Totsy), remembered happy times with him, with his gifts of fresh fruit, birthday presents, and his laughter.

Zeke and Maud's separation grew in 1937 when Maud moved to Arizona with Pearl. He did not agree with that, and he did not follow them as Maud had hoped. Their chasm widened, and he filed for divorce in 1939. The next year he married an attractive lady who had been born with a shortened leg, requiring her to use crutches. She had been widowed four times, which might have raised some questions in a cautious man seeking marriage.

During this period of time, Totsy was aged five to nine and remembered those visits by him. Totsy recalled:

> I know my mother worried about his well-being in his new marriage. I came to understand that he had been a dreamer, thinker, schemer, and a doer. At the same time, we all loved Grandma's kind, sweet, and pure heart, and she was the reason the family was close and had Christian principles.
>
> With Grandpa, there was an atmosphere of sadness surrounding our relationships. He didn't have

Maud and Pearl

his family together, much to his own doing. Yet, he was still struggling while practically having given up hope that his family cared for him. His dreams of prosperity and success were gone. My mother was the only one of his children he kept in touch with. Years later, my younger cousin Danny said Grandma told him she loved Grandpa a lot the rest of her life, that it had been a mistake to leave him and go to Arizona.

Life's struggles had been very hard for EZ, an Arkansas boy who never found the connection he sought with his biological father, who endured more heartbreaking failures than life-strengthening successes, and who was without the right life skills to find himself and keep the relationships he most coveted and loved, things that Maud had in her life.

Some things about him were Maud's opposites. She was the steady, stable, ever-present lifeblood of their large family, his large family. It is clear that none of the children ever stayed particularly close to Zeke except Martha, who always lived in his vicinity. And in contrast to Maud and the children being deeply religious, he did not display a religious bent. He died suddenly of pneumonia in 1942 at nearly 62, on the brink of time before the miracle cure of penicillin could have saved his life.

He went by many names, but EZ Allen Sr. is the name on his gravestone in the Marlow Cemetery. Ezekiel, Zeke, EZ—did he leave a legacy? While he was proud, confident, and knew he had accomplished things, he may very well have answered "no." But in reality, through his and Maud's descendants' accomplishments, he did establish an impressive legacy, which his descendants have recognized. This legacy lies in part within the wide range of successes that his progeny achieved. His family knows the real answer for him.

In another sense, his destiny was that he began a very large family. Did he ever dream that there would be 31 grandchildren in his Christmas Future? He would answer "no" again. Did he ever think that his children and grandchildren would remain close-knit and, as the years unfolded, have numerous, well-attended family

Pearl Allen Andree

reunions? He'd answer "no" again. But his greatest legacy was his choice of life companion, Stella Maud Allen, who loved him always and who kept their family bound in love. While he may have sensed failure, with Maud at his side, he grew a lasting legacy that has continued flourishing. After all is said, with her he owns half the real estate and half the mineral rights.

The Catesby Homestead

THE qualities of Allen family members had their beginnings on the plains of west Oklahoma bordering the Texas panhandle, a part of the country that in the early 1900s was still a wild frontier in the Oklahoma Indian Territory. Statehood did not occur until 1907.

Ezekiel and Maud began married life at or near the old Hall farm in Cleveland County, farming. He was 22; she, 18. They were married June 22, 1902 in an arbor in Dripping Springs, near Noble. A few months after their wedding, Maud became pregnant, and in April 1903 she gave birth to Effie Bernice. Only eight months later, Effie died and was buried in the Noble cemetery. The young couple, married only two years and seeking their future, did what many young people in that day and age did to acquire property and become independent. They homesteaded. They acquired 160 acres of property, a quarter section, by following the government's simple requirements, which were Ezekiel's signature, a modest filing fee, and his promise to work the land. Their homestead was in the area of Catesby, 17 miles northwest of Shattuck in Ellis County.

The young couple made their way westward to this area of the great plains previously shared by members of the Comanche, Kiowa, Cheyenne, Arapaho, and other prairie tribes. The Indigenous peoples had not had the concept of individual or even tribal land ownership. They were nomadic and had always used the land they occupied then moved on, leaving the land fallow. Left alone, the land recovered and wild game moved back in.

Pearl Allen Andree

Zeke and Maud approached the property with a whole new idea. This land was theirs now. Despite the area being called "Indian Territory," the government had ceded more territory every few years to non-Indians. Zeke and Maud arrived in May 1904.

Maud was heavily pregnant and must have also been grieving having to leave her Hall family and their well-established, comfortable Marlow farm some 200 miles away. The couple had set out by horse-drawn wagon to begin developing their new homestead, taking axes, saws, picks, hoes, shovels, plows, and other equipment to clear mesquite from the land, pull stumps and roots out of the earth, and prepare the land for farming. The property was completely wild, and they arrived to face the elements and wildlife.

Following their arrival, Zeke set about building their first home, a sod house, clearing land, and building a fence. Because the land did not provide wood suitable for fence posts, Zeke went into west Texas to the Canadian Breaks, where he cut and hauled fence posts back into Oklahoma to build their fences. These trips took him away for days to weeks at a time, which meant that Maud and the youngsters, as they came, were alone. Because the mesquite burned rapidly, their supply of firewood was often depleted, and Maud had to hitch a horse to the wagon and go out across the prairie to find dry buffalo and cow chips to burn for cooking and to keep the house warm.

Leo, Ira, Ornan, and Martha were all born either in the homestead house or in nearby Catesby. In subsequent pregnancies, Maud went to stay with her family on the Hall farm to give birth. Zeke Jr. was born in Burns Community and Pete in Marlow.

Zeke was a good farmer, but successful farming was always chancy, depending on many factors, weather and pests being chief among them. As the boys grew, Zeke put them to work on the farm, and sometimes he took them on trips for supplies and the like. He was gone quite a bit. Maud kept the farm going while he was gone. Zeke taught Maud to shoot, and she became an excellent shot. The family remembers that she "always shot to kill."

Maud and Pearl

The house was vulnerable to critters, including skunks and rats. The kitchen cupboard Maud brought with her had to be replaced when Zeke shot a skunk that had managed to get into the house. That cupboard was abandoned to the outdoors for several years, and still smelled of skunk.

The chicken coop was sod also. One day, Maud went to collect the eggs and a skunk was hanging in the air in the henhouse, having been caught in a trap Zeke had devised. She got the gun and shot that skunk several times before she realized she'd probably killed him with the first one. No smell resulted because the trap that captured the culprit was hanging in the air, and a skunk cannot emit its odor unless all four feet are on the ground. Maud could be lethal with a varmint endangering her chickens and eggs.

How did Maud persevere with four rowdy boys and a baby girl, and Zeke gone weeks at a time? She was determined. She had grit. She cared. Leo once said, "Mama raised eight children to maturity, all of whom worked at being Christians. She got us to school and she got us to church meetings." She appears to have kept the farm functioning when Zeke was absent as well.

After years of living a hard life in Catesby, Maud missed her Hall family, was occasionally ill, and was declining physically. And in the Marlow area, one of her Hall uncles was a doctor. As Ornan later recounted, the rattlesnake draped over the back of the rocking chair was her last straw there. Zeke conceded their living accommodations had to improve.

Zeke, meanwhile, began having notions that he had some geological ability. The oil boom age had dawned, and it held the promise of greater wealth than he could achieve by farming. In 1913, they agreed to sell the homestead, and they moved to Marlow to stay with Maud's family on the Hall farm.

The couple and their children had become indelibly molded by their decade of pioneering. There was no doubt about the homestead, recorded in the Ellis County Book of Deeds: the Northwest Quarter of Section 34-23N-26W. After the required five years to improve the land, Zeke paid for the patent in late 1909

Pearl Allen Andree

and received an impressive certificate signed by President William H. Taft on January 3, 1910. Zeke and Maud sold the land in 1917.

By the time they left, the older boys, Leo, Ira, and Ornan, had spent their early childhoods with retrievable memories there. Zekie was four, Martha was a toddler at two, and Pete was soon to be born in Marlow.

Maud remained a pioneer at heart and by habit and means, always. She had survived fear and scare, varmints and snakes on the homestead. She kept and used her pioneer housekeeping equipment through later decades. She didn't own an electric iron until the 1940s, nor her first power washer until 1949, at age 65.

The end of Percy Bysshe Shelley's poem "Ozymandias" reads, "Round the decay of that colossal wreck, boundless and bare, the lone and level sands stretch far away." That describes the end of the homesteading in 1913—and the end of Catesby in their lives. Years later, Catesby became a ghost town.

Maud: Dawn of a Family

For her marriage in 1902, Maud had made her wedding dress. She brought a kitchen cupboard and a bunch of chickens to her new home. When she didn't conceive the first month, Zeke got worried that she might be barren. No such luck for Maud; the second month, all was well. A baby girl, Effie Bernice, was born in April 1903.

By Christmas, little Effie was walking. Maud cut up her wedding dress to make a petite dress for her. In January, Maud, who was also pregnant at the time, took the baby on the train to visit her parents. Maud caught measles and gave them to her baby girl. On the way home in fierce winter weather, tiny Effie contracted pneumonia and died. They buried her in that precious dress that Maud had made for her.

Although Maud was pregnant when she had measles, it didn't seem to affect the health of Isaac (named for his grandfather Isaac Hall) Leo, who was born July 5, 1904. Years later, Leo decided he didn't appreciate being called "Ikie," so he changed his name to Wilfred Leo.

Thirteen months after Leo was born, another boy was born on August 13, 1905. He was named Ira Eugene and later nicknamed Stub. Leo and Ira were like twins. They started school the same year, maybe because it was easier to get two kids to school than just one in those times. The two remained close all through Ira's lifetime, energetically and spiritually.

It was hard for me to imagine that Mama (Maud) and Daddy (Zeke) had raised a large family together for over 25 years before I was born, the first decade of that on their prairie homestead.

Pearl Allen Andree

Mama not only valued education and got the boys to school, but also, with them in tow, she actively practiced religion. She didn't talk about that a lot, but she lived it. If a traveling preacher came to the area or a revival was held, whether Church of Christ (one of the restoration faiths) or Pentecostal, she had the older boys hitch the wagon to the plow horse and spent the day in worship and traveling to and from it. Although the Pentecostal services were different from what she was used to, they provided instruction and she enjoyed them.

Mama had a way of disciplining by example and by her kind and caring nature.

To tell my family's story, I've written about each of my older siblings in the separate sections that follow, chronologically after Effie Bernice to the youngest, me. I've always felt indebted to them, as all of them helped me throughout the years I grew up.

Leo and Ira

ONE of the government requirements to obtain the patent to a homestead was to make improvements, such as planting, fencing, and home building. If the homesteader did this, in five years he could own the place. When Zeke and Maud first reached the Catesby land in a covered wagon, Maud had chickens and a kitchen cupboard (also called a "safe.") After paying the filing fees for the 160 acres, Zeke had $3.25 left in his pocket. The first house Zeke built was a little sod 9' x 12' hut with a dirt floor. He later built or moved a wood-frame house on the property to accommodate a growing family. On the Oklahoma prairie, there were no trees and, of course, no electricity, but it was unparalleled in its beauty. It was a farming life. Wagons and teams of horses or mules provided transportation.

Maud and Zeke had few of the niceties of the modern home. There was no electricity, and many times for fuel they used dried buffalo chips, which could have been 20 years old. The chips were good fuel if dry—but when wet, a horrible smell wafted through the house. Laundry was boiled in a big black tub over a fire in the yard and scrubbed on a washboard with lye soap Maud made herself. For a long time, she had no clothesline. Since the prairie grass was waist-high, she threw the laundry over the tops of the grass to dry. When gathering in the laundry, they sometimes encountered bumblebees or other flying bugs and insects to guard against.

Leo and Stub had a dog named Tige. Zeke had obtained a harness similar to what one would use on a goat. The boys decided to put it on Tige and go for a ride. They hooked him up to a washtub and Ira got in the tub. They knew to holler "Git" if they wanted Tige to run, so that's what Leo did. Tige got. After bumping over rough terrain at a rapid clip and finally being turned over with the tub on top of him, Stub walked up to his older brother, shook his finger in Leo's face, and commanded, "Don't you EVER do that again!" Their ages at this time are not known, but they had to be old enough to use a harness, so Leo had to be at least six or seven and Ira a year younger.

Tige wasn't the only animal around to play with; there was also a cat. Tige had much fun chasing the cat. One day the boys decided to have some fun. They knew the cat was conditioned to run if they said, "Sic 'em." They found an oatmeal box that fit over the cat's head, stuck it on, and yelled, "Sic 'em." The cat immediately took off—and raced to the nearest telephone pole, climbing quickly to the top as he usually did when running from Tige. Unfortunately, when he needed later to come down, because of the box he couldn't figure out how, so the boys had to manage that on their own. The boys learned many things about the nature and whims of animals.

Not many buffaloes were left, but there were still buffalo "wallers" on the prairie. Wallers, or wallows, were hollowed-out places where at one time the buffalo had "wallered" in the dirt or mud. The boys were forbidden to go near them because snakes liked to hang out there.

Since Maud raised chickens, she thought it would be a good idea to raise some turkeys, too. Leo and Ira overheard her and Zeke talking about the likelihood of the eggs not hatching. The mother turkey might desert the nest and leave them without warmth. The boys decided to help by sitting on the eggs to keep them warm. OOPS! Disaster, big time—of course it made a huge mess.

Maud always insisted on going to church. If there was no building, services might be held in the schoolhouse. Dave was the horse she rode, holding the baby in her lap with Leo and Ira riding behind her on the same horse. On Sunday, she got the boys dressed in their Sunday best and then concentrated on herself and the baby. One Sunday Leo and Ira escaped and were playing in the hog pen when she found them. Maud was so hurt she cried.

Maud and Pearl

Dave was a true friend to the boys and to Maud. He seemed to know Maud needed him to be gentle with her and the children. Hooked up to the buggy when Maud drove, he went easy to the destination. With Zeke, it was a different story. Zeke worked him.

Zeke's favorite pie was coconut cream. Grocery items like flour and sugar were brought from the store seventeen miles away in large containers and kept on the back porch that had been built to add sleeping space. One of these storage containers held the coconut Maud used for those special pies. She had canisters in the kitchen that she refilled from the stores on the porch. A wooden block had been placed outside the door of the screened porch to step on when exiting the house. Leo and Stub taught Dave to come to the door and use his hoof to pound on the wood block until they came out. They would have some treat for him, and they found out he loved coconut, so that was the treat of choice. The day came when Maud needed to refill her coconut canister, and lo and behold, there was no more in the large container! They got in trouble for that.

When Leo and Ira started school at ages six and five, Dave took them there. They sent him home, where Zeke worked him until time to go back to the school to pick them up in the afternoons. In the wintertime, the boys made snowballs and sent Dave home packed with them. Dave soon discovered a small gully with a meadow not far from the schoolhouse and decided it was much better to spend the day there than to go home and work.

Maud was always eager for the children to be educated, and learning held a special place in her heart. She had only gone to school through the fifth grade, but she had a fine mind and absorbed knowledge like a sponge. Maud considered teaching to be the finest calling anyone could have except for preaching, so for a woman it was fine indeed. Leo and Ira had a male teacher, and in those years, there were already PTA meetings. Often, there were evenings where the children entertained the parents rather than having business meetings. At the first PTA meeting Maud attended, the teacher had taught Ira a little speech to deliver. Ira stood in front of the room and orated in a good, strong voice: "Patience: If a string is in a knot, patience will untie it. Patience can do many things." Here, he paused, looked around the audience assembled, and forcefully added, "DID YOU EVER TRY IT?"

It was about this period that Zeke's stepfather, Robert Allen, came from Little Rock, Arkansas to visit. New babies Ornan and Zeke Jr. had arrived in 1907 and 1909. Zeke Jr., called Zekie, was the baby. Somehow, the family had acquired a baby buggy. Zekie loved being pushed in it, and it usually fell to Leo and Ira to fulfill this exercise. In fact, Zekie loved for them to run with him, and if they didn't, he cried. Grandpa became ill while visiting and it upset him to hear Zekie cry. Leo and Ira were given the task of keeping him quiet. One day they found it difficult to push the buggy in the dirt, and especially to run with it. They finally ran it up to a spot where the land sloped off downhill. They stopped.

Leo looked at Stub. Stub looked at Leo. They gave a push downhill and let go. The buggy made a wild ride over the rocks, but luckily dumped Zekie out early on so he was not hurt. The buggy was roughed up but still workable. However, no one could understand why baby Zekie wouldn't let anyone put him in that buggy again.

Leo saw his first car when he was about six years old. It was a red Buick, and the driver was a broomcorn buyer. Leo ran to see it. The crank was on the side and there were two doors, both on the same side.

Storms came up suddenly in that prairie country. It was a wild beauty. In one of these sudden storms, they couldn't find Leo's younger brother, Ornan. He was just a toddler, and the grass was tall. When they found him, he was in the orchard with a stick, trying to keep the rabbits away from the trees.

The family ate well from the wildlife that ended up on the dinner table, like quail, prairie chickens, and rabbits, even young jackrabbits. Sometimes the jackrabbit was old and tough. Many years later, Leo described them as "so tough you had to stick a fork in the gravy." One time, Zeke and a couple of other farmers found an abandoned house, and by putting grain in the house, they caught 22 prairie chickens. Then they put chicken wire all around the house.

Maud and Pearl

Maud milked the cows when Zeke was away. They had a cow that must have been half wild. One day when Maud was endeavoring to milk her, the cow was giving her a bad time. Suddenly a rope came out of nowhere and lassoed the cow. The voice of a stranger said, "I think you can milk her now, Ma'am."

All the man wanted was to water his horse and have a little grain for feed. Maud fixed him a meal and brought it out to him. It was an action Maud did many times in her life, especially during the Great Depression when there were so many men traveling as hoboes. If Zeke was home, he found a task they could help with, like cutting wood or some such.

Stub had a run-in with that wild cow too. No one could find him until he showed up crying and said, "That cow kicked me in the stomach. I was just holding her tail."

Leo and Ira heard the grown-ups talking about all the predators around, like coyotes, that could attack the domestic animals. They decided to help with the effort. Knowing they would need a gun, they took Zeke's gun and started on their mission. They got as far as the mailbox, which was about a mile from the house, and realized they needed Dave to take them farther afield. They hid the gun in the tall grass and returned to get Dave. When they returned with Dave, they could not find the gun. After looking all over, they gave up but agreed they wouldn't say a word to their dad about their part in the gun's disappearance. The gun was never found, and Zeke blamed about everyone in the county with no results. Zeke loved that gun. He had won it at a shooting match. Leo was a grown man when he told his dad the truth about its disappearance, and Zeke almost whipped him then.

Occasionally Maud and Zeke (if he was home) and the children went to visit Maud's parents, Grandpa and Grandma Hall. The Halls lived near a more wooded area than the boys were used to. One time, Stub went off by himself and got lost in the woods. He was gone so long there was a search party out looking for him. They were worried about snakes and other dangers. Maud's brother Ernest was riding along, searching, when he heard a weak little voice saying, "Gimme a ride, gimme a ride." It was Stub, with no clothes on and unable to tell anyone where the clothes had been left.

The Chickasha Years

LEO AND Ira grew in stature and in favor with God and man. In their teens, they began to have different ideas about the direction of their lives, but were still deeply bound by sibling closeness. It was during these years that Zeke sold the homestead supplies and equipment and moved the family, first to stay at the Halls' Marlow farm.

Once he had gotten Maud and the children settled on the farm, Zeke began one of his lengthy disappearance episodes, this one with more plausibility than others. In the latter part of 1913, he went to Houston to work in the oil fields with his brother Jerry (Neri). He then hired on to go to Old Mexico to drill for oil. On January 17, 1914, he signed the homestead deed over to Maud, except he kept the mortgage to pay himself.

In Mexico, the Revolution of 1910-1920 was going on, and he was jailed. For a lengthy time, no one knew where he was, so in July 1914, Maud recorded the deed in Ellis County, not knowing his well-being. Zeke came back late that year with pay from the oil company and moved the family to Chickasha in 1915.

The Allens settled into town. Maud and Zeke, after a long sojourn apart, were together again with six children. Maud focused on schooling (both private and public) for the older four and cared for Martha and Pete at home. The family lived in Chickasha for four years, first renting on Pennsylvania St. near the Old North School. Zeke found work in a local hardware store. By late in the year, Maud was pregnant again, despite having had bronchial pneumonia in 1914 and having recovered slowly. She was determined her children would get a good education.

Maud and Pearl

In Chickasha, the older boys were schooled and at times boarded at the Catholic school there, St. Joseph's Academy. Years later, Mama said, "I have a lot of respect for the Catholic Church. They've built schools and hospitals to help so many. If I weren't a member of the Church of Christ, I would be a Catholic."

Soon, at the store, Zeke met Art B. Dale, who had a grain-thrashing machine. Zeke began helping Art with his thrashing business, and the two realized they had mutual interests in the oil boom industry developing at that time in Texas and Oklahoma. It held the possibility of making them rich.

Maud was consistently trying to see that her children learned to sing so they could glorify God, and to help them do that, she encouraged them to learn to play an instrument. She and Zeke both were good at singing and Zeke could play any instrument available—fiddle, mouth harp, whatever. He could even play spoons, probably from his roots in Arkansas.

In 1916 Maud had their eighth child, Alma; and the next year she began having serious, even disabling, headaches. The doctor prescribed that she cut her long hair, which she had not previously done, as a means of relieving the headaches. Maud's Hall family had deep roots in the Church of Christ, one of the restoration faiths, whose early tenets included biblical beliefs that women should minimize the use of jewelry and the trimming of their hair. Permitting her hair to be cut was a heart-wrenching decision. She did agree to do so for the sake of her health. It may have helped for a few years, but she let it grow long again and would not have it cut again for nearly 50 years.

In 1917, the Allens built a house at 13th and Oregon Streets, and Martha started school.

EZ and Art got into the oil business together using the "mineral rights ownership" concept. They leased 160 acres and its mineral rights adjacent to a producing well. By reselling the lease, they made a $100,000 profit. The lessor that they sold to would be hopeful of making more than $100,000 profit because of their proximity to the productive well. Leo would say, "Dad could trade the stripe off a skunk's back." Owning mineral rights has remained an important practice to generations of EZ's descendants, who have included them in real estate contracts as often as possible and benefited greatly on occasion.

Leo recalled, "We were making some money. We were living better than we had in the past. We had spurts of wealth interspersed with poverty." Years later, Martha said, "Throughout the oil boom years, when times were good, Dad (Zeke) spent money like we were rich—and when they were bad, he moved the family back to stay with the Halls or to Duncan or Marlow to get going again. We had lots of ups and downs."

The turnstile year for Chickasha was 1918. Ira finished seventh grade, receiving an attendance award. Because of the Great War and his patriotic spirit, Leo wanted to enlist.

Pete was recognized to be especially bright and ready for school before his age group. He was enrolled in the first grade while still five years old and went to school on the first day with his brothers and sisters. When he came home, his mother asked him how the day was. He answered, "Fine, but I ain't goin' back." And he didn't until the next school year started.

Zeke and Art continued their leasing and wildcatting success and formed Allendale Oil Co. in 1918. Then, they made the strategic decision to make their headquarters in Fort Worth, Texas. They moved their families there in 1919.

Twins Apart but Ties Forever

WHEN Leo was fourteen, he decided he wanted to join the Navy. He lied about his age and begged Maud to sign the consent for the Navy to accept him as a sixteen-year-old swabbie, to which she agreed with much crying and tears. Although WWI was over, the Versailles Peace Treaty hadn't been signed. Leo had been in the Navy for six months when they started discharging all who wanted to go home. Leo was homesick and took the opportunity to go back home.

During the Allens' time in Fort Worth, Leo's recollections were that Maud and Mrs. Dale were both involved in the running of the business, contributing ideas and decisions. But, the big oil companies, like the ones run by the Morgans and Rockefellers, began to buy up the little ones. Allendale continued as long as possible but finally went the way of the others.

When Leo was seventeen, he began a lifelong interest in the Bible. He had an eager and intense desire to learn as much as possible. He rode a horse seventeen miles daily to study with a preacher he had met named Charlie Spencer. Brother Spencer had a 160-acre farm where he raised his family, and from time to time he went to outlying areas to hold gospel meetings. He was a family friend through the years. Twelve years later, the two families united when one of his pretty daughters, Ellen, and Zekie dated, fell in love, and married. Leo's studies with Brother Spencer fired his intellect and planted in him a deep faith in the word of God that became a practical guide for his everyday life.

Brother Spencer had one trait that was indeed unique. He didn't consider it right to take money in payment for preaching the Word. He referred to money as "filthy lucre." People paid him with food items, like chickens, potatoes, and other fruits of their labor. He regarded these gifts as coming from hearts of love and accepted them with graciousness and thanks.

In the early 1920s, Ezekiel and Maud bought a house in Marlow, and the children all went to school there except for Leo and Ornan. Ira graduated from Marlow High School and, along with Leo, started working in the oil fields. They worked the same jobs at times and made good money. Leo wanted to invest some money in something, so he bought a twenty-acre farm three miles out of Marlow. It had a shack of a house on it that had never been properly finished, but his intent was to have a place of his own to retreat to when he wanted.

By the time Ira was twenty-one, he had become engaged to a girl named Pearl Harrison. She was only sixteen, so Ira worked hard to give them a good financial start when they married in a few years. It was not to be.

On January 21, 1927, Ira was working on an oil derrick when the cable that carried the elevator up and down broke. The 4000-pound elevator made so much noise as it fell that the other workers could not yell loud enough for Ira to hear their warning shouts. He was crushed, and one loving and loved life was severed from the family.

Leo wasn't at that location that day and learned about it later. It is not recalled who in the family in anguish had to identify Ira, whether Zeke or Leo. Leo had suffered the traumatic loss of his lifelong companion torn from his life. In shock, he remembered painfully, "His death was gruesome. He was crushed, although the watch on his wrist was still intact and working."

A word about the Allen family plot that Zeke had the foresight to purchase using insurance money he and Maud received for Ira's loss. It's in a beautiful old part of the cemetery. Nearby is a Hall family section, where grandparents Ike and Amanda, great-uncle Porter Hall, MD, and Uncle John and his wife Annie and their children rest. As the years went by after Ira's death, first Maud with little Pearl, later Martha and Babe, and later yet Charles and Betty with their children have cared for the family plot. Sadly, in

Maud and Pearl

time it also became the resting place for Zeke himself, and much later Maud as well. The site has become important to Allen family members seeking solace or a sense of connection with those who have gone before. It's not a sad place as it has so many memories of a wonderful family.

When Ira died, Maud was seven months pregnant with her ninth child. Iralene Pearl was born exactly two months later, on March 21. Maud was forty-three and not in good health, compounded by the grief she was experiencing. Her uncle, known to the family as "Uncle Doc," was able to get a permit for Zeke to make home brew in spite of Prohibition. It was their belief that the malt would help Maud recover her strength. She suffered from bad health for at least a year.

Leo continued to work in the oil fields after Ira's death for a few years, until unemployment began to be a way of life in those early years of the 1930s. He worked with Zeke and the other boys on the farm unless he could get a job somewhere else for a period of time.

Whether Zeke could foresee the economic future isn't known, but in 1929 he moved the family out to the 20-acre farm Leo had bought some years earlier. In October of that year came the Crash of Wall Street that ushered in the Great Depression, one of the most devastating economic periods in the history of the country. The move was fortuitous. Zeke and his four grown sons could work to keep the family fed, and Maud had recuperated enough to accomplish the many tasks required of a farm wife. Teenaged Alma could help with two-year-old Pearl as well as with the ironing and other heavy housework.

The farm had almost everything they needed. After crossing the little creek that ran across it, there was an area where they had the potato patch and corn field where they grew, in addition to the corn they ate, a field of broomcorn. They grew peanuts and Maud made her own peanut butter and sometimes peanut brittle candy. Between the house and the creek was a great big peach orchard, along with a few prune plum trees and a couple of cherry trees in another section near the front yard.

Pearl Allen Andree

A barn housed the cows and mules. A chicken coop housed Maud's chickens. Another building was called "the garage," but it wasn't for cars. The only vehicle was a wagon, and the garage was used for working to prepare the corn or saw lumber, and sometimes as a smokehouse. Quite a ways from the house was the pigpen.

Maud planted a large garden every year. The cows allowed them to have a good supply of dairy products. In the fall Zeke butchered a hog and a beef animal. Maud rendered out the meat, supplying them with lard for cooking. She canned meat as well as a generous amount of fruit and vegetables to be used in the winter months. She stored this canned food in a cellar, which was also used for shelter from cyclones that occurred from time to time. There was a berry patch with rows of blackberries and dewberries (like a blackberry but with a bluish color and not quite as sweet).

Along the creek were wild black walnut trees and wild grapes. The latter had to be fought over with the birds for possession. There were even "poke greens," something like Swiss chard that grew wild and were cooked as a healthy substitute for spinach. The red poke berries, however, were poisonous and could only be used as a red dye for coloring fabric.

Maud did the laundry on a scrub board outside. She was glad to have a wringer to use. There was a spot in the yard for a campfire where she kept a big, black cauldron at the ready. She made her own lye soap and would cut some of it up into the pot of water. After scrubbing the clothes, she boiled them in that big black pot.

The house was similar to a shotgun house, except at one place there were rooms on each side of the hall. All the rooms were large. The front door opened to a big entry hall. On the north side of this hall was the front room, which held a heat stove and a couch called a "dufold" as it opened up into a bed. On the south side of the entry hall was another huge room, big enough to hold two double beds. The house had been built with only planks of lumber, so there was no insulation. Maud found boxes from the grocery store to collapse and nailed them to the walls to help keep out the blizzard winds that blew through the cracks in the wintertime. The product advertising on this "wallpaper"

Maud and Pearl

was a source of questions for young Pearl. The box labeled "bathroom tissue" certainly didn't describe the Sears Roebuck and Montgomery Ward catalogs used for that purpose in the outdoor toilet located at the back of the backyard.

At the end of that large entry hall was a big kitchen. The dining table Zeke built stood there, with benches on all four sides. There, too, was the big cookstove on which Maud cooked three meals a day. At every meal, she baked huge biscuits on a sheet that had been the top of a 55-gallon drum, unless cornbread was the bread of choice.

At the back of the kitchen, a screened porch had been added, where another double bed stood. The icebox that occasionally held ice brought from town was there too, and Maud had fixed a window-like space for keeping cool the butter, milk, eggs, etc. It was a metal box that jutted out from the house and was covered with canvas that came down to the floor of the box and trailed in the water she kept there.

Between the house and the road, there was a large expanse of yard. Beautiful green grass grew there, with a number of blackjack oak trees, giving needed shade in the hot summertime.

Leo's Life

SOMETIME in those years Leo began to look west for jobs, as did the other brothers later. Although there always seemed to be a car in the yard that one of them had latched onto, it was never reliable enough to go on a long trip. When Zeke could get away from the farm for a while, he might accompany a couple of the boys as far as New Mexico. Otherwise, the boys hopped a freight train, as thousands of other men did in those years.

When Leo journeyed west, he wrote letters back home. From Arizona, during scorching heat, he wrote: "I was walking across the desert near Gila Bend and saw a man coming toward me walking really funny—zigzagging and hopping some. When he came closer, he said, 'Sure are a lot of sidewinders around today, huh?' and I said, 'Hadn't noticed.' He started pointing them out to me. That man hadn't been walking funny at all compared to what I was doing after that."

He would go home to Oklahoma and go west again, sometimes with one of his brothers. While these were the years his brothers were becoming enamored of their sweethearts, marrying, and starting families, the love bug didn't bite Leo. He was too busy helping in their lives and Maud's. He had friends, some female, and dated, but when anyone asked him why he hadn't gotten married, he responded, "I love all the women too much to starve one of them to death."

He happened to be in Arizona in early 1938, when Babe and Martha, who had moved there the previous December, changed their minds and moved back to Oklahoma in May, and he went with them.

Maud and Pearl

In Oklahoma, Leo became interested in becoming a Freemason and progressed quickly to the level of 32nd degree. He then was qualified to teach other men in the steps. In September 1939, Zeke sued Maud for divorce. Leo realized the money he had been giving his dad to send to Maud and Pearl was not being sent, so he returned to Arizona to be their sole support.

Leo made several contacts within the Masonic community, finding men in Tolleson who were studying the steps. The first lodge meeting he attended was in Phoenix, in the Masonic Temple. He realized he might be out of his social register when he saw the men dressed in tuxedos to come to meetings. There was a smaller lodge meeting in Peoria, a small town near Tolleson, where the local men with whom he was becoming acquainted attended.

One of these men was on the Tolleson Union High School Board of Education and owned a ranch in the area. He hired Leo to work on the Snake Ranch. The work was supervising laborers in the hot Arizona summer sun, and Leo worked alongside them. At the water station there were salt tablets the men took to replace the body salt lost in sweat. In spite of this, one day Leo suffered a heat stroke and had to be brought home. His blue work shirt had a ring of white around the back of the salt lost from his system.

When a position at the high school opened for one of two janitor/maintenance man/bus drivers, Leo was hired. He had a unique way of describing the students on his bus route. One girl was redheaded and freckled, and he said, "She's as cute as a red pup under a red wagon." A boy who was rather clumsy he described as "like a bull in a China closet."

Leo began trying to get accepted back into the Navy after Pearl Harbor was attacked on December 7, 1941. Of course, he was older, as well as being two years older, according to the Navy, than he actually was. In January 1943, they accepted him into the Seabees, the construction battalion that built camps on beaches in preparation for the Marines to land.

When he was inducted in January, Leo was sent to the same training camp as in his youth. He wrote home, "They still can't make me like mutton." In April, he had a leave to come home for a couple of weeks. While home, he accompanied Pearl's Senior Ditch

Pearl Allen Andree

Day up to Canyon Lake. One Saturday night, he took Pearl and six of her girlfriends to a movie in Phoenix. During WWII there were multiple military installations nearby, and on Saturday nights the sidewalks in Phoenix were chock-a-block with uniforms. There was much commentary about "this old sailor with all these young girls with him." One young man attached himself to the group and accompanied them out to Encanto Park before the evening ended.

In June, Leo shipped out from Port Hueneme, California to the South Pacific, where he spent over two years going from island to island before the war ended. He had arranged for allotments to be sent each month to his mother and Pearl for their financial benefit.

While in the South Pacific, Leo had Pearl get and deliver gifts he had in mind for various people. On Mother's Day, it was a single rose in a bud vase for Maud. This was a little tradition he had started while working at the high school since, among other jobs, he was the gardener. A senior girl who had been one among many students on the school bus he drove was good to write to him, and he asked Pearl to get something for her for a graduation gift. Pearl chose to get the graduate an orchid corsage and wrote Leo to let him know about the gift. He wrote back that the day he heard from her, he walked outside his tent and saw an orchid growing wild on a tree. Letters were V-mail, a reduced size of later aerograms. Sometimes words were blacked out due to censorship.

Leo returned from the South Pacific in late August 1945 and needed to start his civilian life again. He joined the Lions Club and took a job caring for a farm his friend Bill Ritchie owned. Maud moved into the house with him to keep house for him. She was very conscious of being where she was most needed.

He had no trouble getting well acquainted with his new brother-in-law, Jimmy Goggin, whom Pearl had married the previous May.

A few things had changed in his social group. Some had moved, and one couple had obtained a divorce. In the years before joining the Navy, when his friends got together, he teamed up with Dutchie, the local single beautician. They were the only single

Maud and Pearl

people in the group, and it was simply a friendship. After the war, the divorced couple still were in the social group, and Leo admired Eva very much, even to the point of asking her to marry him. He had a moral code that prevented him from expecting premarital intimacy. Unfortunately, she apparently saw nothing wrong with intimacy outside marriage. In November 1947, he discovered she was having an affair with the mayor, who was married.

Of his Navy Seabees group, Leo and one other man were the only ones who survived without battle fatigue. One Saturday night in that same fateful November of 1947, he was working at the Lions Club carnival on the elementary school grounds when he collapsed and had to be taken to the VA hospital. It was a nervous breakdown and was diagnosed as delayed battle fatigue. He drew on his moral strength and physical work, exercising the resiliency of a lifetime. The family around him was supportive also, and, of course, a mother's loving care came to the fore.

In the months following, the VA had a lottery system set up for veterans, who could draw a land grant on which to make a farm life for themselves and their family. Leo was fortunate to draw one of the best and largest of the grants. It was near Yuma and near the Colorado River. The river had changed course through the years and formed an area of several acres called "no man's land." Since this bordered his grant, he was allowed to farm it and reap its benefits though he didn't actually own it.

A nearby town was Somerton. Maud moved there with him when the house was ready, and of course she went to church meetings. Leo hadn't been a regular churchgoer for several years, but Maud had ideas. She met a widow lady whom she thought was just who her boy needed. When Leo met Vergin Broadway, he decided she was the one he could "love her enough to starve her to death." Vergin had two older married daughters and two young sons, Everett, aged twelve, and Ronnie, six. Leo and Vergin were married on Armistice Day, a circumstance that caused much teasing. He was 46 and finally had his own family. A baby girl was born to Leo and Vergin in October 1953. She was named Marsha Maudine.

Pearl Allen Andree

After going to Yuma to help Leo, Maud occasionally went to Tolleson to help Alma, who lived there. The family was relocating to various places—California, Texas, and Oklahoma. After Alma went to Texas, Maud moved into a little room on Ornan's property in Tolleson, again because she thought that was where she was needed most. In 1955, Pearl bought a place in Tempe for her, and she lived there for the next 11 years.

Leo and Vergin spent summers fishing in the White Mountains of Arizona. He had sold his land grant, and they had moved to a house in Yuma.

Leo had started smoking when he was only 13, which eventually progressed to chain smoking. He did finally quit, but too late to prevent emphysema. In 1970, he quit smoking in the house, going outside to have a cigarette after dinner. By 1977, he quit completely. Marsha was asked how he decided to quit completely, and she replied, "He watched his best friend die." Quitting added ten years to his life.

He was always ready to admonish a young person not to smoke. Vergin was sometimes embarrassed when they were in the grocery store and he saw a young woman smoking. He would approach her and say, "Honey, if I had a million dollars, I would give it to you if you would quit smoking."

In April 1983, Leo had a heart attack one Sunday evening and was hospitalized. For 24 hours they monitored him and considered a pacemaker. He was recuperating well, and they decided not to put in the pacemaker. Vergin was with him constantly. She wouldn't let them send her home. Finally, on Thursday, they were sure to be sending him home soon and convinced Vergin to go home and get some rest. About 4:00 p.m. he was sitting up in bed, cracking jokes with the nurse, and died with a smile on his face.

Vergin grieved for Leo for about a year. She remarried, and she and her new husband, Mr. Harniss, planned to spend summers in Washington State, where his son was a chiropractor. They were there just a few weeks after they were married when he dropped her off at the son's office and went to do some errands. Sadly, Mr. Harniss had diabetes and suffered a blackout while driving and died.

Maud and Pearl

Vergin returned to Arizona and eventually moved permanently to the White Mountains, where Marsha and Everett lived with their families. Ronn continued to live in the Phoenix area. On her 95th birthday, Vergin's picture was in the White Mountain paper, sitting atop a horse, one of her birthday wishes. Through those years, Vergin was in assisted living, then in a nursing home. Friends and family celebrated her 100th birthday in September 2011. On September 24, 2012, at 11:00 p.m., she passed away.

Marsha remarked, "There's a two-hour time difference between Arkansas (where she was born) and Arizona. That makes it 1:00 a.m., September 25, so she did live to be 101." Vergin had suffered, in her lifetime, the loss of three husbands, as well as her son Everett.

Thoughts on My Dad, Leo

I love hearing the stories others tell about my father in his younger days—the days when he was a scamp and a scoundrel. I am sometimes sad I didn't hear them from him.

I knew him as a farmer, conservative in politics and faith. My memories are usually of his kindness, of me riding an old paint horse bareback through the alfalfa while he drove the tractor. He is forever associated with those distant purple hills and booming thunder during the monsoons. During those times, Dad and I sat together on the porch of our little house in Dome Valley, and he would explain the lightning and thunder so I wasn't afraid. His manly smell of tobacco was a great comfort.

On our many drives to Tolleson or Tempe to see Grandma Allen, we would leave very early in the mornings before the desert heat arrived with the rising sun. But he would say, "Sis, what do you think? Do you think any artist could paint such pretty colors?" The rising desert sun was always Dad's way of saying good morning.

Dad never finished high school but was a well self-educated man. He knew the Bible and the poets as well as he knew his own name. During my high school years, he would sit at the table while I ate breakfast and quote those poets—Kipling, still a favorite of mine, Keats, Tennyson. There was no end to his repertoire of stories and poems. He spoke Spanish with me. He let me teach him organic chemistry because, we decided, if I could make him understand, then I also understood.

My older girls benefited from knowing Be-Pa, as they called him. They put rollers in his hair, and he allowed their free-range play whatever the cost, though Mom took the scissors away when

Maud and Pearl

they wanted to give him a haircut. I truly wish my younger children could have known him as well.

They'd have enjoyed hearing about the time, on his way home from work or some other event, he happened upon a baby skunk and thought what a great pet it would make. So he got as close as he dared then tossed his brand-new hat over it. He laughed till tears ran when he remembered how he and that no-longer-new hat had to live in the barn for a week. Grandma wouldn't let him in the house!

Then there was the baby raccoon he raised to good size. He kept peanuts in his pockets and when he came home, his little friend would search until he found them. Unfortunately his little raccoon grew into an adult, and unfortunately one day he had no peanuts to offer! He laughed when he said he thought the raccoon would tear him up before he could get loose from it.

Dad worked in the oil fields, ranched, farmed, prospected, drove a school bus, and fought a world war where he earned three Bronze Stars and, according to one of my brothers, two Purple Hearts. He changed his name from Isaac to Wilfred, his favorite knight hero character in Ivanhoe, his favorite book. He was a man of intellect and passion, of fierce anger and fiercer love. "Don't you ever start a fight," he said. "Walk away if you can. But if you can't walk away, you finish it!"

I miss this man. I have so many things to ask him. To tell him.

Marsha Allen Ford, Leo and Vergin's daughter, an Allen cousin

Ornan

OKLAHOMA became a state in 1907. A new citizen of that state was born on October 20th of that year. The day started for Maud as most wash days did. It was also butchering day for Zeke. Maud helped with that also, rendering out the lard and helping with the meat preservation process. Her mother, Grandma Hall, was there to help.

At about 7:00 p.m. Maud started tying ropes to the iron bedstead, and Grandma Hall commented, "I thought you were acting a little feisty today." Within three hours, with the help of Zeke and her mother, the third son was born into the family. They named him Ornan Robert (for Grandpa Allen). For many years he was the comedian in the family. As he grew through boyhood, he loved doing gymnastic tricks. One favorite was walking on his hands. When the family moved to Chickasha and there were stairs, he excelled at doing this up and down the stairs. This earned him the nickname Monkey, which was shortened to Monk. For most of his life, this nickname was used by family and close friends.

Ornan's younger brother, Zeke Jr., was his playmate, and they at times tried to contribute to the well-being of various forms of life on the farm. Nails came in wooden kegs and Zeke kept them available for construction projects. Ornan and Zekie overheard talk about putting the current crop of baby chickens somewhere to be kept warm. They decided to help. After dumping the nails out of a keg, they put the chicks in the bottom of the keg. Something told them they would get in trouble if they didn't put the nails somewhere, so they put them back into the keg. The

Maud and Pearl

grown-ups started wondering where all the baby chicks had gone. The mystery was finally solved when the smell became apparent.

They had two dogs that protected the boys from snakes many times. One such time was when they found a snake hole and the tail of the snake was sticking out. Ornan pulled on it to try and get it out, but the dogs put up such a barking fuss that he abandoned the idea.

Another time, they were playing around the mailbox near some wild grape vines. They heard sounds like pups, and when they searched under the vines, they found some puppies. They went home and told their dad they had found some baby pups. He investigated and found them to be wolves!

While Maud's brother, Uncle Ernest, was visiting, there was a flood in a nearby canyon. He was caught in the water and had vines tangled around him. The boys helped get him unwound and free of the dangerous water.

Sometimes Zeke left home on trips to look for work, leaving the place in the care of his boys. Of course, that meant it was in Maud's care also, reminding her of Ike (her father) telling about working on the railroad in Texas for six months and her mother having to take care of everything on the farm. Since Zeke had left home at an early age, he believed his sons could shoulder responsibility early in life.

The rhyme "reading, writing, n' arithmetic, taught to the tune of a hickory stick" was more truth than poetry. Children got whipped for infractions. Zeke used a razor strap and made sure they heard him the first time. If they didn't obey, there wasn't a second chance. Grandpas were adept at this discipline, too. Once at Grandpa Hall's, Ornan was with Leo out looking for the cows when they mischievously got into the watermelon patch. Grandpa whipped Leo the hardest because, he said, Leo knew better.

Ornan learned many things, such as that if you had to build a new wheel for a Springfield wagon, you had to have the wood and iron just right for repair. You had to heat the steel rim, get it red hot, slip it on the wheel with a hammer, and pour water on it to make it tight.

Pearl Allen Andree

One time, he and his older brothers found a very tall cottonwood tree. About halfway up was a knothole. They found a beehive there and took out two tubs of honey. The problem was, it tasted like the tree. They also found that if you dig a well near tree roots, the water will taste like that.

When Ornan was very young, Zeke took the family to Little Rock to visit the Allen grandparents. Ornan was impressed with the hens roosting in trees and wild turkeys roosting with them, giving them protection from predators.

Zeke was an admirer of Teddy Roosevelt. He told Ornan stories of having been a scout for Roosevelt's Rough Riders, although there is no evidence that he was. As Ornan grew old enough to be aware of politics, he asked his dad why, being a Democrat, he admired Roosevelt, a Republican, so much. His dad responded with, "Well, he's a progressive Republican." Zeke also believed himself a relative of Daniel Boone, but whether this was ever proved, Ornan never knew.

The family left the homestead when Ornan was about six years old, and for about two years the family lived on Grandpa's farm northwest of Marlow. In 1915, they moved again to Chickasha for a few years. When Zeke was home, he took the boys fishing on the Washita River, catching many catfish to take home for a big meal. Sometimes they filled a gunny sack with them.

One time, Zeke brought his gun, and since he expected to hunt, it was loaded. One of the boys picked it up and pulled the trigger. After that, Zeke never carried a loaded gun.

On their own on the Hall farm, the boys wandered in the woods, and one time they were hungry and started eating the wild nuts, persimmons, grapes, and mushrooms. The thought occurred to Ornan that some of these wild things might make them sick, so he offered to eat them first to see if they made him sick. As he filled himself, Zekie began to realize his brother was having a feast and the others weren't getting their share. Zekie grabbed the rest away from Ornan and declared, "You can't have any more!"

Ornan was a wiry, athletic, growing-up-fast kid, and after the prairie homestead, the culverts, streets, and neighborhoods of Chickasha became his next playground. He was spongy intellectually as well as physically. He liked reading and memorizing passages from the classics, poems, and Bible scriptures.

In the late 1910s, as previously mentioned, Zeke moved the family to Ft. Worth where he began an oil exploration and drilling company with the Dales. During this time the Allens had a good life. Somewhere along the way they lived near a golf course, and in later years Ornan told stories of how he would sneak around the ponds and swim in them when the coast was clear.

Allendale Oil Company

THROUGH the later homestead years, the Chickasha years, and into the 1920s, Zeke focused on oil and gas exploration and became a self-made geologist. In this endeavor, he was knowledgeable and it was said that throughout the years others came to him for advice. There are family photos of him and the older boys exploring in West Texas as late as 1928. He and Art Dale felt that their Allendale Oil Co. could be successful, even though they would be Davids among Goliaths.

Troubles began as early as 1918. A group of ranchers sued Allendale because their oil leases had leaked into a river that polluted the water supply. It's not known how this dispute was resolved.

An accurate recall is obscure, and only general speculation of the early course of Allendale's efforts is possible but worth trying. Even while in Fort Worth with residences for their families, business offices in the commercial area, their shingle hung out as "Oil Producers and Refiners," and a general sales manager in tow, their fortunes and futures began to falter.

In those times, major eastern oil companies had come to the area, and with their knowledge, experience, and money, they had the power to stifle smaller competition. The major oil companies, like Standard Oil, began controlling the transportation of oil barrels to railroads, by which crude oil could be shipped to refineries. They contracted with independent companies to make barrels, haul them by truck, and preferentially ship their oil, preventing small producers from obtaining barrels or accessing transport. For gas, pipeline companies were formed, but they also

Maud and Pearl

contracted with large producers and excluded the small ones. By such blackballing techniques, many small companies were induced to sell out to the major ones.

Hard times hit Allendale in short order, but not before it had drilled some successful wells and become a successful enterprise.

Oral tradition supported by older members of the Allen clan is that Allendale was approached by Standard Oil and given a serious offer of $500,000 for the business. Sadly, no records or proof of this remains. At the time, Allendale owed their bank $160,000, which would be covered. The offer included $50,000 worth of land, at one dollar an acre, and a furnished house for each family.

As remembered by son Zekie (at that time the errand boy for Allendale), the Allens and Dales spent late nights for several weeks to make their decision, considering their best options but struggling to reach an agreement. Maud favored the sale and country life, concerned her children would become "citified." However, Mrs. Dale liked the city and the potential to become a socialite. She apparently was influential in the final decision together with the men, which was to "stay and ride it out."

But then came calamity. Whether by large oil company domination, under-handed business practices, or stock market decline, Allendale could not sell its oil fast enough and began having to pay storage fees (in those days, often in open ponds or large tanks) while labor expenses continued. With the headwinds of the Depression of 1920-1921, banks called in their loans, and Allendale was forced to declare bankruptcy. EZ and Mr. Dale tried to survive by being paid for other jobs under pseudonyms. But despite their efforts, they could not stay afloat, and their business folded. It's not known when the men parted ways.

Years later, on several occasions Maud told Pearl the story of EZ's brush with history in the form of Erle Halliburton. Mr. Halliburton had invented and patented a technique to cement oil well pump structures, to their underground pipes. Controlling the flow of oil under pressure was sometimes very difficult. Fired in 1919 by an oil company that didn't like his ideas, Mr. Halliburton and his wife moved to Burkburnett, Texas and tried to persuade oil companies and area wildcatters to use his patented oil well

Pearl Allen Andree

cementing and capping process, without success for a while, and his business experienced very lean times. It was during this time, Maud recalled, that Erle approached EZ, who was then wildcatting, about going into business with him and using his patent. But EZ chose not to, telling him that his method wouldn't work well enough. Shortly after, Halliburton successfully cemented an unruly well in southern Oklahoma, proving his method useful, catapulting his company's reputation, and saving what would become a legendary industry leader. EZ's decision was on the wrong side of history. Pete Allen told this same story to his son Lanier and his son-in-law, Dick Cosby, as well.

Some Allendale Oil Company memories have faded into oblivion, but some facts remain secure and recorded. EZ wildcatted at least two successful wells, in Ranger and Desdemona in Eastland County, Texas. He sent Maud and the kids back to Duncan, Oklahoma at the end of 1919, after less than a year's stay in Fort Worth. It's clear that he kept his wells active as long as he could, perhaps hoping he could revive Allendale. Records obtained from the Texas Railroad Commission prove that, indeed, he was an active and sometimes successful wildcatter. His Ellison No. 1 well (Eastland Co.) was permitted to connect to the United Producers Pipe Line Co. in July 1920. Several other wells that were drilled are documented through November 1920. In the oil boom, he had achieved some of the success he craved. As a wildcatter, Zeke was the real thing!

Fort Worth Sequel: The Duncan Years

CONSIDERING their ruinous lack of business success, it must have been very difficult for EZ and Maud to generate enough enthusiasm to pick up their lives again. Their road to survival had immediacy: a one-bedroom apartment on East Main Street in Duncan, the younger boys Ornan and Zeke being boarded at school in Chickasha, and EZ trucking back and forth to his Eastland County wildcat wells, desperate to make money somewhere in the oil patch. Maud endured, somehow.

The forecasted Depression came and settled in and became stifling for business everywhere. Home from school, the boys tried a poultry enterprise. Apparently, EZ adjusted by securing a contract with the City of Duncan to lay water lines in the city streets as they were being paved. The boys got a water meter installation and hook-up contract, probably with EZ's help. Ornan (Monk) returned to Duncan and enrolled in Duncan public school for ninth grade, 1921-1922.

Still, the allure of the hunt for oil kept EZ in its pocket, leading him to travel, explore, and work, but return empty handed, repeatedly. He was home in September 1922 when the newspapers broke the headline news of the family feud in Arkansas called the Enon Massacre and described its terrific bloodshed. On a Sunday morning, he read the headlines and quipped, "Well, I probably lost a couple of cousins in that fight!" referring to his childhood in Arkansas.

EZ moved to Chickasha in 1922, taking Ornan, who went to public school that autumn and then dropped out of school for

Pearl Allen Andree

good. Leo and Ira worked different jobs in the area, but it's not known where they lived. Maud and the other children remained in Duncan. This separation was probably economically necessitated. Other factors that might have contributed are unknown.

What is known is that EZ bought a house on the southeast corner of Arapahoe and Broadway in Marlow in 1923, where the family lived until 1929, and which was owned by the Allen family for years afterward. Five of the children finished their education at Marlow High School. Martha and Babe's family stayed there after returning from Arizona in 1938, and they referred to it as "Grandpa's house."

Yet after 1923, EZ's absences increased in length and frequency for several years.

Nothing the family has kept documents anything about what EZ did or his whereabouts between 1923 and the end of 1925. He's not known to have wildcatted successfully after his Eastland County days. His prolonged absences even dimmed the family's memories of his earlier wildcatting exploits, sadly.

EZ was indeed a wayfarer. He was gone so long on one occasion that Grandma and the children, who didn't know his whereabouts, came to fear that he had died by illness or foul play. Was that disappearance because of his pride having been hurt by the failure of Allendale? Was it his sense of inadequacy in supporting his large family consistently? Was it because of his stubborn determination to have success and strike it rich again? While details of his experiences would be fascinating to know, his journeying remains mysterious.

When he reappeared in the early to mid-1920s, of course he had beguiling stories to tell. He was enigmatic. One oral tradition that's remained in the family without proof is that he'd gone down into Mexico again, during their rebel revolt of 1924, which was risky. Somehow, he'd run afoul of the police during the insurrection. After a lengthy period of dealing with the authorities (read "jailed in Mexico"), he was released. His freedom to roam was restored.

This event and others are reminders of his own father's trips back and forth between Oregon and Grayson County, Kentucky,

Maud and Pearl

which had taken place half a century earlier. Each of his father's trips to Oregon was preceded by fathering a child with Martha. His father never kept the promises that he made to Martha. EZ himself never drilled that last wildcat well that might have made everything right again. Like his father, he seemed to have been true to type, a solitary soul traveling and searching along the black gold trail.

We'll never know the truth of EZ's activities and adventures during his absences. He did come back, though, and settled down. By late 1925, he was home in Marlow to stay.

Ornan: Growing Up Early; A Long Life

IN DUNCAN, the boys, young teenagers, helped lay city water lines, install water meters, and did other "grown men" work because in the early 1920s Grandpa had lengthy absences from time to time. On top of it all, the Depression of 1920-1921 had brought hard times to the family, and they were particularly so for Maud and the kids.

During these years, Ornan and Zekie boarded at school in Chickasha, again at St. Joseph's Academy. The boys were required to study Catholic catechism. During Ornan's eighth grade, he and Zekie boarded for twelve months. They had to work for part of their tuition. They swept the church and worked in the laundry. At Christmas they had no money for gifts, but the two of them discovered they were good at playing marbles. One of their friends was fairly well-to-do, and they could win most of his marbles. He would buy marbles back from them, and they then repeated the system, thus acquiring enough money to have a little for Christmas. They were allowed to be altar boys, helping with communion, and sing in the choir. They didn't have to be Catholic to do these things. It must have been during this time that Ornan took violin lessons. Grandma, later in life, reminisced about how Ornan had learned to play "Wonderful Words of Life" on the violin.

Ornan quit school midway through the tenth grade, but he continued through life to improve his "self-made man" education. He had a love for literature and could quote poetry he had learned, such as Portia's speech from *The Merchant of Venice*, when he was in his nineties.

Maud and Pearl

By 1926, Zeke was back with the family. In previous years, the boys also found odd jobs to get spending money. Ornan and Zekie bought chickens and sold them, either alive or after killing and dressing them, for a profit. They used a red wagon in front of a store. At seventy-five cents a pound, they had a business!

Oil was one business that was booming. Ornan found jobs digging ditches and then was hired as a water boy, for which he got paid better than digging ditches and the work was easier.

From Duncan, the family moved to Marlow. They moved into the place on Arapahoe, where they lived for several years. It was in the 1920s that Ornan worked many different jobs and learned many of life's lessons.

In the 1920s, the jobs involved pipelines in Texas, working for Standard Oil and Shell Oil loading ships with oil down around Corpus Christi, Aransas Pass and Mustang Island, and Padre Island. He was with his dad and sometimes with Leo. One time he had to climb down a hole to hook up some pipes on a ship. On one occasion, they were sawing timber for a project, and the Texas Wildlife Fish and Game Department put a stop to it, as they thought the pipeline might leak and destroy wildlife.

They had acquired a "hoopty" (car) in Kansas that repeatedly had flats, especially if they drove over a stump in the West Texas desert. One of those times, Ornan found a sweater that looked brand new, so he decided to keep it. However, as he wore it, he realized why he had found it. It was permeated with cactus thorns. That broke him from picking up things in the desert.

One time at a pipeline camp they met a sheriff, and the next day when they started driving, he stopped them because they didn't have a driver's license. He held what Zeke called a "kangaroo court" and fined them before they could go on.

In the summer of 1926, Ornan decided to strike out on his own, having returned to the home in Marlow. He didn't tell any of the family but left without a word. On his own, he was determined to work and make his way. He was on his way to the wheat harvest in western Kansas when he stopped in the area of Shattuck and Woodward and found a ball game in progress. He made $5 selling pop and continued on to Kansas. He later hitchhiked to Denver

Pearl Allen Andree

and caught the CB&Q train to Nebraska. Deciding to return home, he caught a freight train south, following close to Highway 81 through Wichita and on to Marlow.

Almost the first people he saw were Zekie and Martha. They asked him, "Why didn't you tell us you were going to the wheat harvest?"

He replied, "Because you would've tried to talk me out of it."

In a large family like theirs, someone was always quoting poems or singing silly songs and making observations of wisdom to remember into old age, like this paraphrased Henry Austin Dobson poem:

The rose waxed full in the warm June air
Her fullness of beauty spread;
The rose is Beauty, the gardener Time,
And she'll soon be dead.

Ira and Ornan sang a ditty about the Green Mountain Boys. It was named "Sydney Allen" and they seemed to think he was an ancestor. It went something like this:

Sydney Allen was a prisoner and he was on time.
He went into the barroom about half past nine.
He went into the barroom with his pistol in his hand,
And he sent Judge Mavis to the Promised Land.
The County Sheriff, who was thin and tall, had him backed
    up against the wall.
He turned to his deputy and this is what he said,
"Just a moment more and we'll all be dead."

Was this a harbinger of the future when wild west movies would be entertainment?

Even in his youth, Ornan thought seriously about life lessons and was morally connected to his Biblical studies. He contemplated things like "a lawyer's greatest plea," being the one Judah (one of the twelve sons of Jacob) gave for his brother Benjamin when the

Maud and Pearl

silver cup was found in his sack of grain, to offer himself to suffer in place of his brother. He compared it to Christ's plea, "Come unto me, all you that are heavy laden, for my yoke is easy and my burden is light."

When the family moved to the twenty acres and the Great Depression was in full swing, he went wherever he could to get work, as all of the boys did. Zeke raised hogs to help with the meat on the dinner table. One time, he wanted to castrate an 800-pound hog, and Ornan helped. They threaded baling wire through the animal's nostrils and wrapped the other end around a tree. With the hog immobile, Dad was able to do the deed.

The men also went hunting to supplement the meat fare. At night they went possum hunting. Ornan put a lantern on his head to help see the possum in a tree and aim his .22 for a good shot. The possum hides were sold or traded for making various possum-leather products.

It was also time to find the right woman with whom to share his life. He found her in a family at church, where she had been all along. Her name was Dorothy Edna Brown. Her older sister Sybil worked in Oklahoma City, and Dorothy went to stay with her after graduating from high school. Sybil encouraged her to go to college, so she entered Oklahoma College for Women. She went one year before deciding to accept Ornan's proposal.

They were married on July 13, 1935. The plan was to have a double wedding with his younger brother, Pete. Unfortunately, Pete was having to spend so much time getting his future father-in-law's permission that Ornan and Dorothy decided they'd better leave and go on their own. The family friend Charlie Spencer was a preacher living on a farm near Rush Springs, and that is where they went. Zeke Jr. had married Brother Spencer's daughter Ellen two years before, so they knew they were in good company. The ceremony was conducted under a shade tree in the Spencers' front yard. Brother Spencer was a preacher who didn't believe in taking money for his services. Ornan chased him around the tree trying to pay him $2, but he never took it.

On April 23, 1937, Ornan and Dorothy had a baby girl they named Bobbie Carlene. In the early part of 1938, they decided to

Pearl Allen Andree

move to Arizona, as the other boys had already done. Sybil had also gone there and was working for a doctor in Phoenix. On Bobbie Carlene's first birthday, she was a healthy, charming one-year-old. She played with her Grandma Maud's long braids as if they were reins on a horse, calling, "Horsie, horsie, giddy up." Dorothy was in the process of weaning her from the breast.

Unfortunately, the living conditions left much to be desired. There was the Arizona heat, already high in April, plus flies that were difficult to keep out of the house. A couple of days after her birthday, Bobbie became sick with diarrhea. They took her to a doctor who recommended mashed bananas and scraped apple, and Sybil's employer insisted she should be put in hospital. Nothing helped. Five days after her first birthday, she died of diarrhea and dehydration. At that time, many similar deaths gave Arizona the highest infant mortality rate in the nation. Bobbie was the first (and for many years, the only) Allen grandchild to die. Dorothy blamed herself for trying to wean the baby too soon.

The funeral was held in the parlor of the local mortuary in Phoenix, and the baby was buried in Greenwood Cemetery. That funeral was one of the saddest events that anyone could have experienced. The family sat around the parlor while the words were said that would not bring peace to their hearts for years to come. Ornan and Dorothy left Arizona for California to wander, camping sometimes under bridges, looking for work and for solace. Ornan lost that carefree, fun-loving part of his heart for a long time to come. He was restless, unable to enjoy or find humor in life. Going to the cemetery with Dorothy to visit the grave was not something he could do.

In March 1939, they were back in Mesa, Arizona, and Dorothy gave birth to their first son, Terrell Wayne. Dorothy determined not to try weaning her children for two years. On March 30, 1941, another boy was born, Jimmie Robert. On March 10, 1946, another boy, Bill, was added to the fold, and on June 4, 1950, Phillip. Some years later, they finally had another girl, Lorraine.

Ornan gradually regained his jovial personality. With a house full of boisterous boys, how could he not? During the

Maud and Pearl

years of WWII, he worked at Goodyear Aircraft as a jig builder, where he received appreciation and respect for his ability to solve problems others thought were unsolvable.

In the summer of 1944, Ornan, Zeke Jr., and Pete began to realize they had put off for too long the teaching of their children about God, Christ, and the church. They decided to start having Sunday services, and it was decided Ornan's house would be the place. Their house was small, and the living room had a double bed in it, along with a dresser. Somehow, they acquired folding chairs and found out about a young man who would come from Phoenix to give a sermon on Sundays.

The preacher, Robert Hawkins, and his wife, Jody, came for the day, had dinner at one of the four houses (Grandma, Pearl, and Alma were in the fourth house), and officiated at a Sunday evening service. Robert had gone to Abilene Christian College in Texas for one year and had married Jody at the end of the year. Ornan's sister Pearl took the children into the kitchen for a Sunday school lesson and his brother Pete led the singing. Dorothy's parents and Sybil lived next door, and two ladies from rural farms that Maud had known came to worship with them. They had been raised in the church but for years had been isolated and unable to attend. As visiting preacher, Robert was paid $25, stayed for dinner, and had some afternoon rest.

Robert was not healthy, and in August 1944, he was diagnosed with tuberculosis. He had to have bed rest for a year. They found another young man, Ray Rayburn, who, like Robert, had attended Abilene and married the previous June. He agreed to take over from Robert with the same arrangements. Sometime during the next year, the Allens and the Browns bought a building and moved into the larger space.

The brothers Leo, Zeke Jr., and Pete had built their houses within a block of each other. The family eventually referred to the area as "Allen's Alley." After WWII ended and Goodyear Aircraft closed, they went back to traveling to California for part of the year for the seasonal work, packing vegetables and making the boxes in which to pack them. The children stayed the greater part

Pearl Allen Andree

of the year in Tolleson schools. Since there were two seasons for lettuce, the fall and spring served this purpose.

When Pearl married Jimmy Goggin in May 1945, Ornan gave her away. A few years later, he also gave his niece Jenny away. He was teased that for a man with no daughters, he gave away a few.

Dorothy's parents and Sybil lived next door to Ornan and Dorothy in Tolleson. Sybil was struck with a debilitating condition that eventually made her bed-ridden, and Dorothy grieved again when they had to hospitalize Sybil. In 1958, their son Terrell was diagnosed with esophageal cancer and had to have major surgery. In Phoenix, the procedure took nine hours. He had a scar from neck to waist and over to his left side, and it was one of the first times that surgery had been accomplished there.

In March 1961, when Lorraine was born, she helped heal many empty places in their hearts. Of course, Dorothy was very protective of her. When Lorraine was a teen, she found the perfect gift to give her mother. It was a wood carving with the astute message, "I'll never get lost; There'll always be someone to tell me where to go." She watched her brothers work on cars and other rough-and-tumble activities through the years.

The Saint and the Counselor

At age sixteen, I flew like a cannonball out of my home and landed at Uncle Ornan and Aunt Dorthy's house for the summer of 1965. Hospitality seemed to be the middle name of each of them. I was glad. It was a summer I've never forgotten.

Aunt Dorothy was generally taciturn, often appearing stern. After she said what she needed or wanted to say and went busily on, she spoke in a characteristic trailing, low-toned muttering that had an emphatic "Listen here, Buster" sound.

Her sense of duty wasn't her choice, it was her essence. She didn't question her tasks nor the material shortages to do them with, nor the inconveniences or hardships endured as she did them.

Before and after that time, she was the primary caretaker for the severely ill and disabled within her family, whom she loved. She simply showed up, filled the room with her saintliness, and stayed. When Grandma visited that summer, I saw a prelude of what was to come.

For the time that she spent attending at home and at bedside, no one except Ornan could keep up or continue assisting alongside her, such that she became one of the Allen family legends.

It's practically unimaginable that as a young mother she had lost her precious first child, one-year-old Bobbie Carlene, to acute fulminant infection, and survived the torment of that. But she had, and she went on to have a large family and a long life.

Dorothy and Ornan were always poor. She could cook something from nothing, superbly. Relatives dreamed about eating her wonderful pies, as I did. Not having enough money was obviously frustrating and worrisome to her at times. Still, her religious nature remained embedded, as did her principles about what was good, what was right, and basic values. She was the Saint of Example.

Also innately religious, Uncle Ornan had the classic type-B personality, without a sense of hurry or urgency. This, despite a long life of hard work, a generally limited income, and difficulty making ends meet. In theory he could be vexed or irritated and even angered, but in reality that was a rarity.

Through his myriad jobs, employers, and coworkers, he had many life experiences. With a sound mechanical mind and quick hands, in the melon sheds he took the older, slower box-making machine while Pete used the newer one.

Once settled in their new home in Ashland, Oregon, Ornan inherited a large garden in the backyard and grew luscious, large Beefsteak tomatoes and a bountiful grape arbor, among other things.

When it happened, I had a glimpse of a bygone era, an indelible memory for me. Uncle Ornan was leaning on the fence talking to his neighbor, who was partially obscured. Occasional snippets of the exchange revealed that his neighbor was upset and negative about a number of things. Ornan responded in a consoling tone, several times offering his characteristic declaration, "Lord have mercy!"

What actually happened? Uncle Ornan listened a lot, and patiently. He conveyed compassion. Whatever his own views, he showed tolerance of his neighbor's. I realized that Uncle Ornan had made the choice to be helpful and caring to his neighbor.

Danny Goggin, Pearl and Jimmy's son, an Allen cousin

"What'd You Boys Do?!"

THIS happened to my cousin Danny and me in the summer of 1965. Knowing that accurately recalling events from that time would be impossible, I will try anyway. It's wonderful to think of the experiences of my youth. My father, Ornan, would call me a rapscallion at times. This event would certainly have earned me the title of rascal. Danny may have earned the rascal title also, but I admit I may have talked him into something we both knew we shouldn't be doing.

Family was everything at this time of my teenage life. Grandmother Allen and Cousin Danny were visiting in the summer of 1965, making times even more exciting. My mother, Dorothy, was intent on being a good host. She wanted to treat her guests to experiences unique to southwestern Oregon. This particular day she decided to make blackberry cobblers or pies. Cousin Danny and I were delegated to fetch the berries. With the smells coming from her kitchen, how could any teen of right mind deny the request?

Danny drove the car as he was 17 with a driver's license and I was 15 with the job of navigator. I am not so sure we dressed appropriately for the occasion. I think I wore my usual summer attire of a T-shirt, Levi cutoffs, and tennis shoes. The invasive blackberries of western Oregon have thorns. These thorns made the berries very hard to pick. I was told to direct Danny to an area my mother and I had gone previously. My navigation was not perfect, but we ended up in the general area my mother was talking about.

We found a promising spot, so we stopped to check the berries. As we looked down the ravine, we felt we had found blackberry paradise. Rays of sun twinkled through the clouds and trees, highlighting huge blackberries everywhere. We grabbed our picking pails and set to work.

As can be expected, we had to taste some of those huge blackberries. That was a mistake! They were so juicy, so sweet, and so hard to resist eating. More berries were going down our hatches than into our pails. After eating so many berries and being stuck with so many thorns, we made a change of plans. It was time to go home with our less than bountiful harvest.

Needless to say, Mom was less than impressed with our blackberry picking expertise. To our relief, Mom, without stern admonishment, killed us with kindness. She said, "I have some green grapes. I'll just make pie with them." She did and it was fabulous. On that day and many others, Danny and I were touched by the kindness of an angel, which was my mother.

Phill Allen, Ornan and Dorothy's son, an Allen cousin

Letter to a Cousin Back Home

3rd Marine Division C Company San Francisco
Da Nang, Viet Nam

Thanksgiving, November 24, 1966

Dear Danny,

    I hope college has started out okay for you.
    I've been here a short while, but there's no doubt this is war. I've been in the vicinity of death and seen some bad injuries. Some close calls for me, too.
    I'm in a motor transport battalion for supply line, moving food and ammo from the port up toward Phu Bai.
    Jim called me recently on a special phone line, but I was in combat getting shot at, so I couldn't talk!
    Here is where you see history, that mankind keeps messing up peace with hate and lust for power.
    It's strange to think, since we are not that old, that I may not make it home alive. I love MaryEllon and want to be with her again.
    I have my hope and faith in God. I think about the blessings we have that God has given us. Keep this in mind, Danny, and I look forward to seeing you again.
    Pray for me. I need that.

Your cousin, Bill

William H. (Bill) Allen, Ornan and Dorothy's son, an Allen cousin

Pearl Allen Andree

Postscript: Bill Allen was injured and came home. He married MaryEllon, and they had four children. He finished college and had a career in business and finance management. He was a church leader. Married 52 years, he passed away after illnesses of multiple myeloma and recurrent metastatic melanoma in 2021.

Maud and Pearl

~~~

After Dorothy's parents and Sybil passed away, Ornan and Dorothy decided to pull up stakes and move to Ashland, Oregon. They were able to buy a historical house and some apartments near Lithia Park, where the Shakespearean Festival was held each year. For a few years, Ornan worked at the County Courthouse in Medford. Their children loved living in that place. In fact, Bill gave Ornan the impetus to stay there when he remarked to his dad, "I'd like to stay here," when they were in the park one day.

In January 1966, Maud had a stroke and was not able to live alone. She spent about a year with her daughter Alma in Texas and then went to stay with Ornan and Dorothy in Ashland. Again Dorothy was a caretaker, and a better one could not have been found. The rest of the family came to visit Maud and sometimes spell Ornan and Dorothy so they could have a little trip, usually a fishing trip.

Ornan could still walk on his hands at 75, plus climb a tree to pick big juicy blackberries from the vines that had also climbed the tree. Dorothy, however, began to have trouble with her arthritic knees. It was difficult for him to convince her they needed to put Maud in a rest home, but she finally realized it was necessary. Maud was about 92 when she entered a nursing home right across the street from the church building. Dorothy visited at odd times and let them know her thoughts on keeping Maud dressed and clean, especially on Sunday mornings when she wheeled her across the street for services. On Sunday, August 14, 1977, Dorothy noticed Maud was not feeling well (Maud could not talk at that time). When she returned Maud to the home, she told them they needed to have a doctor check her out. Maud had pneumonia and passed away on August 16. As it so happened, this was also the day Elvis Presley died. It was speculated that if he made it to the Jordan, Maud Allen would have taken his hand and walked him across. Every year when they celebrate at Graceland, a wonderful woman's life is also remembered by her family.

July 13, 1985 marked the fiftieth anniversary of Ornan and Dorothy. The years ahead were filled with enjoying their home and visiting with their children and grandchildren and a family

Pearl Allen Andree

reunion when the occasion presented itself. In 1986, Pearl was getting her longed-for degree in Tempe, Arizona and sent them an announcement. Ornan was legally blind and didn't drive, but he said, "You know, I'd like to go to that."

Dorothy responded with, "All right, let's go." She drove them from Ashland, Oregon to Tempe, Arizona, only to find that Pearl had not attended the big ceremony but rather a smaller one in the Fine Arts Theatre. Pearl explained over the phone the directions to her house, about twenty miles away. Unfortunately, Dorothy misunderstood the directions and mistakenly got on the freeway going in the wrong direction. She said to Ornan, "Why is everyone honking at me?"

He said, "You must not be going fast enough." It is not known how God directed them off that freeway and onto the right road, but they arrived at Pearl's unscathed. However, when their children heard about it, they considered it a wake-up call. When there was a family reunion two years later in Pinetop, Arizona, their granddaughter, Heather, drove them there. It began to be apparent that Dorothy was in the throes of Alzheimer's disease.

With live-in caregivers and son Bill taking over the finances, Ornan weathered this storm as he had other calamities. Dorothy passed away in December 1994, seven months before their 60th anniversary.

About this time, Bill's wife, MaryEllon, decided that now that their children were grown and going on with their lives, she would resuscitate her nursing skills and go to medical school to become a doctor. She was over 50 and was told acceptance into a medical school in the United States probably would not happen. Not being deterred, and with Bill's business profession on hiatus, she applied to the University of Mexico in Guadalajara and was accepted. They accepted the responsibility of caring for Ornan, pulled up stakes, and moved to Mexico. Bill spent time with his dad and tried business opportunities, while Mary studied medicine. Bill arranged for a real estate agent to sell the house and apartments in Ashland, bought a house in Guadalajara, and Ornan settled into Mexican life. The house was near a park and Ornan

Maud and Pearl

spent time there, walking with his two canes and communicating with people he met, in spite of the different language.

When Mary completed her medical school requirements, she did her residencies in Texas, so they returned to the States. Bill had worked into a business of his own, buying furniture and things in Mexico and shipping them to their daughter Becky, who had started a shop in Abilene called Relics. After San Antonio, Mary was doing a rotation in Abilene, and they had settled into a home life there. Ornan was living his indomitable life as always and getting older each year. Although legally blind and hard of hearing, he was always eager to go somewhere if it was suggested. One steadfast friend constantly was their little dog, Lucy. In October 2003, his four boys (Terrill, Jim, Bill, and Phillip) came to help him celebrate 96 years by taking him fishing.

MaryEllon and Bill saw to it that Ornan had the best of medical care, but in January 2004, doctors diagnosed him with esophageal cancer and predicted he would only have a few more weeks. He was in the hospital where Mary was working, and they brought Lucy to keep him company. His boys and Lorraine came to be with him, and when nieces and nephews found out the situation, they came too. His sister Pearl was in the area, and she came to Abilene to visit one last time. He was like a potentate enjoying his subjects as Lucy lay on the foot of his bed. Someone was always available to take Lucy for a walk and see that she had food and water.

Years before, Bill had asked his dad where he wanted to be buried, and Ornan specified Ashland, where Dorothy was laid to rest. Bill found out that air transport was exorbitantly expensive. The mortician told Bill it was still legal for family members to transport the deceased. Since Bill owned a large four-door pickup, they put Ornan's casket in the bed of the pickup. This man who had traveled all over the western part of the country finding work in his younger years during the Great Depression traveled to his eternal destination in splendor. Bill, Mary, their son B. J., and Lucy occupied the spacious cab, and they took Ornan on his last trip to Ashland, Oregon from Abilene, Texas. Riding shotgun in nephew Dick Curtis' car was Ornan's son, Jim.

Pearl Allen Andree

Ornan's funeral in Oregon was like a family reunion. His life was celebrated in style. Lucy joined the mourners at the cemetery, walking around as if saying goodbye to her friend.

Ornan and Dorothy were a couple "without a lot of money because they had given so much away." Dorothy had cared for so many others after Bobbie's tragic loss—Sybil, Maud, and of course her own children. Ornan and Dorothy's door was always open, and they always loved having company. Together, they modeled universal things to the grandchildren's generation, the Allen cousins. Richness wasn't something you had around you that others saw; rather, richness was what you were made of inside.

Zeke Jr.

(Note: he was named after his father with no middle name. The family does not know if his given name was Ezekiel Allen, or Ezekiel Allen Jr. Informally as he grew up and for the purpose of contrast, family and friends called him Zekie or Zeke Jr. Before and after his father was gone, he too was called Zeke or EZ. For this section, Ezekiel is Dad and his son will be referred to as Zeke Jr. or Zeke.)

EZEKIEL Jr. was born June 30, 1909. He was the baby for two years and had to be taken care of or watched by his older siblings. As he grew older, Maud encouraged him, as she did the other children, to sing and play a musical instrument. The instrument she chose for him was the harmonica. He lost interest in it and wasn't interested in singing. His talent lay in the direction of memory, learning dramatic poems and saying them with flair.

Like Ornan, Zeke boarded at the Catholic school in Chickasha, Oklahoma for a few months in elementary school. He was good at sports and in high school he excelled at playing football. He set some records that were not broken even by the early 1940s.

Zeke had a winsome personality but developed some bad habits that he dealt with throughout the years. He began smoking in late childhood and continued for the rest of his life. He smoked sometimes secretively, if not slyly, because his family persisted in trying to get him to stop. Some of his high school friends were not the best influence, and when the Depression hit and there was no work, he did some bootlegging with them. Unfortunately, he began to drink but kept that hidden, too.

In 1930, he was 21 and found it impossible to get a job. His solution was to travel to Little Rock, Arkansas, where Grandpa Robert Allen had a construction company. There were also cousins in his age bracket with whom he could socialize. One weekend, one of them asked if he would like to go up in the mountains (the Ozarks) and meet some of his other cousins. Zeke was glad for the opportunity. They had a car, but there weren't many roads at that time, so they had to park and walk up and down the hills. Coming to a flat meadow area, they heard a shot. The cousin halted their trek. After a while, they heard another shot. The cousin said, "Okay, let's go."

Zeke responded, "Whoa, what do you mean? There's someone out there shooting at us!"

The cousin replied, "Oh, that was just the 12-year-old lookout. If they didn't want you here, you wouldn't have heard the second shot."

Zeke was handsome with movie-star good looks. He had the "Allen eyelashes"—long, black, and curled. The family was acquainted with the Spencer family in Rush Springs. Brother Spencer was the preacher Leo had studied the Bible with. When Zeke came back to Oklahoma, he began visiting the Spencers on their 160-acre farm. The attraction was a daughter named Ellen, a pretty auburn-haired girl about four years younger than Zeke.

It isn't known whether one or both were afraid of Mr. Spencer's reaction, but Zeke and Ellen eloped to get married and kept it quiet for a while. When their friends found out, they insisted on a shivaree. The couple tried to hide from their friends, even hiding behind the couch in the living room, which was placed at an angle, leaving a space big enough to hide in. Zeke's little sister Pearl was worried and sat in the room trying not to say anything. She had heard the grown-ups tell of scary things happening at shivarees, like dumb practical jokes being played on the bride and groom. Fortunately, when they were found, the friends just partied with them.

Maud and Pearl

Their first child was born on August 13, 1934. They named her Rita Jo. She was a beautiful little girl with blond curly hair and big brown eyes that possessed those Allen eyelashes. Zeke worked on farms, and for a while they had a small, furnished, two-room house as part of their pay.

In 1936, at the beginning of the summer, Zeke's sister, nine-year-old Pearl, visited for a week. Ellen was sick in the mornings, so Zeke got up and fixed breakfast after taking some saltine crackers to her. One morning he was making pancakes, and while he was turned away, Rita, not quite two, reached up and clasped the batter bowl, bringing it down onto her head, batter and all. She got a spanking, and Pearl felt so sorry for her that the incident was recorded for posterity in a penny postcard to her mama.

Zeke and Ellen decided to take a chance on moving to Arizona. Zeke had traveled some out west, as his brothers had, and was sure he could find work there and hopefully improve their income.

Leo was in Borger, Texas at their sister Alma's, and Zeke and family picked Leo up to accompany them. They had very little money and Leo spent his last 42 cents on a lot of bananas. That irritated Ellen, as she felt they should use the money for more practical things. They found cotton fields after entering Arizona, and Leo and Zeke picked cotton for a few days. Zeke didn't like picking cotton and figured they surely could find different work, so they moved on. At one point, Ellen spent their last ten cents on a tall can of Campbell's soup. Zeke felt it was good to spend it on something to eat, even though it was all they had at that time.

A daughter, Carol Lou, was born that November while they were living in Tolleson, Arizona, the Lettuce Capital of the World.

Pete and Zeke and their wives were now living in Arizona much of the time, in "cabin courts"—the motels of that time. One day, Ellen and Dorothy had to do some shopping and left Rita with her daddy, who was outside doing some work. The time was getting near supper time and Rita, at the age of five, decided it must be her responsibility to fix dinner. She had watched her mother make biscuits, so that's what she did. They were in the

Pearl Allen Andree

pan, ready to go into the oven, when she realized she didn't know how to turn the stove on. She knew to go outside and ask her daddy to come and start the oven! The biscuits were quite good. This may have been a harbinger for the future. She never lost her talent for cooking. Later in life, she was a major chef at family reunions and church camps.

It was apparently in this period that something life-changing occurred for Zeke (concealed for decades). He woke up intoxicated on the couch, discovered by his girls and clearly upsetting Ellen as well. He decided not to drink again, and he did not. The lone exception was making a hot toddy when someone was ill. He kept a bottle of whiskey in the icebox as a reminder of his decision.

There were two seasons for lettuce, fall and spring. The brothers found work—they were familiar with farm work—and they packed the lettuce in wooden crates in the big sheds close to the railroad tracks. At the busiest times, they worked 12 hours a day. Those times were called "being in the snow." Thanksgiving nearly always found them at this busiest time. Their wives had dinner ready so the brothers could hurriedly come home to eat and go back to work for the rest of the day.

During the off-season, they traveled to California for work packing melons, fruit, and vegetables. The workers who did this were called fruit tramps. Because the brothers were good workers and learned quickly, they gradually became box-makers. The crates were made on machines, and they became proficient at this. Later, the brothers were upgraded to carpenters. They were able to buy lots and build houses on them in Tolleson.

"We Were Broke, and I Mean Broke!"

ZEKE and I were secretly married in October 1933 and were discovered after our marriage license was found by his mother. By then, I was pregnant with Rita, who was born August 13, 1934.

Because it was the middle of the Depression, work was hard to come by in our area of Marlow-Rush Springs, Oklahoma. Zeke had previously found work in Arizona and wanted to return there. In early 1936, we traveled with 18-month-old Rita. I was pregnant with Carol. We picked up Leo on the way out of the state.

What little money we had was spent on food as we camped out in the elements along the way. We were broke, but made it to Buckeye, Arizona and the men got work in a cotton-picking camp. Nothing derogatory, that's what it was called. But Zeke got tired fast of cotton, so we went on to Tolleson to work in the lettuce fields.

Soon after, Pete came, followed later by his wife Dorothy and their daughter Dawn. In September, my daddy sent my older brother, Ed, to check on me. He worked picking cotton, but he later left it too. Zeke, Rita, and I had a one-bedroom house, and Ed slept in the garage.

I began labor with Carol and drove to the lettuce fields to get Zeke to help with the birth. Carol was born at home on November 10, 1936. Zeke left to seek a job with the All American Canal in Yuma, but the hiring was corrupt and he didn't have a good feeling about it. I stayed behind with my brother Ed and the two girls.

Money stayed scarce, so Zeke's next stop in seeking a job was in Kanab, Utah. We stayed there for several weeks. We left with

Pearl Allen Andree

$12, using one of them to fill up our tank with gas, and returned to Tolleson!

Back in Tolleson, we were delighted to see Monk (Ornan) and Dorothy again. They left California to join the rest of the family. We were family and in the hard times we found ourselves together in Tolleson. Many good memories were made during those hard times.

In Oklahoma, another story was happening: Grandpa and Grandma Allen had separated. Grandma was hurting and Pearl probably didn't know. I wrote and asked her to come and join us in Arizona, which she did.

We would stay nearly broke for awhile, but we made "nearly broke" stretch.

Ellen Spencer Allen, Zeke Jr.'s wife, an Allen daughter-in-law

Maud and Pearl

~~~

Zeke once told his son Earl, "In March of 1942, Daddy became deathly ill. All of us brothers had more or less disavowed him after he divorced Mama. Word came that he wished the family would visit. We were reluctant, but decided one of us should go, and Ornan was the one chosen."

Earl later reported, "As I was growing up, Dad said a number of times that he regretted having not gone himself. It was clear that it remained a lament for him."

The year after Pearl Harbor was bombed, 1942, Zeke and Ellen added a son to their family. Ellen didn't want to be pressured into naming him Ezekiel because she didn't want people to call him Zekie. She wanted to name him Glenn Earl. Mama wanted them to name him Ezekiel, and in the excitement of the new brother, Zeke asked Rita, "Wouldn't you like for your brother to be named for your daddy?"

Innocently she answered "Yes," and Ellen finally consented to naming him Ezekiel Earl, demanding he be known as Earl. That was all right with everyone except Mama. She did call him Zekie.

During WWII, Ornan, Zeke, and Pete all had jobs at Goodyear Aircraft. Whether or not this oral tradition is true, Earl recalled that Zeke once told him that Leo "had words" with the draft board chairman. "Dad said Uncle Leo put the fear of God in the man, that he would go into the Navy, but none of the three brothers would be called up."

During the war, the children spent the whole school year in Tolleson. In the summer of 1944, Zeke participated in establishing the local congregation of the church. The family took turns having the minister for Sunday dinner. One Sunday, by way of apology (not for the cooking, as the Allen women outshone all others in culinary arts), Zeke told the preacher, "It isn't much, but if we can stand it all of the time, you can stand it part of the time." This came from a man who entertained family and friends from time to time with the dramatic regaling of poems like "Dangerous Dan

Pearl Allen Andree

McGrew," "The Face on the Bar Room Floor," "Casey at the Bat," and similar works of literature.

One of Zeke's post-war jobs in Tolleson was interesting: running a city garbage crew that used prisoners. About that, he said, "I didn't carry a gun because I was afraid the prisoners might make me eat it!"

After the war, Zeke and Ellen decided to move back to Oklahoma. They went back to Tolleson for a family visit in 1950. Rita had been baptized in Tolleson when she was twelve, as had other young people. One of these was Gary Lauer, who lived next door to her aunt Pearl. A large family group was at Pearl and Jimmy's one day, including Leo and his wife, Ornan and his family, and Pete and his family, along with Maud and Alma and her family. Rita was now a pretty sixteen-year-old, even wearing the ring of a boyfriend from back home. Gary had grown to be a tall, good-looking boy, and an old crush resurfaced.

The nieces, including Rita and Carol, and other church teens asked if they could have a party. The girls would bake cookies and the boys would crank the (homemade ice cream) freezer. The hot August day required the evaporative cooling system to run full time. The girls baked the cookies before Alma, Pearl, and Jimmy started making tacos in the kitchen. They planned a noon meal for about thirty people, including the younger children, who were running in and out the front door.

The kitchen crew was sweating profusely, trying unsuccessfully to get the children to stop opening the front door so the air could be drawn through the kitchen by the back door window. Pearl was seven months pregnant with Pat but didn't think that would cause Jimmy and Alma to be so hot. The cause finally became apparent when they realized that after the cookies had been baked, the girls, instead of turning the oven off, had turned the knob the wrong direction, to the highest temperature! The cookies were delicious, though, as was the ice cream, so the party was a success.

Ellen was carrying that Oklahoma boy's ring in her purse so it wouldn't get lost. Gary was a Boy Scout, and the following May he was participating in their Memorial Day activity of parking cars

Maud and Pearl

at nearby Luke Air Force Base when he collapsed at about 5:00 p.m. with polio. He had to be in an iron lung machine for eight months and lived another eight years. His Christian life touched many and was the model for a minister friend's writing a piece on "Why Must We Suffer?"

The family continued to live permanently in Oklahoma City.

Earl once told a story about when he was a young child:

> Grandma had come to visit us in the early 1950s, maybe the fall of 1952, and she stayed with us one or two weeks. Rita Jo had gone off to college and Carol Lou was in high school. I walked home from grade school to eat lunch, latchkey. There was Grandma.
>
> I said, "I'm hungry."
>
> Grandma said, "There's lima beans on the stove."
>
> What I wanted was a peanut butter sandwich. So I said, "I don't like them."
>
> Grandma responded, "Then you're not hungry."
>
> I ate those beans because I was hungry. I still don't like lima beans, but I'll eat them if I'm really hungry. I think Grandma taught me a lesson to take what's available and be happy that you got it.

Zeke and Ellen went on to have varied yet complementary work careers. He always had a spark of entrepreneurial spirit. Fancy that! As time passed, Zeke, who had a number of sales jobs, would create an idea of selling specialized products to niche markets, like cleaning products such as ScotchKlean, or janitorial supplies to bowling alleys. When things did not pan out, he returned to employment and paid back his debts. Ellen went to work at John A. Brown Company (later bought by Dillard's) and later worked for First American Title, where she was working at the time she retired.

Rita Jo attended Abilene Christian College in Abilene, Texas, excelling in theatre arts. She married Bill Grieb, a veterinarian. Carol Lou married Harry Canning, and Earl joined the Air Force after graduation from high school. Earl was stationed in Germany when he met Christa, an East German girl, but he had to get permission from his commanding officer before getting married. This permission hinged on Zeke's permission. Zeke did not consent to the marriage, but Earl waited till his maturity age and married her anyway. Christa came to the United States with her husband.

Their family grew with the arrival of grandchildren. Bill and Rita Jo had Allen, Jo Ellen, and Matthew; Carol Lou and Harry had Susan, Richard, and Karen; Earl and Christa had Esther and Heidi.

Zeke (and Ellen as well) was wise and witty. On several occasions, he took Earl along to visit a friend who was an immigrant blacksmith with a heavy Scandinavian accent and an old country way of talking. The blacksmith's name is unknown. Amazingly talented, he had heating methods to make fireplace irons in a variety of colors. Zeke's quote of the blacksmith was, "Don't ask me, 'can I?' Just tell me vhat you vant." The gentleman gave Zeke and Earl a special gift, a ball peen hammer initialed and engraved with the date 1820, which Earl has kept.

One quip of Zeke's that he often repeated was, "Figures don't lie, but liars figure."

In March 1973, Danny was staying with Zeke and Ellen while doing a clerkship at St. Anthony Hospital. He learned his internship match was not his first choice and reacted very disappointedly. Zeke consoled him with support and by quoting Robert Frost's poem, "The Road Not Taken," in which the one less traveled made "all the difference."

Zeke was religiously faithful throughout his life and had leadership roles in his church congregations. To Maud, he was always loyal and attentive, making episodic trips to see her in Arizona and Texas and, together with Ellen, hosting her in their home from time to time. Before she left Alma and Lee's home near Sunray and went to Oregon to stay with Ornan and Dorothy, Maud was visited by Zeke and Ellen. At one point, she tried to say something, thought it came out funny, and began laughing

Maud and Pearl

so hard that she became tearful. Alma came over and interpreted, explaining, "Tears don't mean that you're hurt." Everyone laughed.

Post-retirement, Ellen worked in sales at the Dillard's in a nearby mall. Zeke and Bill tried their hands at hydroponic gardening in their own greenhouse, raising many crops of beautiful tomatoes. Zeke's smoking became a health issue. He lessened the amount he smoked but developed an aneurysm, emphysema, and eventually a heart condition. In December 1987, he died at the age of 78.

To Ellen from Pearl: A Birthday Note

I KEPT a copy of this greeting to my sister-in-law Ellen, which referenced some happenings and memories from my growing up years. In doing so, I combined my childhood and my adult perspectives about her, reflecting on the quality of the person that she was.

~~~

I was six when you, Ellen, and Zeke were married. You were my first sister-in-law. I remember you and Zeke hiding behind the couch from your friends at your shivaree. I was frightened for you, afraid that you might be thrown in the lake or something like that.

I remember visiting your mother at the Spencer home. While Mom (Maud) and Mrs. Spencer visited, Oleta played with me, I think in a sand pile. At any rate, she was very nice to me.

I thought your hair was the most beautiful color, and I wished I could grow up to have the same color hair.

When Rita was born, you lived in that little house across the creek from us, and I loved going to visit. Your home was always immaculate, but comfortable, too.

A child can usually recognize when adults don't want him or her around. Never did I sense that in you.

There was the week I visited with you on a farm where Zeke worked. That was when Rita pulled a bowl of pancake batter down on top of herself. When older, I realized you were in that first few months of pregnancy with Carol. For years I kept a postcard you wrote to me that summer before I visited you.

Maud and Pearl

Growing up, I couldn't have had a better role model.

Jimmy and I, and then Bill and I, have enjoyed many an excellent meal and beautiful hospitality in your home—the most recent about three years ago. I wish I could be there for this Big Birthday Shindig.

HAVE A GREAT ONE!

Martha

AFTER losing little Effie, Maud had those four boys and then, at long last, she had another baby girl. Martha Amanda was born on July 29, 1911. With four older brothers, Martha was to have a lively personality.

When Martha was five, Maud was told by her doctor to cut her own long hair in order to relieve her severe headaches. Since it was the current fashion, Martha begged to have her hair cut also. A few days later, she begged again—to have it reattached!

It was at this age that she had a little girlfriend who invited her to go to church at the Baptist Church during a revival meeting. The song leader asked if there were any hymn requests from the audience. She and her friend were sitting on the front row, and Martha piped up, "Could you sing 'Little Liza Jane,' please?"

Martha was a beautiful child, and as she grew into her teen years this became quite apparent to the boys who came to the house with her brothers. Leo recalled, "She was the prettiest girl in Marlow at age 14 in 1925—too pretty for her own good. All the boys chased her, such that she might have gotten an elevated view of herself."

Zeke, especially, being only two years older, had many friends attracted to her. One boy particularly was smitten. His last name was Townsend, and his nickname was Tinky. He must have had a charismatic personality because he was able to persuade Martha to elope and get married. Since this was the roaring 20s and Martha had discovered that she enjoyed dancing and having a good time, Tinky must not have had much trouble with the persuasion.

Maud and Pearl

The mystery remains as to why Maud and EZ didn't have the marriage annulled. They had both grown up in a period of time when early marriages were not uncommon, and regardless of her heartbreak, Maud would have hoped the union would last: a "what's done is done and there's no going back" idea. Maud was very angry, however, at the Baptist preacher for marrying them. "He knew better than to do that. He just wanted that five dollars."

In July 1926, Martha turned 15 and had finished her sophomore year in high school. She started working at the telephone office to make a home for herself and help support Tink, who was a freshman that fall at Oklahoma University in Norman. Martha decided to surprise him with a visit. She was surprised to find him with another girl. The marriage had lasted six months when they divorced, and Martha's life moved on.

The family had a busy year in 1926. Leo, Ira, and Ornan (Monk) were in the working world, Zeke was still in high school, and Maud was pregnant with her ninth child.

The year 1927 became traumatic and tragic. Ira was killed in January, and in March, Maud had her baby, a girl she named Iralene Pearl.

Martha met Babe Robertson, and they were married in December 1929, just after the big market crash. EZ and Maud didn't like that and wouldn't have much to do with the young couple for a while, but soon everything was fine. His full name was Henry Earnest Robertson, but the nickname was the name by which he was known.

Babe was a farmer and had been married and divorced. He had a daughter who lived with her mother, but no one in the family knew this, not even his and Martha's children, until much later in life. There was a possibility that the girl was actually the child of a married brother and that Babe's marriage to the girl's mother was to save the brother's marriage.

Babe liked to play the fiddle, and his cousin played the guitar at country dances. Martha loved to dance, and they made a good match. The country dances were held in closed school buildings, along with pie suppers. They married in Jacksboro, Texas in November 1929 but were concerned the marriage might not be legal. They married again in Duncan, Oklahoma on December 16, 1929, making sure it was legal this time.

Babe, the youngest in his family, had grown up farming Robertson land near Marlow with his father. Because of the Depression and the Dust Bowl years, part of this land had to go back to the bank. After this, Martha and Babe moved east from Marlow to the Bray community and farmed.

Their first child was the first Allen grandchild, a boy they named Charles Walter. In childhood, he was called Sonny Boy or sometimes just Son. He was born on December 16, 1930.

Babe was good at farming, and he and Martha worked hard to provide as well as possible during those years of the Great Depression. Their second child was Margaret Louise, born October 25, 1932. Nicknames were becoming a family tradition, and since Sonny Boy couldn't pronounce her name and was cautioned to "Be careful with your baby sister; she's just a little tot," that's what he called her. This was shortened to Totsy and became her name throughout the family and through the years. Even in her eighties, cousins still used the name, especially at family reunions.

Parents and Grandparents

MY MOTHER had the unfortunate experience of being a very mature and attractive teenager who fell head over heels for an older gadabout, married him, but had to divorce soon after. Grandpa and Grandma both supported her lovingly during this difficult time. She married my father, Babe Robertson, in 1929. My dad was the opposite of fly-around: he was steady, principled, and diligent about work.

Mama once told me a story that Daddy had told her. First I have to say, my daddy really liked Grandma Allen—which was interesting, because Mama was known to have felt that at various times as she grew up, Grandma seemed to favor the boys.

It was true that Daddy later helped Grandma get out to Arizona, where she wanted to be. We lived there briefly, too, before returning to Oklahoma. Daddy made the remark, "I can starve better in Oklahoma than I can in Arizona."

In this story, Daddy made observations about Grandpa on an occasion when the Allen family gathered for a meal. Daddy himself had grown up the youngest of six brothers whose father was a farmer. He saw Grandpa as a dreamer, but also one who busily planned, made decisions, and acted on them. Everyone was in the kitchen, Grandma was hard at work cooking, and Grandpa was talking with the boys. He had known Grandpa little himself, but knew Grandpa had done some things successfully and had also failed at times. He saw that Grandpa was a man who had achieved things his way.

      Margaret (Totsy) Robertson Scott,
      Martha and Babe's daughter, an Allen cousin

Pearl Allen Andree

~~~

On January 13, 1935, another girl was born, and they named her Martha Anne. True to form, this became Mart-an and then Tanny, the nickname that followed her through life.

Babe and Martha visited the rest of the family on the 20 acres from time to time. Babe, whose honed barbering skills later gained area renown, and my brothers and EZ cut each other's hair, saving the two bits (25 cents) they'd have to pay a barber.

It was during this period that Babe accidentally stepped on a rusty nail. Strong men rarely went to a doctor; and besides, it cost money, so he ignored it until all indications were that it was extremely serious. Sure enough, by the time he saw a doctor, his foot had turned gangrenous and there was some possibility it would have to be amputated. He had to use crutches until they were able to fight the infection enough for him to be out of danger of losing his foot.

Maud, of course, loved having them visit. When Tanny was about six months old, Martha had to have surgery and Maud took care of the children, especially Tanny. It was a time of canning for Maud, tomatoes in particular. Tanny could be seen sitting on the kitchen floor eating about as many as Grandma was canning. Her cheeks were red and looked like she had eaten so many they had become tomatoes.

The family made ice cream in the big gallon-sized buckets as often as possible, and Babe and Martha did the same at their house, having friends over to enjoy it with them. The morning after, there might be melted ice cream in the container and the children could have a milkshake. People didn't have refrigerators, just iceboxes, and it was difficult to buy ice in the country. Sometimes ice trucks came to rural areas, especially if they knew people who bought it as regularly as possible. Two big, twenty-five-pound blocks were needed for making ice cream.

Maud delighted in having her children and grandchildren around. Through these years, Alma and the boys were getting married and starting families. The Allen boys had decided to go west for work, so Babe and Martha decided to try it also since

Maud and Pearl

times remained bad in Oklahoma. They packed the truck with what they could and put a mattress in the bed of the truck for the kids. Since Maud had worried about Pearl's health for several years and knew the sun and climate would strengthen her, she prevailed on them to take her and Pearl with them. "Okies goin' West!"

They arrived in Tolleson, Arizona on December 16, 1937. Babe acquired work for someone on a farm right away, with a house on it all could move into. Charley, Totsy, and Pearl were enrolled in the three-room schoolhouse nearby. Totsy was just barely old enough to start first grade. By the end of the school year, Martha and Babe had decided Arizona was not for them, so they returned to Oklahoma in the summer of 1938. Maud and Pearl stayed in Tolleson.

After they moved back, Babe and Martha lived at the Allen place in Marlow. Then they both worked a stint at the Sale Barn there, Babe in sales and Martha cooking and running the concession on sale days. A year and a half later, they moved back to Bray and Babe farmed land owned by Mr. Hitchcock. In the 1940s, they bought 180 acres from him for $5,000 and the mineral rights for 120 acres of it. They grew watermelons, corn, cotton, broomcorn, and peanuts, plus raised milk cows and chickens. Babe added part-time welding and carpentry work.

Mom, Dad, the Farm, and the Relatives

Picture this: a crying child, a doll with a broken nose, and my cousin Dawn holding a glass baby bottle. This is my earliest memory with my Allen family. When mentioning this to Mama, she said it happened during Christmas 1937, when we had just moved to Arizona. I was two years old, soon to be three in January. I was crying, brokenhearted because my cousin Dawn had broken my new doll's nose trying to feed it.

Another memory is of my Uncle Leo. I have a picture of us sitting on the running board of an old truck holding my doll on his knee. Mom said it was taken at the bus station where we'd taken him to go into the Navy. I was about eight years old. He wrote letters as he could, and when we received a letter it was a cropped photostatic copy. I thought of him more as a playmate than an uncle because he would talk to me and, more importantly, listen to me. I would tell him what to do. Then he asked me why he should have to listen to me. I would reply, "Because I'm the boss!" For the remainder of his life, he called me the boss. The last time I saw him was at Mom's funeral in November 1981. He still called me the boss! I listened to him and my dad talking late into the night as I fell asleep.

I didn't realize what a wonderful mom I had until I became a mom and found firsthand just how difficult it is being a mother! She worked alongside my dad in the fields, cooked for field hands, but most importantly, took care of her family. She sewed our clothes, worked to earn money to pay for our piano and drama lessons, and was a great cook and baker. She loved her ceramics and homemakers club, was in a bowling league, and loved to play golf.

Maud and Pearl

When I was around age four or five, Daddy had a billy goat large enough for me and my sister to ride. But that goat did not like Mama! One day, Mom and I had to go somewhere and as we were getting ready to go, she saw the goat had escaped his pen and was waiting by the front door. She did not want to get butted, so her plan was for us to stomp through the house to the back door, and when the goat went to the back door, we would tiptoe back to the front door and run for the truck. Well, that goat was back at the front door waiting for us. I don't even remember if we ever made it to the truck. I just remember us laughing till we cried!

I have a sweet memory about cousin Jenny, Aunt Alma, and Uncle Lee. Our parents liked to get together and play cards or dominoes, so Jenny and I would play until we fell asleep. One night at our house, Jenny and I thought it would be fun to swap clothes. When Uncle Lee and Aunt Alma left, they picked up sleeping Jenny, went home, and put her to bed. The next morning I woke up wondering why I was at Jenny's house! I walked to the kitchen where Uncle Lee and Aunt Alma were eating breakfast. Uncle Lee said in his booming voice, "What the hell are you doing here?" They took me home and collected Jenny. My parents may not have discovered the swap until then. Jenny also gave me my nickname. We were close in age and learning to talk at the same time. She tried to say Martha Anne and those garbled words became Tanny!

These early stories began my lifetime of wonderful Allen family memories.

Martha Anne (Tanny) Robertson D'Orville,
Martha and Babe's daughter, an Allen cousin

Wartime, 1941 to 1945

OUR family, like most families, after suppertime usually would gather around the radio in the evenings to listen to *Fibber McGee and Molly*, Daddy's favorite *Bob Wills and the Texas Playboys*, and other programs till bedtime. One evening we listened as President Franklin D. Roosevelt came on to tell the American public that the Japanese had bombed Pearl Harbor and our country had declared war against Japan. This news was just the beginning of the headlines for four years as our country changed and dealt with living in wartime.

Gasoline rationing meant the farmers were priority for growing food for our country, so our Dad bought a gasoline pump and gas was delivered to our farm. Any gasoline that went into the car had to be bought with ration stamps. Car tires were in short supply, and some food items such as sugar were rationed. Nylon hose and elastic were hard to find, and Tanny remembers Mom making her some underwear with buttons instead of elastic and some of our panties had drawstrings. Everyone was saving scrap iron and the farmers had plenty of old equipment that was sold at the scrap-iron yard. Everyone simply was doing without.

At school, each student had the opportunity to help the war effort by buying war bonds at ten dollars each. We would take dimes to the teacher till we had a ten-dollar bond, and it would draw interest. But we didn't cash them in till the war was over. Some of our neighbors moved to Oklahoma City to work at building airplanes.

Our neighbors' children were going off to war, and they were sending airmail letters to their loved ones. But soldiers' lives were changed. For example, after the war Wayne Alexander was alcoholic. Dad was asked by the Alexanders to go get Wayne from the bar, because they didn't have a car.

Life was filled with "Sister" and I getting the cattle up and other chores, studying, and doing homework. It seemed like all we heard on the radio was war news. Finally, in August 1945, the news came on the radio that the war was over. We had won the war! Our neighborhood teenagers wanted to go to Marlow and join in the festivities of celebrating the end of the war. Some had been working in the fields, and as the word got around, we cleaned up and dressed in our best red, white, and blue and had signs on the pickup doors declaring "We Won!" The pickup bed was full of kids as we joined in a parade up and down Marlow's main street, waving and yelling, "We won."

Margaret (Totsy) Scott and Martha (Tanny) D'Orville,
Martha and Babe's daughters, Allen cousins

Pearl Allen Andree

~~~

Babe and Martha's was a close-knit family. They sold cream in Marlow on Saturdays, bought groceries, and went to the Saturday night movies. Charley, Totsy, and Tanny all attended school in Bray, Martha visited Grandma Hall from time to time through her elderly years as she developed hardening of the arteries.

Charley, the oldest and only son, was expected to help Babe with the farming. Totsy told an exciting story that fortunately ended well, that happened when Charles was 15, and she was 13. Charley had a good command of the horses when he hitched them to the wagon, and they obeyed his get-up and whoa orders. In the story, Totsy went with him to gather corn, but when they crossed Highway 29 to go home, an oil field truck flew by, scaring the horses. They took off, running wildly. Charley's whoas no longer worked, and Daddy ran out to the road, yelling and waving his hands. Finally, the horses ran astraddle a tree and stopped. Once the scary runaway was over, Charles started laughing. He was pretty good at dealing with adversity. I thought he was my Superman. Actually, he did always have my back!

Babe tore down an old, stately home and, with Charley's help, built the family a new house. While doing this, he learned how to plumb and wire a home since electricity had arrived in 1946. Their prior electricity source had been a wind charger that powered storage batteries. Soon, Babe was wiring everyone's houses for little or nothing. And he kept on meeting the future, becoming the area's forerunner for things like indoor plumbing for water and later electric-powered engine pumps for water wells.

Once Babe had learned welding from an extension course, his innovative fixes became the talk of the rural neighborhood surrounding Highway 29, and what had to be driven by to be seen. He welded old tanks together to stand 20 feet tall, and then the windmill pumped a pulley chain of water-filled cups up to supply his water tower, which supplied water to the animal troughs. Totsy was right when she once said, "Daddy was ingenious at fixing things!"

Maud and Pearl

He also placed an old military cooking pot with a spigot on the bottom on the back platform of a peanut thrasher. The kids filled it with buckets of water from the well by the house. To this, he attached a bucket with holes drilled into its bottom, creating a sprinkler that became the family's shower! Of course, in the hot summer, the shower was pleasantly warm. Fortunately, the bathers, who stood on a wooden platform from the old home, were on the opposite side of the thrasher-tank and not seen from the road. A few neighbors and friends from Marlow came out and stayed overnight just to shower.

Charley didn't like college and joined the Air Force for four years. After returning home, he married Betty Smith, and they had four children. Betty was religious, practical, and later a caregiver for Martha and Babe. She deeply respected and was upfront about Martha's role as the first and oldest daughter of EZ and Maud. Charley worked with Babe in the plumbing, heating and air conditioning, and electric pump installation business, and he later added pipe fitting as a skill set. Add to that his many years of work, including as fire chief at the Marlow Fire Department.

Margaret went to work after finishing high school, moving to Lawton, where she rented an apartment. After she left home, Tanny sometimes visited her. On one such visit, 16-year-old Tanny met a soldier named Henry at nearby Fort Sill. They kept trying to elope and finally did get married. Margaret felt guilty for not having taken better care of her baby sister.

After working for two years, Margaret entered Oklahoma State University in Stillwater and followed a home economics curriculum. It was there that she met Melford, who was working toward an agricultural degree. They were married in 1954 and embarked on a very full and busy work and family life together.

Tanny's adult life took a different-than-expected course. She and Henry moved to his home area of Biloxi, Mississippi after his military service. They began a large family of six children, but their marriage was difficult and they divorced.

After her divorce, Tanny wasn't interested in dating. Her friends invited her out to eat, and with her permission invited another friend, Glen, to dinner as well. During the meal, Tanny mentioned the children, and Glen asked her if she had some. She looked him straight in the face and said, "Six of them!"

Glen wasn't fazed. Conversations and Sunday dinners through the summer became frequent. At Thanksgiving, Glen asked Tanny what her holiday plans were, and she told him that she and the kids were staying home and having a family meal. Glen invited himself over for the meal.

Tanny and Glen had been married about a year when her oldest son, Mike, was in a serious motorcycle accident, and she decided to go to work to help pay medical expenses. She began as an elementary school librarian in the Biloxi Public School System. Her medical insurance covered Mike's expenses, but she really enjoyed her work and decided to work longer, which she continued doing until retirement. Her unplanned career, ending as Assistant Media Specialist for the school district, stretched over three decades!

After leaving the Navy, Glen was a shipbuilder for Ingalls Shipbuilding (Northrop Grumman) for 35 years and was able to take early retirement, as did Tanny. Both shared community involvement in Girl and Boy Scouts (Glen for 55 years), school parent activities, and Little League, and Tanny taught Sunday school. Glen attended church regularly with Tanny and later converted. While Glen remained an inveterate gardener of varied vegetables and flowers, both he and Tanny enjoyed a lot of traveling after their retirements.

Glen had a very pleasant, unpretentious, conversational style, to the point that one wondered if he had been an Allen who had become a D'Orville who then married an Allen. Tanny felt "Glen and I were happy together. He was respectful of me and fatherly toward my children. More of my life was with Glen, and he raised my children."

In their hearts, Martha and Babe were always farmers. They nearly perfectly complemented each other on their farm. Babe tilled, sowed, and harvested the fields. Both shared the farm animal chores and gardening. Martha cooked for and fed the hired help and excelled in homemaking.

Maud and Pearl

Babe and Martha stayed in the Bray community. Their home was a "home away from home" for children and grandchildren as well as siblings and other relatives and friends. From 1954 on, they were both active in their church congregation, the Owens Prairie Church of Christ, where the musically inclined Babe led singing. Besides the hymn "Blest Be the Tie That Binds," his other favorite song was "Sing and Be Happy," the chorus of which is:

Sing and you'll be happy today,
Press along to the goal,
Trust in Him who leadeth the way,
He is keeping your soul;
Let the world know where you belong,
Look to Jesus and pray,
Lift your voice and praise Him in song,
Sing and be happy today.

Martha and Babe both worked and stayed active into their later years. Babe had done fairly well contracting plumbing and heating and air conditioning jobs, but when he tried to retire at seventy, his neighbors wouldn't let him!

Health issues began to plague both of them. Martha developed diabetes with an accompanying heart condition. They had smoked, and each began having lung problems. They celebrated 50 years of marriage on December 16, 1979.

About two years later, Babe made breakfast one morning and called Martha to get up a couple of times. When she didn't respond, he checked more closely, and he found that she had passed away while reading a book. She died in November 1981. Babe was grief-stricken, and even though that sadness lingered, he was able to remarry, briefly. He died of cancer three years after Martha.

Martha and Babe had worked hard so that they could leave a generous amount of love, money, and land to their three children. They were both buried in the Allen family cemetery plot where Ira, Zeke, and Maud had been laid to rest.

Mama and the Windy Chicken Story and Mr. Killer the Rooster

WHEN I think of Mama, I remember her love, laughing with us kids, enjoying her friendships with our neighbors, and her Home Demonstration Club. She taught my sister and me to sew and cook. We went to the State Fair every year and ate Mom's fried chicken picnic dinner. Daddy, a fiddler, loved hearing Bob Wills and the Texas Playboys sing and play, then we went home in that '41 Chevrolet late at night. Mama made the best beans and cornbread in Stephens County, but her specialty was that fried chicken. This reminds me of a chicken story.

When I was about ten, it was my job to take care of the chickens. I remember my mom ordering chickens from an ad in a farm magazine, so the mail carrier delivered them. We knew the approximate date they would arrive and started preparing their house ahead of time. On a nice, warm day in late February, we cleaned the small room for the baby chicks and placed newspapers on the floor. Electricity had not arrived in our community, so we used a kerosene heater called a brooder to warm the room. We were ready when we saw the mailman's jeep coming down the gravel road.

We got a big box with 100 noisy baby chicks and took it to the chicken house. My sister and I were so excited to watch the new chicks. We changed the newspapers each day, put fresh water in the waterers, and cleaned out the feeders and added feed. Mama had ordered "straight runs," a mixture of male and female, fifty of

Maud and Pearl

each, and when the roosters got big enough, we started having fried chicken.

As summers go in Oklahoma, the wind sometimes gets up, and this particular day the wind was blowing the windmill so hard, the water in the cattle tank overflowed, so Mom wanted it shut down. She told my brother, Charley, to go lock the handle closed. She told me that the door on the chicken house had come loose from the nail and was banging back and forth and needed to be rewired to stay open for the chickens. So Charley and I headed out.

As I got near the chicken yard gate I noticed a rooster known to be mean watching me and getting ready to "welcome" me into the chicken yard. I picked up a big stick in my left hand as I opened the gate with my right hand. Stepping inside the yard, I hit at the rooster with my left hand to keep him at a distance, but he was staying right with me and jumping at me. The door was banging back and forth wildly, and I was trying to catch it with my right hand while keeping my eye on the rooster. The rooster jumped at me and the door banged and hit him in the head and knocked him down. I was so frightened I didn't realize what had happened.

He was dead! I quickly wired the door open and surveyed the situation. Too scared to touch the rooster, I headed for the gate and saw Charley coming toward me, dying laughing. He picked up the rooster to take to the house. I feared reprimand, but Mama had seen the whole thing and said, "That mean rooster had it coming for a long time. It might have hurt someone really bad. Guess we'll have rooster dumplings tomorrow."

Years later, I told this story to my grandkids and when I finished, a granddaughter said in a very serious voice, "Mimi, was that rooster's name KILLER?" So posthumously he was named Killer the Rooster.

Margaret (Totsy) Scott, Martha and Babe's daughter,
an Allen cousin

Pete

AT HIS birth on October 23, 1913, he was named Huber Ernest. As a toddler he expressed decided opinions, and Grandpa Hall announced, "He's so stubborn he should have been named Peter, like the Apostle." Great-grandpa Hall was named Peter, which may have been another reason for Huber Ernest to be called Pete throughout life by friends as well as family.

At an early age, Pete showed musical ability. Maud's purpose to encourage her children to play a musical instrument motivated her to buy a harmonica for Zeke. He showed no interest in it, but Pete picked it up at about the age of four, taught himself how to play, and made it his own. In later years it became obvious that he inherited EZ and Maud's singing and musical ability.

When the family moved to the 20 acres, Pete liked a neighbor girl, Dorothy Cook. The first time they met, she was 8 and he was 13. When he tried to get acquainted, she hauled off and gave him a donnybrook! So began Pete and Dot's love story. More than 60 years later, he told Charlotte's husband, Dick, that the first time he saw her, he said, "That's the girl I'm going to marry." They were married over 71 years.

Pete went to school in Marlow, and in high school he played football. In the rural community of Stover, the young single crowd got together and put on plays at the Stover Elementary schoolhouse. One play was "The Haunted Rocking Chair." In it, Dorothy played a mammy and Pete played her son. Her name in the play was Petunia and for years afterward, Pete's brother Leo teased her by calling her that name.

Maud and Pearl

The rural activities also included baseball games in a meadow and feats of machismo like who could drink the most well water from a gourd dipper in the least time. In one ballgame, Pete was knocked in the mouth with the ball and lost four front teeth. Friends devised a stretcher to bring him home. Pete also went with Dorothy in the afternoons to get the Cooks' cows in for milking, and then she went with him to bring in the Allens' cows.

Pete graduated from high school in 1932, so he went into the labor pool at the height of the Depression. During that time period, he rode the horse from the farm to his job at a gas station. He worked all week there and slept on a cot at night. At week's end, he rode the horse home. He repeated this routine weekly to earn money. Also like his brothers, there were times he hitchhiked and rode the rails out west to get work.

During this time, Dorothy attended school in Rush Springs.

Pete lived a long life and exemplified character traits of goodness, honesty, and a deeply religious nature. On his 80th birthday, his youngest child, Jerry, who was also musically gifted, wrote a song to honor him.

The Print of His Shoes

Written for Pete Allen on his 80th birthday by Jerry Allen,
©1993

Verse 1
He was born in 1913 in Oklahoma town,
Stella Maud's youngest son, a fine young man all round.
Stella bought him a French harp one day,
He learned all the fiddle tunes his dad could play,
Soon folks were steppin' to the music he made, or listening to his cowboy songs.

Chorus
Eighty summers gone and past, a life of loving built to last,
Eighty winters come and gone.
Now he's building wooden toys with his hands, growing gardens on the land, and singing songs of praise to the Lord.

Verse 2
He rode the rails and picked the fruit from Oklahoma to Washington,
Sang for his supper, fought for the union to help workers' rights be won,
Married Dorothy, moved to Arizona, raised a family in Allen's Alley,
All the kids around know Pete's name, he'd fix their bicycles with his tools.

Maud and Pearl

Chorus

Verse 3
The first things I remember about him were his work and songs,
The sweet machine oil mingled with sawdust of melon crates and boards.
His voice leading singing or quiet at home, the tunes on the French harp he would blow
I'd follow him around wherever he'd go, trying to step in the print of his shoes.

Chorus

Verse 4
Eighty years still finds him strong and working with his hands,
Driving a tractor, a child on his lap, showing them the land.
He'd never tell a lie or cheat another man, he's always ready to lend a hand,
Kids follow him around and walk with this man, trying to step in the print of his shoes.

Chorus

Pete the Balladeer

In the early 1930s, at the height of the Depression, the Allen brothers had to go freight-hopping west to find work. Being resourceful, they sang well, Pete especially, and sometimes they sang together with friends to earn meals and make money. Pete's 1933 trek out to California and Washington has been documented by oral history. Ornan was known to be with him because Ornan missed catching the last boxcar near Sacramento, and Pete and the others had to wait for him at the next stop. Someone played guitar, it's unknown who, and Pete played the harmonica. "Zebra Dun" was one of the favorite cowboy songs they sang. "Red Wing" was Pete's favorite folk song, which he would either sing or play on the harmonica, or sing funny alternative choruses.

Pete's son Jerry said, "I'm sure the whole big family in Arizona later sang those songs."

And his granddaughter Lisa Cosby recalled, "Grandpa Pete always sang 'Red River Valley' when he played music and sang at our get-togethers!"

Ballad of Zebra Dun

We were camped along the plains, at the head of the Cimarron,
When along came a stranger, who stopped to argue some.
He looked so very foolish, we began to look around,
We thought he was a greenhorn, just escaped from town.

We asked if he'd had breakfast, some bacon and some beans,
And then he began to talk and tell about foreign kings and queens,
About the Spanish wars, a-fightin' on the seas, with guns as big as steers and ramrods big as trees,
About John Paul Jones a-fightin' old Rascul, who was the grittiest cus to ever tote a gun.
Such an educated feller, his thoughts just came in herds,
He astonished all those cowboys with them jaw-breakin' words.
He just kept on a-talkin' till he made the boys all sick,
And then they began a-lookin' round, for to play a trick.

He said he'd lost his job, upon the Sante Fe,
And was goin' across the plains, to strike the 7 J,
He didn't say how come it, some trouble with the boss,
But he said he'd like to borrow, a nice fat, saddle hoss.

Now this tickled all the boys to death, they laughed down in their sleeves,
Why, we'll lend you a fine horse, just as fresh and fat as you please.
Old Shorty grabbed the lariat, and roped the Zebra Dun,
Turned him over to the stranger, and waited for the fun.

Pearl Allen Andree

Now Dunny was an outlaw, who'd grown so awful wild,
He could paw the white right out of the moon when he got riled.
Old Dunny stood right still, as if he didn't know,
Till the stranger got him saddled and ready for to go.
When the stranger hit the saddle, old Dunny quit the earth,
He traveled right straight up, for all that he was worth,
A-kickin' and a-squealing, and a-havin' wall-eyed fits,
His hind feet perpendicular, his front ones in the bits.

You could see the tops of mountains, under Dunny ever' jump,
But the stranger he was glued there, just like a camel's hump,
He sat abroad ole Dunny and twirled his black mustache,
Just like a summer boarder waitin' for his hash.
Well, he thumped him in the shoulders and he spurred him when he whirled,
Just to show those flunky punchers, I am the wolf of the world.
And when he had dismounted, once more upon the ground,
We knew he was a thoroughbred and not some gent from town.

Now the boss who was a standin' round, lookin' at the show,
Walked right up to the stranger, and told him he needn't go.
If you can handle a lariat like you did old Zebra Dun,
You're the man I've been a-lookin' for since the year of one.
And when the cattle got to millin' he was Johnny on the spot,
He set them to nothin' like the boiling of a pot.
And there's one thing sure I've learned since I've been born,
Ever' educated feller ain't a plumb greenhorn.

—Traditional American Cowboy Song

Red Wing

There once lived an Indian maid;
A shy little prairie maid
She sang all day, a love song gay
While on the plain she'd while away the day

She loved a warrior bold;
This shy little maid of old
And then one day, he rode one day;
To a battle far away

Oh the moon shines tonight on pretty Red Wing
The breeze is sighing, the night bird's crying
Far oh far beneath the stars her brave is sleeping
While Red Wing's weepin' her heart away

She watched all day and night;
She kept all the campfires bright
While under the sky, at night she would lie;
And dream about his coming by and by

But when all the braves returned;
The heart of Red Wing yearned
For on that day, her warrior brave;
Had fallen in the fray

Pearl Allen Andree

Oh the moon shines tonight on pretty Red Wing
The breeze is sighing, the night bird's crying
Far oh far beneath the stars her brave is sleeping
While Red Wing's weepin' her heart away

First Humorous Chorus, Charlie Chaplin

Oh the moon shines tonight on Charlie Chaplin,
His shoes are crackin', they need a blackin'
And his little brown pants they need a patchin',
Where he's been scratchin' mosquito bites

Second Humorous Chorus, Hoboing

Oh the moon shines tonight on moving freight trains,
The breakie's sleeping, the engine's creepin'
Far oh far down the tracks the caboose is comin',
With hobos bummin' their way back home

—Original written in 1907 with music by F.A. Mills and lyrics by Thurland Chattaway

Pete and Dorothy

PETE picked cotton in Parker, Arizona. At night he slept in a bedroll thrown on the ground. Finding work took him as far as Washington State. In 1935, he knew Dorothy was graduating from high school, and he was in a hurry to get back to Oklahoma and ask her to marry him before some other man beat him to it. He had saved rattlers off the rattlesnakes he had killed and gave her a large matchbox full of them, perhaps to show her what he'd gone through to get back to her. Also, an American Indian woman had made a belt of a snake skin for him to take to Dorothy.

The story of their wedding is family legend. Ornan and his Dorothy were planning to get married the same day, July 13, 1935. The two couples planned to go to Rush Springs and have Brother Spencer, Ellen's dad, marry them in a double ceremony. They had planned without Mr. Cook's input.

Since Dorothy was only sixteen, she had to have her parents' permission. Pete went up to the North 40 to ask Mr. Cook for permission to marry his daughter. After stalling a while, Mr. Cook told Pete to go back to the house and ask her mama. She maintained she couldn't make a decision like that and sent him back up to the North 40. Since they kept him going back and forth, Ornan and Dorothy decided to leave and go on to Rush Springs.

After many trips, Pete's persistence paid off. Mr. Cook finally said, "Well, if nothing'll do you, go ahead, but you ought to take a fool's advice." They drove to Duncan and were married in the living room of a Presbyterian minister. Dorothy must have been planning this day for a while as she arrived at the 20 acres in her new pink dress with a pair of shoes dyed to match, carrying

Pearl Allen Andree

the shoes in her hand as they'd had a flat and she had gotten out of the car to help with the tire.

When love stories are told around Valentine's Day, their love story tops them all. That marriage lasted over 71 years.

Pete and Dorothy were a team. At first, they lived on a farm where Pete worked for the owner and there was a house for them. Their first child was born there, a girl named Dawn Marie, on June 30, 1936. During her pregnancy, Dorothy walked five miles daily to visit with her mother.

In a few months, they decided to go west. Pete went first alone and found work so he could send for Dorothy and Dawn. When Mr. Cook put them on the train, he remarked, "Probably everyone on the route will know Pete's expecting his family."

In January 1939, another daughter was born, and they named her Charlotte Ruth. She was born in Tolleson. With work and frugality, they were able to buy a house on Madison Street in Tolleson, paying a small amount each month. Pete added a bathroom and garage, and it remained their permanent address for over a decade. A son was born on July 14, 1940 and was named Edwin Lanier. Lanier Dark was the name of a friend of Pete's when he was growing up. A younger brother of that friend, in later years, became a well-known baseball player nationally, and the young Lanier treasured an autographed baseball from Alvin Dark.

Life was not always easy, but they weathered their storms together. One such storm occurred when Charlotte was about four and had mumps followed closely by measles and complicated by pneumonia. At one point, the doctor told them prayer was their only option. Maud was also extremely concerned as she remembered her first baby's death. Dr. Philip Johnson was who the Allens called in times of sickness, and he made house calls from Phoenix even during wartime when gas rationing was in effect. Charlotte survived but had a long recuperation period. She remembered having to drink large amounts of milk during her recovery, an unpleasant memory.

Pete and Dorothy's children were able to attend most of the school year in Tolleson because of the lettuce seasons, but the family left to follow the crops during summer.

Wartime West of Oklahoma: Arizona and California

I (CHARLOTTE) was just six when WWII ended. I don't have many memories of conditions at home and in the town of Tolleson during the war. Dad worked at Goodyear Aircraft, and this plus having a family protected him from the draft. We had our usual vegetable garden in the yard and chickens in the backyard for eggs and meat, while neighbors added Victory Gardens to their yards and raised chickens and rabbits to save farm-raised produce for the military. I definitely remember that sugar, butter, and gasoline were rationed. Instead, we used oleo margarine, a white spread of hydrogenated vegetable oil sold with a tiny capsule of dye, which we hand-mixed into the margarine after bringing it home.

Residents had blackout curtains on all of their house windows to prevent aerial surveillance. Every time the lights were turned on, those curtains were drawn.

Everyone worked really hard, and families stayed close. My Aunt Margie lived with us for awhile. Daddy brought things like puzzles home from the plant for Christmas presents. I was six when he built our bathroom. During the war, for us as children, home on Madison Street was a stable place to be because we didn't migrate with the crops in summers.

I was most aware of the day Uncle Leo came home from the Navy. He simply came strolling down the street, having made his way from his point of discharge to Tolleson and Allen's Alley on his own, unannounced!

Pearl Allen Andree

~~~

As does Charlotte, I (Dick) have WWII memories as well. Like Pete, my father George initially had a work-protected job at Douglas Aircraft in Long Beach, California, but later he was drafted. He hitchhiked home a couple of times from specialty schools in the Midwest or Gulf states before shipping out to the Pacific. He'd suddenly appear at the door or come walking across the field in front of our house.

See's Candy was a deluxe chocolate, a luxury hard to get because the ingredients were rationed. Mom saved her sugar ration stamps for it and on occasions when available, we had to drive a distance in our old Rockne car to purchase some. The lines formed before dawn, it was cold and boring, and I could hardly stand standing up. Our relatives who got boxes of See's candy as Christmas presents were very lucky indeed, because our little family never got a bite!

I remember the end of the war in Europe and Japan because of the car-honking celebrations in the neighborhood and on the highway. I remember Dad's discharge. Mom, my sister Ellen, and I hugged him ecstatically when he was discharged directly from his ship docked at Terminal Island in the Los Angeles harbor, still in his uniform. Dad's ship had been a landing craft, designed to land men and equipment on beaches under fire, very dangerous ships to be on in battle. His ship had missed several island battles by only a day or two, had gone on to Japan, and was in Tokyo Bay at Armistice. We all knew we were lucky to have him home safely.

The war was disequilibrating for me. Four of my uncles went away to fight. One was wounded at the Battle of the Bulge and hospitalized six months in Wales before returning to his unit. I remember what we were doing the day that President Roosevelt died. Although young, I had grown through the worst and best of times, the modifying of life to comply with the scarcity of things, to do without.

Charlotte and Dick Cosby,
daughter and son-in-law of Pete and Dorothy, Allen cousins

Settling the West: Peaks and Valleys

During the WWII years, the steady job at Goodyear Aircraft meant Pete and his family were year-round in Arizona. As already mentioned, they participated in the founding of the local church congregation in 1944. After the war, Pete and Dorothy began to think about moving permanently to California, as they were once again following the seasonal work.

At the beginning of 1950, they had a surprise visit from the stork. In the ten years since Lanier's birth there had been new findings about blood types. Dorothy had always blithely stated, "A train could run over me and I wouldn't lose my baby."

When the doctor had her blood work done, they found she was Rh-negative. The doctor said, "You get your husband in here as soon as possible for a blood test." Turned out Pete was Rh-negative also. Pete had type O blood and he and Dorothy had already donated blood at times when needed and continued to do so in their future years. The new member of the family was a boy they named Jerry (Gerald Lynn), who was born on November 4, 1950 in Phoenix.

In the early 1950s, they decided to move permanently to Brentwood, California, about 60 miles northeast of San Francisco near the delta. Pete's carpentry skills were good enough that they did not have to move from place to place and he joined the Carpenter's Union. They bought four acres and the whole family built their house from the ground up. Initially they spent $5000 on building materials and built three bedrooms, a bath, and a garage.

They had a cow and planted a large garden, including fruit and nut trees. They canned and froze food for future use. Pete

Pearl Allen Andree

experimented with melons. He created a thirty-tree pistachio orchard of four different types by obtaining discarded but fresh, pruned branches from neighboring farms and grafting buds from the branches onto rootstock he purchased cheaply. He and Dorothy were well-known for producing and giving food to those who needed it. He considered the soil on his four acres the best in the USA.

The children were growing up. The church congregation was an integral part of their lives. Whether it was the influence of a preacher or because Pete, like so many Christian fathers (especially of daughters), simply became paranoid about the social life of his offspring, he became rigid about the activities in which they were allowed to participate. They were not allowed to go to movies or school dances.

Dawn and Mike were high school sweethearts, going steady for two years before graduating and receiving scholarships to the University of California at Berkeley. Three weeks after classes started, Dawn found out she was pregnant. They both quit school to work and start their family. Six children and 65 years later when Dawn passed away, they had shared their lives together successfully.

Charlotte and Dick met at church camps before each attended and then dated at UC-Berkeley. They married before Dick entered medical school at UCLA. They had three girls: Jo Ellen, Lisa, and Kirsten. One of the many things Dorothy taught her daughters, as the Bible says, was "how to love their husbands." Or maybe it was the example of their parents' love for each other that gave the children a good foundation for marriage.

Sports were encouraged by Pete, so Lanier played football in high school and was very good at it. Later, when a college freshman at age 19, he developed epilepsy, which may have been related to a fall as a child or a concussion while playing football. With treatment, it was controlled and he accepted it as something he just had to live with. He went on to a career of accomplishment as chief perfusionist for heart transplant surgeon Dr. Richard Lower, first at Stanford and later at Medical College of Virginia. He went to college for two years at Harding College in Searcy, Arkansas, and finished his college education at Chico State University. At

Maud and Pearl

Harding, he met Alice Jenkins, also a student there. They were married and later had three girls.

While Pete and Dorothy, individually and as a couple, epitomized action-oriented, highly functional individuals, their family was touched by tragedy multiple times in the form of suicide, involving their daughter-in-law Alice, several grandchildren, and a great-grandchild. These dumbfounding and overpowering losses, which have not been the only such losses in the family, have reverberated throughout the years in the most sorrowful places of Allen hearts.

It cannot be said sensitively enough, but Alice's loss seemed related to a deepening melancholia, which occurred at a time of ascendency for both her as a mother of growing-up daughters and for Lanier with his pioneering role assisting Dr. Lower in open heart and heart transplant surgery in America. In spite of the success and the upward trajectory of her family, Alice one day sat in her car, where she was overcome by carbon monoxide fumes and died. It was a universal reminder to be attuned to a loved one seemingly walling off, or disconnecting, from family, whether due to significant stresses or for no apparent reason. Eventually, Pete and Dorothy were very glad that Cynthia later came into Lanier's life. They had a son, Lee Lanier.

Charlotte and Dick had three beautiful daughters. The oldest, Jo Ellen, chose to attend college at the University of California, Davis, near home. A successful student, she was awarded a year in Vienna, Austria, her junior year; but during her sophomore year, she met a handsome, charismatic pre-vet student and fell in love. She became less enthused about Vienna because her boyfriend was completely against it. Was he becoming excessively possessive, wanting to control her decisions? Or, was he grossly immature, unable to see her as an equal a distance apart? Or was he pathologically jealous, given Jo Ellen's exceptional beauty and the length of time she'd be at a distance and meeting others?

Nevertheless, Jo Ellen agreed with her parents that this wonderful opportunity was too good to turn down, so she traveled with fellow students to Vienna, and began studies there. Yet as the fall semester unfolded, she was besieged by his daily, lengthy

Pearl Allen Andree

phone calls begging her to come home, which were in denial of why she was there.

Charlotte and Dick made multiple, reasonable suggestions for him to adjust to her absence with a visit to see her, and for her to finish her academic year. They even visited her in Europe themselves to support her. But to no avail. Jo Ellen cut short her Vienna studies, as the controlling boyfriend inappropriately demanded, because she was very sensitive to his neediness. Once home, she was lovingly welcomed by her parents, who knew that her confliction about staying had become an ordeal for her.

They got engaged and planned a beautiful wedding that occurred in August. Immediately, her husband changed their honeymoon plans, insisting their first night be spent at his parents' house, which had to have disappointed her greatly. For the subsequent nine months, Jo Ellen seemed to be confined. It also seemed that her husband had become extremely possessive and controlling. She was not able to see friends, her parents, or her sisters, or have phone conversations with them.

She could attend college and work part-time. Dick and Charlotte were only able to have a very few brief conversations with Jo Ellen at Dick's medical office. Finally, after nine months, her husband agreed that her paternal grandparents could be invited for dinner, which was wonderful in that as with everything she did, Jo Ellen was an excellent cook. But on the day of the dinner, he changed plans, telling her that he would not be home for dinner.

Rejected and disheartened, she did not answer the door when her grandparents came. She had taken her life. A note was found in her handwriting. Oddly, when the police arrived, her husband and his parents were finishing packing his and Jo Ellen's possessions to take to his parents' house, where he also went to stay. Charlotte and Dick, away on a trip, had not even yet been notified of this ultimate tragedy.

What did Jo Ellen agonize about before the turning point of her young life? Hopelessness and despair about lack of control to have a livable life? Abject isolation? Or that her husband was a Mr. Hyde and not a Dr. Jekyll? It will always remain a mystery and an unknown. For her parents, sisters, grandparents, and the

Maud and Pearl

entire Allen family, forever since words were not enough, shock remained, and love could not do enough.

This story has been shared to give universal warnings about the potentially destructive and worst traits of human nature and about unrequited love, and because sharing with others can be the balm that can save. When one sees a person that one loves or cares about whose behavior changes with some form of struggling or withdrawal, there is a fine line about whether or not to intervene. Kindly inquiring about their life circumstances may help, by providing them a space to talk, and encouraging them to share their story.

Marty was the youngest of Dawn and Mike's six children, and in his late teens, unfortunately, he had the onset of a severe mental illness. Marty was very friendly and likable both within and outside the family. He was a smart, handsome, and muscular person who excelled at playing football in high school. In junior college, he played some football, but seemed to lose direction and motivation.

The first evidence of his severe mental illness happened when he was 21, when he revealed to his family that he'd been having intrusive, terrible thoughts. In the several years that followed, he was diagnosed with schizophrenia and hospitalized multiple times. Medication helped him, but once better, he stopped them too soon, then worsened. He didn't like the way he felt when taking medicine, though it effectively controlled his symptoms. This cycle is a familiar one for those with chronic mental illness. For Marty as well, his paranoid thinking sometimes adversely affected his decisions.

Over time, Marty developed fears of having done something wrong (he had not), having caused misfortunes for others (like miscarriages) that he had not, and that he might hurt someone, which were agonizing fears for him. Always kind-hearted by nature, he was afflicted by undeserved, emotionally painful guilt, as his sister Denise described. His family stayed as supportive and helpful as possible.

On one occasion in late 1986, his sister Kelly recalled that he seemed happier and he wanted everyone to come to dinner and be together at Dawn and Mike's. They enthusiastically were glad to host that family gathering. He planned a hunting trip with Mike, being the only son who'd not yet done that. In retrospect, his mood change and increased vigor may have reflected an inner, walled-off, tragic resolve.

Right after getting back from the hunting trip, he took the old family F-250 truck south toward Los Angeles on I-5. In the vicinity of the Six Flags Magic Mountain, near the Grapevine, he turned around, northbound, and parked. He intentionally dove under a big rig truck, dying instantly.

Despite his family's love and support, his illness was devastating. In those several years, the alienation from most friends, the tormenting thoughts, and subsequently the onset of a permanently painful sense of loss for those who loved him, had occurred. Marty's family did the best they could to help him and keep hope in his life. Instilling that hope, shoring it up, and persistently pursuing solutions for him to try, were all things his parents and siblings did for him.

For the loving family and friends of those afflicted with such illnesses, the pursuit of hope—for better treatment response, for finding better forms of relief, and hopefully for finding the key to unlock what may be a walled-off, unknown inner sense of doom—is what can be done. Thanks to Marty's family for sharing these universal reminders and truths about chronic severe mental illness. They are testament to how important endearing family love can be.

A renowned psychiatrist, Dr. Walt Menninger, once said that for a variety of serious mental illnesses, where life is lost, those illnesses have in fact been terminal illnesses. Individual friends, loving families, and treating professionals themselves realize that they are coping with life-threatening illnesses.

Less than 30 years after Alice's loss, her middle daughter, Dominique, a nurse with military service and firearms training, was struggling with major losses and changes in her life. At this point she tragically took her life with a firearm. The news of her suicide was a completely unexpected shock for her family.

Maud and Pearl

As an older child, and despite her mother's earlier grievous loss, Dominique had been a vivacious, spritely girl.

It seems that often the suicidal mind, even if not affected by the haze of drug use, has reached the point of perceiving a hopeless future. Yet the effect that person's death has on loved ones left behind who have always loved, nurtured, related to, and held important that person, is lastingly devastating. Dorothy kept framed pictures of each of those dearest ones in a special place, on top of a chest of drawers in her and Pete's guest room. She always kept them close and nearby, as she did in her heart.

After a very early start in their lives of their romance for all time, Pete and Dorothy lived quite lengthy and extremely busy lives together. Only after becoming encumbered by aging and disabling physical problems did they agree to leave their four-acre Brentwood farm. They lived in an assisted living center for about three years before Pete passed away, almost exactly on his 93rd birthday in 2006. Dorothy lived another two years. They were an inspiration to all who knew them and role models to younger family members. They rest in peace near the home area they loved so much.

Pete, Dorothy, and the Little Grandsons

WHEN I was a young boy about eleven years old, and my younger brother Marty was eight, we helped Grandpa build a hayloft for his cattle. He and a friend put down the decking around an opening to drop the hay into a trough below. We kids were given a bucket of bent, rusty nails, and our job was to straighten them with a hammer, which we did.

Years later, I found out that Grandpa had gotten the lumber through a bid and salvaged it from old Camp Stoneman in nearby Pittsburg. He'd removed it himself, board by board. I realized that explained the bent nails. Grandpa did not like to waste anything!

~~~

It would be an absolute understatement to say that my grandparents were religious. They were very religious. They had a high moral code and a similar standard for conduct.

When Marty and I were still little, Pete and Dorothy took us camping. We went in their F-250 with a camper on the back north on Highway 101 to somewhere in the redwoods. We stopped next to a creek and Marty and I went down by the water to play. Grandma was making sandwiches and Grandpa was checking something on the truck.

Some hippies were camped on the other side of the creek, and some of them removed their clothes and came down to the creek to swim. About that time, Grandma came out of the camper with the sandwiches and saw the naked people.

Oops!

Maud and Pearl

She yelled at us to come back to the camper, and for Grandpa to start the truck. We left immediately.
We boys thought the whole thing was very funny.

Mark Devine, Pete and Dorothy's grandson, an Allen cousin

Motel and Tevye Meet on the Fiddler's Roof

CHARLOTTE had pneumonia at age four, a time when her family lived on Allen's Alley. A Phoenix doctor made several house calls, finally informing Pete and Dorothy that they might lose her. The only thing left to do was pray, and because she wouldn't eat but was thirsty, the doctor advised milk. Her parents then made a remarkable decision to give her fresh farm milk, which, unlike pasteurized store-bought milk, they knew had a thick layer of nutritious cream on top. Every day for over two years, Pete drove to an area dairy farm and back to get her that whole milk. Charlotte recalled, "I was still carrying a thermos jug filled with milk through the first grade." Charlotte survived and later blossomed into an attractive young lady.

Charlotte added, "But at age 70, I began to have a cough, and a chest x-ray showed a mass. Fearing cancer, I had surgery. It was an aspergillosis granuloma, an infection that only grows within a lung cyst or pocket—for me, probably a lung scar from my illness as a toddler."

Off to college, Charlotte met Dick again, a former acquaintance at church camps. They graduated and married. Dick was accepted to the University of California at Los Angeles (UCLA) School of Medicine. Off they went, broke. As Dick said, "We had no money, no job, and no wealthy relatives."

Charlotte's three pregnancies led Dorothy to exclaim, "What will you do?!" Charlotte remained supportive and worked full-time while Dick worked when he could as a medical student and

Maud and Pearl

traversed financially modest physician jobs of internship, military duty in Germany, residency, and nephrology fellowship. He worried that Pete and Dorothy might begin to raise their eyebrows, but that never happened.

Dick recalled, "but from the start, they accepted me eagerly and engulfed me quickly into their wonderful family, which of course began with their beautiful and pillar-like daughter, Charlotte."

Not long after marrying, Dick had his mettle examined by Maud, who was visiting Pete and Dorothy. After a length of easy conversation, she invited him to a back room, whereupon she revealed to Dick that the Allen name came into the family years after Ezekiel and his sisters had been born.

Dick had a Eureka moment. "I fell in love with her that day! What a privilege to have been welcomed by the Allen family matriarch and entrusted with the sharing of family secrets. She wanted me to find a way to encourage Allen family members to openly discuss the Allen family secret, and not be ashamed of it."

Later, Dick formed a very close friendship with Charlotte's brother, Lanier. Dick said, "I came to feel that I had gained a new brother through our marriage. Then I added sister Dawn and brother Jerry and their loving families."

Modest about his talents, Dick may have felt fortunate to become an Allen, but he was also gobbled up by the family and became its surefire second medical resource: wise, discerning, informed, and, in the presence of Charlotte, succinctly framed.

Charlotte and Dick Cosby,
daughter and son-in-law of Pete and Dorothy, Allen cousins

Lanier

THE story of Pete and Dorothy moving to Brentwood began the journey of the rest of their lives. Their son Lanier, responded graciously and very helpfully to requests for additional memories and experiences about Pete and Dorothy's family. With Lanier's permission, I've chosen to include his description of his growing up, his survival of Alice's and Dominique's losses, and raising his own family together with Cynthia, including his son, Lee. His own story is interlaced with Allen family heritage, while he has modestly reflected on himself and his children at the end of his career. His narrative, which he first wrote in 2006 and completed in 2009, is presented in the next section.

But first, more about Lanier himself. He grew up to be a monolithic Allen grandson, a son to Pete and Dorothy, and an Allen cousin. From very early and throughout his life, Lanier worked harder than hard work: he has exemplified responsibility. His curiosity has killed many cats; but once when it did not, it spawned his genealogy interest, which has lifted the Allen family to more understanding, acceptance, and pride in its unifying roots.

Lanier and Dick, a nephrologist, became close and came to share, with Charlotte, the genealogy inquisitiveness. Dick has been able to articulate Lanier's part in American, and indeed world, medical history. As an aside, it's also worth noting that Lanier did all that he did while coping with a chronic seizure disorder that required Dilantin medication and dosage adjustment for the breakthrough seizures that episodically afflicted him.

The following is Dick's description of what Lanier accomplished. Happenstance was part of Lanier's destiny.

Maud and Pearl

After college in 1963, he got a job as a research lab assistant in the new Stanford Palo Alto facility, headed by renowned cardiac surgeon Dr. Norman Shumway. One of Dr. Shumway's top residents, Dr. Richard Lower, became Lanier's dog lab supervisor. There, Lanier perfected the complex protocols for safe cardio-pulmonary bypass machinery use in dogs, and later humans.

In 1965, Dr. Lower finished his training and became head of the new cardiac surgery program at Medical College of Virginia (MCV—now VCU Medical Center) in Richmond, and he took Lanier with him. Of course, that also meant Alice and, eventually, their three daughters. Again, Lanier developed that program's dog bypass technology to perfect human bypass surgery, which made Lanier a part of the cardiac surgery team, the chief perfusionist. Top surgeons from around the world came to MCV to study their setup. One who did this was Dr. Christian Bernard, who went back to South Africa and performed the world's first heart transplant in December 1967. After several such surgeries by Dr. Shumway at Stanford, in May 1968, Dr. Lower, with Lanier providing the bypass support, performed the first heart transplant at MCV. Historically, it was the world's sixth such surgery ever.

For so many years, including the losses of Alice and Dominique decades apart, Lanier carried such a huge load on his shoulders: chronic illness, single parenting, and the rigorous demands of pioneering in a life-or-death field of medicine. Yet, he stoically endured in a modest, unassuming way. What follows is another remarkable thing about him, as he tells his life story and simultaneously that of the Allens' westward reach. He writes in a direct, memorable, Huckleberry Finn style. He's aptly entitled it with his childhood places.

Years in Tolleson & Brentwood

Our family lived most of each year on Madison Street in Tolleson, Arizona, which was ten miles west of Phoenix at the time. It is now part of Phoenix. Dad worked in the packing sheds in that area and in California. Dad and Mom (Pete and Dorothy) owned their small home in Tolleson at the time, as did Uncle Monk (Ornan) and Uncle Zeke. In the early 1940s Uncle Leo also lived in Tolleson, but by 1948 he lived in Somerton, Arizona. I think Mom and Dad bought their place in the early 1940s, shortly after I, Lanier, was born on July 14, 1940. I was born in Salinas, California while Dad was packing lettuce.

The family moved around a lot during the summers as Dad and Mom both followed the crops. Dad stopped following the crops for a while during WWII and worked at an airplane factory in Goodyear, Arizona, which was also only ten miles west of Tolleson. He was supervisor of a crew that installed the interiors in the aircraft. At the end of the war, he went back to the outside work in the packing sheds. Of course, Mom didn't like that, but he couldn't stand the inside work. Dad and Uncle Monk started following the crops again.

In the summer, we followed the melon crops in California from south to north. We started out in far southern California, sometimes in Somerton, Arizona, and came up through the San Joaquin Valley, ending up in Brentwood. We stayed in either tents or small Quonset huts that were provided for the workers. By that time Dad and Uncle Monk were making the boxes that the melons were packed in. There was pretty good money for the time in doing that.

Maud and Pearl

The first summer I remember being in Brentwood was the summer of 1946. Dad and Uncle Monk had bought large Army tents in Stockton, California. In Brentwood, the boss of the H.P. Garin Shed where they worked, Fran Walden, let Dad set his tent up behind the packing shed. I don't remember where Uncle Monk set his up. Fran also let Dad have enough pine 2 x 4s each year to make a floor for the tent. That made it a little better for the girls and Mom. Dad was able to store the tent in the loft of the shed each fall after we no longer needed it until the next summer. Our whole family lived in that tent every summer and fall through late October until 1949.

We started school in Brentwood and then transferred to schools in Tolleson in late October most years. I remember that in the fall of 1946, all of us children rode the train back to Arizona with our Mom so I could start school in Tolleson for my first year of school. My first partial year of school in Brentwood was the second grade in 1947. Mrs. Story was my teacher. My third grade teacher was Mrs. Carpenter. I loved living in the tent during those times because it was like camping out. On the other hand, my sisters, Dawn and Charlotte, and Mom all say that they hated it.

One thing I remember about living in the tent is Charlotte being afraid of the mice. They were all over the place. Of course, I didn't help that situation any by catching mice and running after Charlotte while holding them by the tails. As a young boy, I thought living in that tent was the way life should be. I was able to ride the freight trains and sometimes ride in the engines. There were large piles of sawdust for me to play in, as well as old trucks and wagons.

One problem with the sawdust piles was the nails in them. One time I was stupidly jumping up and down in one without any shoes on. One of the four-penny nails stuck into the bottom of my foot and Mom and Dad had to take me to Dr. Geyser to get a tetanus shot. That was not a pleasant experience.

Another thing I remember is putting large nails on the train tracks and letting the train run over them. That flattened them enough so that I could make a simple knife out of them. All I

Pearl Allen Andree

needed was to put a simple handle on them and sharpen them a little. It was a young boy's heaven, but not for my sisters, I'm sure.

Today, the area where the H.P. Garin Shed stood is a shopping center with a Safeway. It is right across the street from the old grammar school seventh- and eighth-grade buildings.

In the summer of 1949, when I was in the fourth grade, Mom talked Dad into renting a small cottage behind Bill's Market & Bar, north of Brentwood. It was on the left side of Highway 4 just before you get to Lone Tree Way. Uncle Monk and his family lived in a cottage next to us that summer. During that time, I remember Mom and Dad and Uncle Ornan going striped bass fishing at Frank's Track in the Delta and coming home with quite a lot of fish. I remember Dad taking us kids fishing quite a lot in those days. Sometimes we went bank fishing and other times out on a boat. There were lots of places to go fishing within ten miles or less.

In the summer of 1950, Mom and Dad rented a nice little house at the top of the hill above Davis Store & Camp on the left side of Highway 4 as you travel north. Davis Camp is built right along the north bank of Marsh Creek. Apparently, it was during that summer that I made a famous family saying.

As I remember it, Dad was home from work that day for lunch and all the family was sitting around the table when someone brought up the question of what the baby would look like when it was born. The discussion went back and forth and then someone said that they wondered if the baby would be pretty. I piped up and said, "I don't see how it could help but be pretty, as pretty as the rest of us are." I was ten years old at the time. That statement still gets a laugh out of the family today, 56 years later.

In the fall of 1950, we went back to Arizona a little sooner than usual because Mom was due to have Jerry in November. I remember going to school in Tolleson that whole school year.

I don't know whether Mom gave Dad an ultimatum or what, but in the summer of 1951 Mom and Dad moved the household to Brentwood to stay. They sold their home in Tolleson. All of the Allens were moving out of Tolleson. Uncle Leo had moved to Somerton, Arizona in about 1948, and Uncle Zeke had moved his

Maud and Pearl

family back to Oklahoma in about 1949. Mom and Dad moved to a small rental house just off of Dainty Avenue and directly behind the Pool's house when we first moved to Brentwood. I don't remember how long we stayed in that little house, but I think we had moved to another rental house on Sunset Road by the time school started in the fall of 1951.

That house backed up to Marsh Creek and was just across the creek from Davis Camp. Enough property came with the house to have a large garden on both sides of the driveway. It was just across the road from a large field that they grew corn in every year. It had a fairly large tree in the side yard that Dad hung a swing in for Jerry when he was old enough. Dad taught me a lot about gardening while we lived there. He bought a rototiller, and we tilled our own garden with it, as well as other peoples' gardens for a small fee.

I got my first bicycle while we lived there, in the summer of 1952 for my birthday. It was a three-speed English race bike with narrow tires. I rode that bike all over the area. It was the best birthday present that I ever received as a child. I had that bike and used it until 1972. I used to ride it back and forth to work at Stanford, California and here in Richmond, Virginia. I also rode it all the time I was in college in Chico, California.

I don't remember whether it was in the winter of 1951-52 or the winter of 1952-53 that we had a big flood while we were in that house on Sunset Road. I remember that Mt. Diablo had a large snow pack on it at the time it started raining. It rained so long and so much that there were bad floods all over the state at the same time. There was bad flooding in Yuba City and Marysville, as well as in Brentwood. The flooding in Brentwood was caused by Marsh Creek, which starts up on Mt. Diablo and winds its way all the way down to the Delta and into the San Joaquin River.

I can remember looking out the back window of the house (which is where I slept) and watching the water get higher and higher. We put everything up as high as possible and then we all left the house and drove over to Ab and Norma Pool's house on Dainty Avenue. By the time we left our house, the water was already coming into it. From the water marks, it looked like it got

Pearl Allen Andree

up to about four feet deep in the house. We had a small shed out back with canned goods that Mom had canned and other things that floated a couple hundred yards down the creek bank. We had to wade to the car before driving to the Pool's house. The Pool's house was several miles south of ours, but it was only about one mile north of a point where Marsh Creek crossed under Dainty Avenue as it meandered its way down from Mt. Diablo. Their house sat down in a depression at the side of the road. At that place Marsh Creek had pretty high banks, so everyone thought the water would stay in the creek banks there.

They were wrong! We had all just gotten to sleep when we were awakened and told that we had to evacuate. The creek had broken out of its banks just south of us. This time I remember wading out in waist-high water. We all went over to another house in the town of Brentwood where there was no fear of being flooded out again. That was some night to remember.

It was several days before we could go back home, but when we did, we found mud six to eight inches deep in the house. The current had been so strong that it washed a shed that was out back down the creek bank about 100 yards. A lot of family things were lost or ruined in that shed. We all worked at cleaning it out, and it seems like just as we got it cleaned out, the creek flooded again. I think it flooded us out three times that winter.

In the spring of 1953, Mom and Dad bought a four-acre mini-farm back over on the west side of Highway 4 from Davis Store & Campground. It is on what became Lone Oak Road. I think back then it was just an extension of Grant Street. The fellow they bought it from had started the groundwork for the foundation of a house and had a pole with the power run to it, with a PG&E meter on the pole. The rest of the property was in alfalfa, with a ditch down the southern edge and Marsh Creek running along the eastern edge.

Across the dirt road to the north was another alfalfa field of about 30 acres. Across another dirt road to the west was another alfalfa field. While I was in high school, I worked for the man who owned both fields, loading and stacking hay when it was in season. Across the ditch to the south of the property was a 40-acre

Maud and Pearl

cherry orchard owned by Jack Mayhorn and Nat Boring. Right across the dirt road from that cherry orchard was about a 20-acre peach orchard owned by Vernon Turles. Down that same dirt road and around the corner were some more alfalfa fields owned by Carl Jackson and his brother. I worked for all of these people, both digging and repairing ditches and irrigating as needed.

Alongside Vernon Turles's peach orchard and all along the 13-acre field of alfalfa to the west of Mom and Dad's place was an irrigation ditch that brought the much-needed water to his place to irrigate the alfalfa, as well as vegetables later. That ditch was about a half mile long and was always springing leaks. In later years, after I left home, Dad was able to have about a 20" irrigation pipe laid that whole distance. That saved him a lot of trouble.

As soon as possible that first summer, Dad and Uncle Monk and Clarence Rennels shot the lines for the foundation of the house, and we started to build the house. We all had to use picks and shovels in that hard clay to dig down for the foundation. I spent that whole summer in 1953 digging trenches for the foundation and irrigating the alfalfa, along with my cousin Terrell Wayne and my sisters, Dawn and Charlotte. You could say that building that house was a family affair. Dad bought the right to tear down an old apartment in Richmond, California along with another man about that time. They shared the lumber. That lumber was mostly what Mom and Dad's house was made out of. It was good lumber. The 2 x 4s were actually 3 x 4s, and the 2 x 8s and 2 x 6s were very hefty. Most of the hardwood flooring, doors, and windows also came from the apartment. All of the framework also came from there. Dad bought an old one-and-a-half ton flatbed Ford truck to haul that lumber from Richmond to Brentwood. I remember spending a lot of time helping him haul that lumber. The one negative thing about all of that was the pulling of nails. The whole family all got their fill of pulling out old nails. Dad insisted that all of the old nails be pulled out. We had lots of five-gallon buckets full of rusty nails. We also saved a lot of sheetrock that was eventually used in the house.

With all the family working together and the help of a lot of friends and neighbors, we were at a point in August of 1954 that

Pearl Allen Andree

Dad thought we could move in. The house wasn't nearly finished but it had outer walls, doors, windows, and a roof that didn't leak. We had running water and flushing toilets and a bathtub with a shower. We also had a telephone for the first time in my life. The garage and patio had only sand floors and no doors. What else could a 14-year-old boy want? Now, the girls and Mom were a different matter. I don't think they were wild about moving in then. You will have to get Charlotte and Dawn's opinions.

That fall was an eventful one. Dawn and Mike got married in September, against Mom and Dad's wishes. I don't think they ever wanted any of us to get married.

The dirt road was dirt all the way up to what became the end of Grant Street. It became really muddy during the heavy rains that fall and spring. Dad let me drive the old DeSoto or the old Ford truck up to the end of Grant Street at Highway 4. I parked at the Pentecostal church and we walked across Highway 4 to Davis Store to catch a school bus. Charlotte rode with me many times to keep from getting all muddy. Sometimes other neighbor children also rode. To me, it was a blast learning to drive in that mud. I think it was about one year, or one and one-half years, before the pavement was brought down to the corner by Mom and Dad's house.

Dad and I also built a small lean-to down by the creek with a holding pen for a couple of milk cows. He bought a couple of cows from someplace and started a mini-dairy farm. We also went out to Cloverleaf Dairy and bought a couple of three-day-old calves. I was never very good at milking, so I never did like to do it. I loved teaching the little calves to drink and feeding them, though.

Sometime during my sophomore year, I believe, Dad and I, and probably with some other help, constructed that huge barn that is behind the house and built a chicken pen in and around it. We constructed laying boxes for the hens and built four rabbit hutches. At one time we had 70 hens that were laying eggs. If you know how prolific rabbits are, you can imagine the number of rabbits we had. We also fenced off about two acres for pasture and made a water trough for the cattle.

Maud and Pearl

In my sophomore year, I started playing football, so I had to plan my time well to get all of the animals taken care of. Working on the house, taking care of the animals, and studying took up a lot of my time, in addition to the football. The whole family was continually working on the house for the next three years of my high school days. In the spring and summer, we grew a huge vegetable garden and started a blackberry vineyard. It was a great experience for me.

During that summer after graduating from high school, I had a job in Turlock, California driving a forklift at a peach cannery. I also had some other part-time jobs as fillers. That fall of 1958, I went to college at Harding College in Arkansas and started my life away from home. In June 1959, I came home for the summer and got a job at the paper mill. I worked all shifts on a rotating basis. Dad and I and a couple of friends also poured a lot of concrete that summer to finish off his garage, driveway, and patio. At the end of that summer (fall of 1959), I went back east a little early to be in my friend Gary Ackers's wedding and to go on a float/fishing/camping trip with another friend, Earl Chester, in Pocahontas, Arkansas. I met my first wife, Alice, during my freshman year, and during our sophomore year in 1959-1960, we got more serious and decided to get married in Tulsa, Oklahoma, at her mother's house, in September 1960. I worked at the paper mill again during that summer of 1960, with a little break for Charlotte and Dick's wedding on the 18th of June. Mom and Dad did not want me to get married, so I went back to Tulsa the last of August and Alice and I were married on September 3, 1960.

Alice and I spent all of school year 1960-1961 at Harding, where my major was pre-med with a minor in math. Due to financial difficulties after marrying Alice, we returned to California in 1961 to work and go to school. After spending six months working in the paper mill in Antioch, California to save money for school and to pay for the birth of my oldest daughter, Lori, I returned to school, this time in Chico, California. I spent my last year and a half of school at Chico State Teachers College, now Cal State University. I changed my major to physical science in the School of Education, with a minor in math.

Pearl Allen Andree

Because of the birth of my first daughter, Lori, and the necessity to support my family, I had decided to go into teaching instead of medicine. Following graduation with a BA in Physical Science from Chico State in 1963, and with a desire to stay near the medical field, I went to work at Stanford University for Dr. Norman Shumway and Dr. Richard Lower, who designed the technique for heart transplantation as a resident under Dr. Shumway. I was a research assistant in the Cardiac Research Laboratory, operating the heart-lung machine while we were doing heart transplants on dogs. I was very lucky to get in on the ground floor of a very new profession. In July 1964, I went with Dr. Richard Lower to the Palo Alto VA Hospital, where we continued our research on heart transplantation and started the Clinical Open Heart Surgery Program. We did the open-heart cases with Dr. Lower doing the surgery while I operated the heart-lung machine. In those days we were called pump techs, but now those same technicians are called perfusionists. In August 1965, I moved with Dr. Lower to Richmond, Virginia to the Medical College of Virginia where we started a Heart Transplant Research Program and Clinical Open Heart Surgery Program.

My second daughter, Dominique, was born in September 1965, shortly after we arrived in Richmond. In May 1968, we performed our first clinical heart transplant. My third daughter, Michelle, was born on October 30, the same night we did our fourth heart transplant. During the next several years, we did a large number of open-heart cases along with quite a few heart transplants. In October 1970, my first wife, Alice, died, leaving me with daughters aged two, five, and nine.

In October 1972, I married my second wife, Cynthia. She was working in the operating room as a scrub nurse at the time. That is where we met. She has raised my three daughters as well as our son, Lee, who was born in June 1975. For many years after our marriage, Cynthia was the supervisor of our Cardiac Research Lab.

Lori, our oldest daughter, went to college at UVA, where she met her first husband, Andrew Serrell. They had two boys, Sean and Ryan. Sean graduated magna cum laude in biomedical

Maud and Pearl

engineering from Syracuse University. He will attend Boston University Graduate School in the fall of 2009.

Our middle daughter, Dominique, went to nursing school at VCU and married Joseph Hudert in August 1990. She was a pediatric airborne nurse stationed in Ft. Bragg, North Carolina during Desert Shield. Dominique and Joe were both sent to Saudi Arabia and Kuwait during the Gulf War (Desert Storm). Joe has been in Iraq and Afghanistan several times since then. Dominique died in 1995 in Chester, Virginia. She and Joe had no children.

Our youngest daughter, Michelle, went to nursing school in Rochester, New York. She married Tony Arduini in November 1988. Both were in the Marines at the time of their marriage. Michelle was out of the Marines by the time of the Gulf War, but Tony was still in active service and was also sent to Saudi Arabia and Kuwait during Desert Storm. Michelle is an emergency room nurse and she and Tony have two boys, Josh and Alex, currently ages fifteen and seven. They live in Midlothian, Virginia, southwest of Richmond, and both work for National Security & Door Company.

In October 1991, the governor of Virginia gave state employees an offer I couldn't refuse. It gave me 31 years full retirement with a good retirement income. I retired with full benefits at age 51, and I'm still retired. I love it! I wish everyone could have that chance. I have no problem staying busy. I fish and hunt a lot and garden. I also do a lot of woodworking, mostly hand carving. My greatest love now is genealogy. I've been doing that since 1987. Cynthia was finally able to retire also in January 2004. She is also loving retirement.

A Memory of My Father, Pete Allen

WHEN I was about four years old in 1953-54, my parents, Pete and Dorothy Allen, were building their house on Lone Oak Road in Brentwood, California. It was time to dig the septic tank and my father hired two Mexican men to dig the hole. I was watching them and I think one of the men spoke to me in Spanish and I must have ignored him. My father called me over some distance away and he looked me in the eyes and said, "I want you to treat those two men with the same respect with which you treat me." I had not done anything terrible, but my dad must have picked up on something in me he wanted to correct. I got the message and began a lifetime of learning about racism and my father's attitude against racism.

I remember in 2006 at my father's funeral when he was 93, several black ministers attended and they spoke about Pete Allen's effort to bring fellowship between black and white congregations. I had known of his efforts, but it was moving to see those men come and honor him. Recently, when I shared this story with Aunt Pearl, she told me that her mother, Stella Maud Hall, my grandmother, was always quick to speak up when she heard racial-disrespecting remarks and that Grandma did not have the idea of keeping strangers at a distance. She was kind and welcoming to everyone.

In this I can see the thread of kindness and respect flowing through the generations of our family. Kindness and respect are great treasures that impact all who experience them. I'm grateful to my father and my grandmother for passing down that wisdom and treasure by their examples.

Jerry Allen, Pete and Dorothy's son, an Allen cousin

Alma

ALMA Mae Allen was born June 17, 1916. From the first she must have been a feisty little thing. A family snapshot shows her at three, having cut her own hair—bangs particularly. Perhaps cutting her own hair set a precedent, as throughout her life, if she saw something she might like to have, she found a way to make it. Silent movies were becoming a part of the culture, and Maud enjoyed going to them. Unfortunately, taking Alma was frustrating as the girl spent most of the time there urging Maud to go home.

Alma became a "little mother" to all things small, animal and human. As she grew, she became Maud's helper around the house. She was nearly eleven when Pearl was born and helped by rocking and singing to her. She often sang "By-low Baby (Daddy's Gone a Hunting)." As Pearl grew, she heard the song as "Bylo's baby." This translated into Pearl calling Alma "Bylo." It became a nickname that Alma's friends called her as well as the family.

She also became the person to put Pearl to bed at night. It was standard procedure to tell her three fairy tales. These were always the same: *The Three Bears*, *Little Red Riding Hood*, and *The Three Little Pigs*. Pearl memorized them and occasionally corrected Alma when she drifted from the regular script. These were about the only times Alma got irritated at her protégé.

One of Alma's chores was ironing. She became quite expert at ironing men's white shirts when her brothers started dressing up to take their girlfriends on dates. The irons were flat irons heated on the big wood range. She also had a curling iron that was heated on the stove when she wanted to use it on her hair. She also

Pearl Allen Andree

became adept on the treadle sewing machine and began making dresses for Pearl out of flour sacks that had floral designs on them.

In high school Alma needed a coat. When she asked EZ for one, he went out and bought some material and gave it to her, saying, "Make yourself one." She had no pattern and no training in how to make a pattern. When the coat was finished, the two sleeves were not the same. She had tried to make a popular sleeve design and it had gone awry. When she learned how to use a pattern and could buy one, she made dresses for her mother.

Alma went to Marlow High School as her brothers had. After moving to the farm, she rode the school bus into town. She excelled in speech and debate and did well in competitions. Unfortunately, one time she overheard some teachers discussing upcoming division competitions (where they had to go to another town) and she heard them saying, "Alma's the one that should go, but she doesn't have nice enough clothes." How it must have hurt. She also excelled as a cheerleader for the Marlow Outlaw football team.

Due to religious opinions in the town churches, there was a junior-senior banquet rather than a prom. Because of Prohibition, the only places young people could go to dance were places where alcohol was available under cover, and Alma, like Martha, liked dancing. She became friendly with a third cousin, Naomi Pearce, and they went where they could dance. This disturbed Maud, but with everything else going on in her life (her sons leaving, EZ's sporadic income, and hard times), she couldn't demand the curtailment of Alma's social life.

Enter the CCC. The Civilian Conservation Corps was made up of young men working in an environment similar to the WPA (Works Progress Administration). These were government-funded departments to aid recovery from the Depression. Lelon "Lee" Curtis was one of those boys, and Alma met him when she and Naomi were going to various dances. Alma wanted to become a nurse after high school, but nursing school was like college in that it cost money. Her alternative was getting married, and that's what she did.

Maud and Pearl

Legend has it that Lee was on a horse singing to her when he proposed. That would fit, as he envisioned himself a Texas cowboy. When the family got together, such as when making homemade ice cream and having neighbors visit, Lee entertained with his singing. The men sang and played harmonica, fiddle, juice harp, and other instruments, but Lee was the first romantic type that the family experienced.

Lee and Alma were married in May 1934, just after her high school graduation, and they moved to Borger, Texas, in the Texas Panhandle, where his family lived. If Alma thought her life would be easier away from the poverty of family, she became disillusioned in the following years. Lee was a gambler, and for many years, either his folks, her folks, or Alma herself put the food on the table. Lee had no trouble getting jobs; he just had trouble hanging onto his pay long enough to get it home.

Their first child was Virginia Lee, born on February 17, 1935. She was called Jenny Lee and was a beautiful child. Alma was an excellent seamstress and was able to take a small piece of fabric that someone gave her and make a beautiful little dress from it. In 1936, Maud finally got a coat to replace her 17-year-old fur coat, and Alma cut up that old fur coat, salvaging the good pieces, and made a fur coat for Jenny. When she was two, Jenny had 28 dresses (one hand-crocheted by Alma) in the closet. She looked like a Vanderbilt child when Alma dressed her up.

A son was born in September 1936, a month premature, in Borger. After that, the doctor said Alma shouldn't have more children. Their son was named Richard Leland and was called Dick or Dickie. Later in adult life he was nicknamed "Shorty" for obvious reasons.

The family lived in a little house on the same lot as the Curtis family. Maud and Pearl took a bus trip to see the new baby and spent Thanksgiving with them. Jenny had learned to climb, figuring nothing should be out of reach for her. There was a small fishpond in the yard, only two or three inches deep, that they had enclosed with chicken wire about four feet high. One day they found Jenny blithely sitting in the pond with the goldfish.

Pearl Allen Andree

Sometime in 1937, Lee and Alma moved to Oklahoma and were living there when Maud and Pearl moved to Arizona in December of that year. When Babe and Martha returned to Oklahoma in May 1938, they lived for a while in the house in Marlow where the family had lived before moving to the farm. When Babe and Martha found a more permanent place (on a farm), Lee and Alma moved into the old house, probably rather dilapidated by then.

It was at this time that Jenny did some more climbing. She climbed to the very top shelf in the kitchen where Alma had put the rat poison, which contained arsenic. Alma found her making "pies" and feeding them to Dickie and herself! Fortunately, Alma got them across the street to the hospital to get their stomachs pumped promptly. The next Sunday Dickie was sitting with his uncle Leo and saw the nurse. He told his uncle, "I don't like her."

In early 1939 Alma had gotten pregnant again. The house where they lived was only a half block from the Weeden Hospital, where long-time family doctor, Dr. Tally, practiced. Miss Mary Maudina Curtis, at the embryonic age of six and a half months, arrived on October 6, 1939. She weighed two pounds, three ounces, and her case was later presented and reviewed in a medical journal. For that period of time, she was truly a miracle baby.

Lee constructed a homemade incubator, which Totsy recalled seeing, that had three glass sides. Because of Mary's tininess, a light bulb was installed within it to provide warmth. When they were allowed to take Mary home from the hospital, Alma was told she wouldn't be able to nurse the baby, and her reply was, "Don't tell me I can't nurse my baby." While Mary was still in the hospital, Alma had already begun nursing her.

Jenny Lee described vivid memories of her early childhood in Marlow after Alma and Lee moved back there in 1937. "I remember what I did," she chuckled, "not so much about the others." She continued:

> Mama was busy keeping up with Dickie. I recall one house we lived in that was two stories, made with redwood shingle siding, and was near Red Bud Park,

Maud and Pearl

east of downtown. Under the staircase was a closet, inside of which was a chest of drawers.

I remember several things that happened just before or after Mary was born, which was in late 1939. So I guess it was the winter of 1939-1940. The first thing was, I knew Christmas candy had been put in a drawer in that closet. Upstairs, we would all take a nap, Mama, Dickie, and myself. But I didn't. When they were asleep, I went downstairs, got one piece of candy, then went back upstairs and laid down. I did that a number of times. Another thing was that Mama had some dinnerware that she prized, and she kept it under a chest of drawers upstairs. Hidden, she thought! But I snuck around and pulled those dishes out and played with them. Then, I put them back in the right spots where they had been.

And something else. Mama, Dickie, and I would walk from Red Bud Park into town. There was a drugstore on the corner. Mama and Dickie would go on, but I'd hang back. Then Grandpa showed up, maybe from his office nearby, and he bought me an ice cream cone! I loved that, and he treated me several times that way.

Jenny told another funny story that happened then or the winter before. "Those winters were bitterly cold. Once, Mama made a pan of fudge, which she set out on a cold winter day. But that night, a mouse came along and froze near its bounty!" Jenny laughingly added, "Since it was the Depression, I'm sure that fudge didn't go in the trash."

In March 1940, Alma took the three children to see Maud in Arizona. Whether she was just homesick for her mother or was leaving Lee to get a job and struggle on her own is not known, but she did get a job. She made a new friend, Catherine Cochran, who owned a maternity home in Tolleson. Since Alma had always wanted to be a nurse, it was a perfect place for her to start learning.

Pearl Allen Andree

Lee came west that summer on his way to Marysville, California, where his family was. He stopped in Arizona to pick up Dickie and took him along. Several months later, Alma took Jenny and Mary and joined him, as he had obtained a job operating big equipment with the company building Shasta Dam.

Jenny Lee once said, "When World War II began and President Roosevelt was telling the nation, I remember exactly where I was. I remember the bedroom where I was, in our house up that hill in California, with the radio on in the living room."

In January 1943 the Navy accepted Leo's application to reenlist, and since he wouldn't be working at the high school anymore, Maud and Pearl had to give up living in the house on campus. They moved back into the two-room house that Leo owned. About three weeks later, Alma and Lee and the three children came back from California and moved in. Lee and Alma took over the little adobe room Leo had used. One of the two rooms was large enough for two double beds and the three children slept in one of those, with Maud and Pearl in the other. Alma obtained a job at Goodyear Aircraft and over the next two years she transitioned back into working again in the maternity home with Catherine Cochran.

By early 1944, Lee had built two more rooms onto the existing house, and the probability of Tolleson getting a sewer system was expected, which improved living conditions considerably.

Jenny, Dickie, and Mary grew up in Tolleson. Many years later, Jenny Lee smiled and reflected, "When I think of Grandma, I think of so many things. She got along with everybody. And Pearl was the older sister that I never had but always wanted."

In the late 1940s, Lee and Alma purchased their own lot on Washington and built a two-story cement block house on it. It wasn't completely finished on the inside but they could move into it. Maud mostly made her home with them and helped with the children. Lee was interested in cockfighting and built an outbuilding where he could raise roosters. Of course, they had to have refrigeration, so he installed a window unit. An evaporative cooler was more economical for the house, and it was efficient enough. The cockfighting satisfied Lee's gambling urges, but he hadn't forgotten his dream of owning horses. In the early 50s, he went to the Texas panhandle, where he acquired property to pursue that dream.

In the meantime, Jenny and Dickie were growing up. Jenny married Doug Evans when she was only sixteen, although she wasn't out of high school yet and it wasn't a marriage of necessity. She did graduate. A baby girl named Gloria Lee was born from the union. However, the marriage disintegrated.

Dickie quit school and went to Texas where his dad lived, and Alma and Mary followed not long afterward. When Dick was 16, he decided to take a job on a shrimp boat in the Gulf of Mexico. While working that job, he had an accident and had to return home to recuperate. When he had healed, he decided to join the Navy, where he stayed for four years. Thanks to the GI Bill of Rights, after the Navy, Dickie attended college for four years. Dickie had a quick smile and a happy-go-lucky demeanor.

Dickie's success at getting an education was an example of his ability to overcome the early trauma of difficulty in school. His fifth-grade year in Tolleson was one of many turnovers of teachers because of the war. They all tried to make Dickie right-handed. Finally, a local woman who had been a teacher in Massachusetts decided to renew her teaching certification to help with the shortage. She helped him use his left hand and his grades improved.

Years later when his young cousin Patrick spent summers with Alma and Lee in Texas, Dickie and Pat played a lot of the board game Monopoly. Patrick said, "Boy, Dickie is a really good Monopoly player!"

His mother replied, "I knew there wasn't anything wrong with that nephew's brain. In Tolleson, I would come home some weekends and we played the game. He became a whiz at it. He had to be good at math to do that." Dickie and Patrick became the champions of Monopoly at future family reunions.

Dickie married Norma Jo, a nurse, and worked at various jobs. He participated in Lee's business of raising quarter horses for racing. They had a boy, Marvin, in 1961 and a daughter, Sabrina,

Pearl Allen Andree

nearly two years later. Many years later, in 1980, they had yet another daughter, Shanda. Marvin was short like his dad and, growing up around his grandpa's horse farm, became a jockey.

While jockeying, he had several serious falls and, in addition, a severe episode of equine encephalitis. One night he failed to negotiate a curve while driving near home and was tragically killed, still a young man. Dick and Norma Jo endured the tumults of Marvin's alcohol misuse, marital ups and downs, and his tragic, untimely loss. But after years of medical bills and other financial strain combined with Dick's "other side" of anger outbursts with Norma Jo, the couple did divorce. Norma Jo later remarried, while Dick later ironically died accidentally the same way that Marvin had.

Sabrina writes about her grandmother Alma:

> Grandma was great at making her grandkids feel special. She taught me how to roller-skate with some skates she bought me. She put on her old roller skates, and we skated in an old house they bought and moved to the farm for ranch hands. It had wooden floors that were great for skating.
>
> One year my mom and dad did not have much money for Christmas, and Grandma got me an Easy-Bake Oven, vacuum cleaner, and refrigerator. It was one of my favorite Christmases. We had a blast cooking. She was a very fun grandma. She died when I was in third grade, but I remember she would take us to the farm for about four weeks every summer. We did things like fishing and horseback riding. Life was always fun and an adventure. She always took us to church every Sunday when we were at the farm, which was most weekends... which turned out to have a great influence on my faith today.

Sabrina and her husband Rocky now own two Papa Murphy Pizza places in Amarillo. They have a daughter, Savannah, and a son, Chance.

Maud and Pearl

When Gloria was a toddler, Jenny took her to Texas. Lee and Alma were enraptured with their granddaughter. Sometime in the late '50s, subsequent to her brief early marriage, Jenny went back to Arizona and met Don Ague, who was in the Air Force and stationed at Luke Air Force Base. They were married in the chapel there.

While they were still in Arizona, an incident happened one hot day. Jenny had acquired a pet skunk that had been deodorized. They were visiting Pearl and Bill and forgot how hot a car can get in an Arizona summer. The pet skunk expired, and Jenny was properly hysterical. They gathered Pearl's children around and had a proper burial for the pet skunk.

Jenny, Don, and Gloria Lee were living in Florida some years later, when Gloria was about 15. Jenny was back in Texas visiting family when, tragically, Don committed suicide. Jenny returned to Florida where she and Gloria stayed for awhile before they moved back to Texas.

Having had a challenging start in life due to her premature birth, Mary lived an entire life, full and busy, always with a gentle spirit and imbued with her mother's pleasantness. After she graduated from Sunray High School and attended West Texas State, taking typing and bookkeeping courses, she moved to Amarillo, where she met and married Dale Jackson, inheriting a stepson, Gary. They moved to a farm that Alma and Lee had bought near Warrensburg, Missouri and managed it, and Curtis was born there in 1964. Later moves were back to Sunray and then Amarillo, where she assisted Dale in managing the business aspects of service stations that he operated. Daughters Lynette and Debbie were born in 1969 and 1975. In the 1970s and 1980s, she had additional jobs in a nursing home and at First National Bank to supplement family income. In later years she doted on her grandchildren and her beloved pets.

Mary had an engaging lightheartedness and was full of fun and laughter, a joy to be around. She was readily available to talk to and was one who listened. Her family said that she was gracious and giving to a fault, having sometimes overextended herself. Her son Curtis described her as "having passions for swimming,

Pearl Allen Andree

football, and caring for pets, especially dogs. Except for the goat. We had a goat while living in Missouri that I actually rode like a horse several times. My mother had a large garden and one day the goat got through the fencing and into the garden and proceeded to have a feast. I never saw that goat again."

In June 1973, Alma and Lee drove to Oklahoma City to visit with her younger sister Pearl's family, who were visiting from Australia with Zeke and Ellen and heading to Dan's graduation from medical school in Galveston.

Ellen told Pearl about a lot of stress that Alma was currently experiencing. Alma's granddaughter Gloria had married a neighboring boy named Roy Dean. Alma was visiting one day and Roy Dean whipped their little three-year-old girl. Alma intervened with the statement, "No one's going to treat my grandchild like that!" and took her home with her. She forced them to go to court to get her back, while her daughter Jenny supported Gloria and Roy Dean. Alma had gained a lot of weight, which happened in her life whenever she was under intense emotional strain.

In October, Pearl and Bill had been back in Australia for several months when Pearl received a letter from Ornan's Dorothy telling them that Alma had been stricken with a cerebral hemorrhage two weeks before. She and a friend had a ceramic shop in town, and Alma awoke one morning with a bad headache. She called her friend to tell her she felt too bad to come in for work. While talking, she asked her friend to call the emergency medics for her, and she couldn't hang up the phone. At the time, 9-1-1 wasn't in isolated country areas, and Lee was out in other parts of the property. She lived three weeks in the Dumas, Texas hospital before she died. All her siblings were able to visit her before the end, except Pearl.

Alma Remembered

Our grandmother always seemed determined for us to have happy, interesting, and memorable experiences as we grew up. She had a ready smile, a knack for making each of us feel important, a fun-loving spirit, and a kindheartedness.

However hard it was on her, one time she loaded up her Buick with several of us and took us across the country to Disneyland! And we saw other sights that kids don't forget.

She tried to teach my cousin a lesson: "Marvin, don't pick on him; he may get bigger and get even." Later, I finished teaching that lesson for her.

She had a room in her home that she used for her ceramics hobby. Sometimes we may have broken more than we finished, but she remained lighthearted.

We had to learn things, she knew. She taught us card games and played with us. Trouble with math? She played grocery store with us, then we laughed about our troubles.

Roller skating went from hard to easy in a vacant house on the ranch. By the way, in what part of her past had she learned her whiz-around skills?

We lost Grandmother way too soon from a massive stroke. One certainty about her was that we always went to church with her on Sunday in Sunray. We've grown up, and we still feel she's at church with us.

Sabrina Curtis Gafford and Curtis Jackson
Alma and Lee's grandchildren, Allen cousins

Ezekiel (Zeke) and Stella Maud Allen
married June 22, 1902
Dripping Springs, Oklahoma

Robert and Martha Bowling Allen and children
Left to Right: Bertha, Emory, and Norris Jerry "Neri"
Little Rock, Arkansas, 1904

Hall children and grandchildren
Left to Right: Eula, Dona, Maud holding Ira, "her baby," Herman,
Ernest, and Emma holding Leo
Location unknown, possibly Hall Marlow farm; photo dated 1906

Mary Angeline Hinkson and
Maud Allen, sisters-in-law
Shattuck, Oklahoma, about 1906

Maud Allen's clear handwriting:
"Independence School near Catesby,
Oklahoma. Edd (and Mary) Hinkson
built this house. Leo's and Ira's first
school was at this place."
Indian Territory, Oklahoma
circa 1900–1910

"My Sweet Little Boys,
My Darling Boys"
Maud Allen wrote
Leo age 6, Ira 5, Ornan 3,
and "Zekie" 1
1910

Writing to a granddaughter, Stella Maud Allen wrote
"Cousin Bessie Hinkson, her mother Aunt Mary Angeline Hinkson,
and Grandmother Martha Bowling Allen, your Great-grandmother."
circa 1915-1920

Ira Allen, eighth grade perfect attendance
Chickasha, Oklahoma, 1918

Martha Bowling Allen
Little Rock, Arkansas
circa 1915-1920

Amanda Augusta Campbell Hall
Marlow, Oklahoma, late 1940s
She passed away in 1951 at age 90

Porter Hall, MD, Maud Allen's uncle
with his clinic staff
Marlow, Oklahoma, 1922

The Wildcatter
Ezekiel Allen, Secretary-Treasurer
Allendale Oil Co., Oil Producers and Refiners
General Offices 221-30 Burton Building
Fort Worth City Directory, telephone Lamar 102
1920
Sketch ©2024 Louis Daniel

Ezekiel and Maud Allen
Fort Worth, Texas, 1919

Maud Allen and children
Back L to R: Leo, Ira
Middle: Ornan, Zeke Jr., Maud, Martha
Front: Alma, Pete
Fort Worth, 1919

Martha Amanda Allen, age 11
Maud Allen wrote on back:
"I wouldn't give a purty for this picture of Martha,
Mother's Day, 1923."
Marlow, Oklahoma

Ira Allen, age 20
Duncan, Oklahoma
about 1925

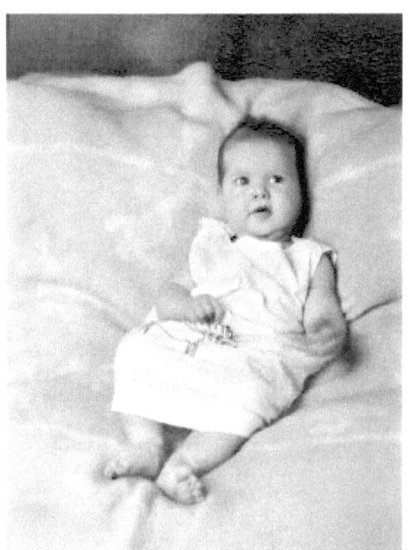

Pearl, age 9 months
Marlow, Oklahoma
Christmas 1927

Looking for Black Gold
Zeke Jr., Ezekiel, Ornan Allen
El Capitan, Texas, 1928

Pete Allen, high school football
Marlow, Oklahoma
about 1931

Mothers
Maud Allen and her mother,
Amanda Hall
Marlow, Oklahoma, mid-1930s

Four Allen Generations
L-R, back: Martha Robertson, Maud Allen, Amanda Hall
front: Charley Robertson, "Son"
Note: Sketched by Louis Daniel from the only known photo of the
20-acre farm (seen in background) kept by the Allen family
Marlow, Oklahoma, about 1934

Ellen Allen surviving hard times with her and Zeke's children
L to R: Rita Jo, infant Earl in Ellen's lap, Carol Lou
Tolleson, Arizona, early 1943

Pete Allen
Wellington, Texas
1939

The Great Depression through a Young Pearl's Eyes and Ears

From my earliest memories, the Great Depression engulfed everything. During the 1930s people lost farms, homes, and jobs. The central states—Oklahoma, Texas, Arkansas, and those surrounding—were especially hard hit.

You may have heard of the Dust Bowl. This was an area where drought caused crops to die and winds to carry off the topsoil of much good land.

During these years many families moved to Arizona and California. My family was one of these.

We lived on a twenty-acre farm just outside the Dust Bowl. Its location saved our bacon. But with four grown sons and one grown daughter plus me, a child, jobs were needed. My brothers started hitchhiking out west for months at a time to get work.

For a time they were employed as laborers building Parker Dam. In that same area, they picked cotton. Near the Colorado River, the fields of cotton provided them with farm work, with which they were familiar. At night they unrolled their bed rolls and put them down under the stars near the fields. They met many creepy-crawly characters that way, like scorpions, tarantulas, and diamondback rattlesnakes. My brother Pete collected rattles he took off the snakes he killed. I've heard that each rattle designates one year of life. Some that Pete saved were twelve rattles long.

Leo wrote home this story: "Thought I was living next door to the Hot Place and today I proved it. There was a knock on the back door and when I went to open it, there was this little

Pearl Allen Andree

man wearing a red suit and horns stuck out of his head. He had a pitchfork in one hand and a cup in the other. He wanted to borrow a cup of flour so he could bake some biscuits!"

They also wrote back about oranges growing on available trees. To my mother that sounded like heaven.

Three of my brothers were ready to get married and knew they couldn't get well-paying jobs in Oklahoma, so gradually they took their new families to Arizona.

The town best for work was Tolleson. The farmers there planted two crops of lettuce a year, one in the spring and another in the fall. My brothers worked in the packing sheds, loading lettuce on boxcars to be carried to grocery stores all over the US. Mama said she wanted to go there.

Pearl

(Authors note: For my own memories, I will change the point of view. From here forward, Zeke Sr. will be Dad and Maud will be Mom or Mama.)

IT WASN'T much, but it was all we had, that twenty acres during the Great Depression. I find that in my adulthood, I treasure the memories of that place and time, and the people we knew.

The youngest of nine children born to Ezekiel and Maud Allen, my view came from a different angle, perhaps, than that of older brothers and sisters. Mom had eight children by the time she was thirty-two, and I arrived eleven years later, in March 1927. My birth, fraught with peril to Mom, followed by two months the death of her twenty-one-year-old son Ira—surely a traumatic time for the entire family.

Sometime in 1929, Dad moved the family out to Leo's twenty-acre farm several miles from Marlow. Leo had bought the place with money he made in the oil fields to have a place to batch. Perhaps Dad foresaw the Great Depression. Whatever the reason, it proved to be a good way to weather those lean years.

The house was truly a shack. I don't believe a paintbrush had ever sullied its sides.

Mom always referred to March 21 as the first day of spring. I was grown before I realized that first day actually changed with the year. Mom was quite ill for my first year and there is a snapshot of a cousin, Ruth Berry, holding me in the back yard. I think she must have come to help take care of me and help Mom in her weakness.

Pearl Allen Andree

Ruth was deformed in some physical ways but had overcome these to become a talented artist. Her legs stopped at her knees. One arm stopped at her elbow and the other had a hand with only a thumb plus the next two fingers, which were grown together. I don't remember being around her after I was old enough to remember names and appearances, but I was told a lot about her.

When the discovery of thalidomide babies' deformities surfaced in the '60s, I remembered Ruth. I wondered if her mother unknowingly used an herb or other substance that could have caused Ruth's similar malformations.

Ruth Berry

THE original watercolor hangs in my living room. Most people probably wouldn't pay particular attention to it, but it holds a special place in my heart.

The one work of art in that five-room shack hung on a wall in the front room. Small for the large wall, about 8"x 10" and framed, it showed a snow scene of an old house with one tree stripped of its leaves. Seeing it may have been the moment I began to appreciate art. I asked Mama who painted it and she answered, "Ruth Berry."

"Who's that?"

She told me of a cousin, deformed from birth, who learned to paint. Then she showed me that picture of Ruth. She showed me a snapshot of a young woman holding me as a baby. The baby quilts draped down over the lower half of her body, and her hand and stub arm were hidden, too. She had a pretty face, much favoring my sister Martha, who was of corresponding age. Her hair was dark and styled in the 1920s mode—short, straight, curving toward her face. It is one of the few baby pictures I have of myself and has a place in the family album.

Since making one's living by painting is uncertain, Ruth joined the circus as a freak. She fell in love with an extremely tall man who was also traveling with the circus as a freak. They married and had a son who was perfectly normal. Another picture I have of her is a professional studio photo with her son at about age ten, and they were the same height.

I haven't seen Ruth Berry since I was old enough to remember the occasion. She must have come to help Mom during

Pearl Allen Andree

her year of illness after my birth, and that's when the snapshot on the back steps was taken. There was a rumor several years ago that she was living in Florida.

In 1980 we were in Oklahoma to bring my daughter Lilly home from college for the summer (on the way back from Florida where granddaughter Audrey Barnes had just made her debut into the world). Visiting my sister Martha, I chanced to mention that old painting—how I remembered it as the one work of art in a cold and poverty-stricken world, and that I wished I could find it and would like to have it.

She responded, "I have one of Ruth's paintings and you can have it. I don't have any place for it."

She immediately went into a back bedroom and brought out a framed long and narrow painting, much bigger than the one I remembered. The glass was broken and the frame had come apart, but it was a Ruth Berry painting. We carefully wrapped it in layers of newspapers and placed it in the back of the car.

Back home I took it to a frame shop and spent $55, probably the most I ever spent on a painting, to get it properly matted with non-glare glass, and it's beautiful on my wall.

An autumn scene, the trees with oranges and golds in a forest setting, the painting is more cheerful than the winter scene of my childhood.

I am grateful for a cousin whose artistic talent conquered her deformities and sparked in me a love and appreciation for art.

I gave the painting to Leo's daughter Marsha because, as a child with her Mom and Dad, she met Ruth and a second husband.

Extended Family Remembered

Mom was one of nine children and her brothers and sisters still lived within traveling distance in the early and mid-1930s. Her three younger sisters were schoolteachers. Two had married and Aunt Emma was an "old maid." There were cousins near my age, and we could play if we could get together.

Aunt Eula was married to Ernest Bird and had three girls. The middle one, Hazel Marie, was near my age, and Anita Florence was a little older. Uncle Ernest was a journalist and tragically died of a heart attack while working on his car one Saturday. The funeral was terrible, especially because Hazel became hysterical. She was only seven but had to be taken out of the building.

Aunt Eula then had to work to support her family.

Hazel took tap lessons, and I took expression lessons, which were paid for with Mama's egg money. Hazel taught me some dance steps and I passed along tips on readings to her.

Aunt Emma was the principal at a rural school where they furnished her with a house. She sometimes came into town on Friday, picked up Hazel and me, and kept us for the weekend. If there was a pie supper or box social at the school, and there usually was, she had the necessary items fixed for us to take. Invariably, we were the entertainment for the evening.

Doris Jean (Hall) was a part of this cousin group. Her parents were Uncle John (Mom's brother) and Aunt Annie. She and cousin Anita had beautiful red hair. I think Hazel and I were envious of that. When we visited, it seemed to me that Aunt Annie was always sick. She was an invalid for many years. I didn't think she'd live long, but I believe she outlived Uncle John. My brothers told me in later years that the reason her house was always clean was that Uncle John cleaned it when Annie was feeling poorly. I never saw Mama lying around even when she was sick.

Aunt Effie was Mom's older sister and was dearly loved by her. She let us girls do her hair. It was long, thick, and black. She didn't feel well a lot of times and lay on the bed while we combed and brushed away. One time she let Anita cut her hair, and it was not a good job. Turned out, she really was sick with cancer of the uterus and died when she was 57. Mom started thinking she would expire at age 57, too.

Aunt Effie was married to Jim Wilkinson, but they were divorced by the time of my memory. In spite of this, Uncle Jim lived in the other building on the lot. Before we had cars it was the carriage house, but had been made quite comfortable, probably by him (he was a carpenter, I think, though he had been an itinerant preacher earlier in life), and Aunt Effie kept it clean for him. This family also stayed at times with Grandpa Ike and Grandma Mandy.

This family had strife and difficult circumstances over the years. Their two children were grown. Geneva was a nurse living in Chickasha. Hall, whose childhood friend was Wiley Post, had mental illness problems later and, subsequently, long-term residential care.

Uncle Ernest (Mom's brother) was married to Aunt Winnie. Their daughter was four or five years older than I and was named for Mom and Alma: Alma Maud. I loved to visit them at their farmhouse because it was always so clean. Aunt Winnie sewed, crocheted, and did other handwork, so there were always lovely things she'd made lying around. Of course, there was much more time in her life to do those things, having only one child, and probably Uncle Ernest helped with a lot of the farm toil.

I guess my favorite uncle was Uncle Lem. He married Mom's sister Dona. I thought he was the handsomest man around. Not only was he tall and good-looking, but he smoked cigars. I still like the smell of a good cigar! Uncle Lem liked to hunt and fish, and when he went on those trips, he'd bring Aunt Dona and the boys up from Paducah, Texas to visit Grandma.

Maud and Pearl

Their sons Neil and L.B. were about a couple of years older than I, and I liked playing with them. I got really worried, though, when I was about five and Neil announced he planned on marrying me when he grew up. There was a cousin of Mom's that had a severely retarded child and Mom said it was because she had married a double cousin. I feared someone might make me marry my cousin Neil. It gave me the creeps.

Mama's cousin took care of that poor child all her life. The second child of this cousin of Mama's, a boy, had a good enough IQ to graduate from eighth grade and probably was able to function at a low-skill job. The third child was a girl and quite intelligent. She was my age, so we played together occasionally. Her father owned the town's barber shop, and once in a while Mom took me in there for my Buster Brown haircut. His name was Alfred Pearce.

Then there were Alec and Annie Grissom. I think Annie was a cousin of Mom's. Apparently, Alec made good money on the farm. He must not have had faith in banks, or lost that faith during the Depression, because he buried his money in the backyard! They had no children, but Annie had insisted on buying a brand-new model T Ford sedan. She still had it, and drove it, when I was a child. It still looked brand new. Alec never drove it, and it was believed he never even rode in it. I loved going to their house. It was like Aunt Winnie's, spic and span with all those needlework creations around.

Despite the hardships of my childhood, I had a large extended family and grew up surrounded by cousins to play with and aunts and uncles to look up to and from whom I was able to learn a lot about life. Again, these interactions had much to do with Mama's loving nature.

You Can't Go Back

THE farm, as previously described, had nearly everything we needed. The house itself, upon entering, had certain features.

In the big entry hall, the only thing there was the cedar chest that my mother kept all her valuable linens in, that she didn't feel she could use in this old farmhouse, and the rocking chair that my daddy sat in and read. Again, all he had to read was the Bible, but there are some pretty racy stories in that.

There were those advertisements on the cardboard boxes in my bedroom, like Noxzema and Coty depilatories, that taught me a lot about adult life. I asked Mama what some of the things on those boxes meant and she wouldn't tell me.

By 1937, I found myself far away in Arizona as a child of ten. Every once in a while, I thought about that 20-acre farm in Oklahoma. You know how you say, when you grow up, you're going to be rich... Well, what are you going to spend your money on when you're rich? I was going to be a famous movie actress—or a petroleum engineer. Either way, I'd make lots of money, and I would go back and buy that 20 acres and build a beautiful house on it. As I grew older, there were other houses to build that were more immediate, and a family to raise, so I never did get rich enough to buy that 20 acres.

Some years ago, I did go back. I was visiting my sister and I said, "You know I'd like to go and see what the 20 acres looks like."

Martha said, "You'll be disappointed."

I said, "I know that, but I want to go anyway."

Maud and Pearl

We drove out there, and we parked on the road because the driveway that used to be there wasn't there anymore. We got out of the car and walked up what had been the driveway onto this land. I stood there and couldn't believe my eyes, or that there could be such a change in my lifetime. I stood about where the house had been and looked toward the road. Instead of grass and trees that had been in our front yard, it was all sandy soil, almost as if nothing had ever grown there. I looked over in the direction of the creek and tried to imagine what it had looked like as a child. I could almost see that cherry tree that I used to spend so much time in.

Then up closer to the house, I remembered the fire over which my mother had kept a big, black pot that was always filled with water on wash day. She scrubbed the clothes and then put them in the pot to boil with pieces of her homemade lye soap to get them good and clean. In the summertime, we put the beds outside because it was cooler and we'd look at the stars, shooting stars especially, before we went to sleep outside.

The barn wasn't there anymore, the old garage was gone, and of course there was no evidence there'd ever been a chicken coop or a pig pen or even the peach orchard. It was all barren, like that place in the Bible that says that fertile land was turned into desert and nothing ever grew there again.

Yes, it's really true that you can't go back.

Yet, many of my earliest memories came drifting back.

Daddy moved us out to the farm when I was only two, so my earliest memories are of life on that farm. I can remember, when I was three, Mama getting up on Sunday mornings, fixing breakfast to get the rest of the family out of bed (and sometimes it was fried chicken), then getting me and herself dressed and the two of us walking three miles to town to church. If I got tired, she picked me up and carried me for a ways. We stopped at Grandma's and she joined us. Many times, someone invited us to their home for dinner.

I remember one Sunday, and I may have been four, we went early enough to go to my brother Ira's grave because the next day was Decoration (Memorial) Day. Mama worked pulling weeds

Pearl Allen Andree

and making his grave pretty with the flowers on it. The couple that were the caretakers invited us for breakfast, and we still went to church!

I had two books in those years. The main one was a collection of Mother Goose rhymes. It was an inch thick and was about 8" x 10." I memorized all those rhymes and then I looked at the pictures and recited the rhyme. I thought I was reading. The other book was about Peter Rabbit and I had to get someone to read that to me. A man Daddy did business with gave that book to him to bring home to me.

Daddy rocked me on his lap and sang to me (like Burl Ives) and I relished those times. He sang songs like "It's a Long Way to Tipperary" and "The Preacher and the Bear." He was a good singer and his roots were the hills of Arkansas. When Martha and Babe visited and Babe brought his fiddle, sometimes Daddy picked it up and played it.

Discipline

Some of my earliest memories involved discipline, the Daddy kind. Older siblings received the full force of EZ Allen's discipline. I only caught it twice, but as you'll note, I remember clearly both times. Both were for disobedience, pure and simple. As Pete has explained, Dad made sure you heard and understood the command—once. He never repeated a request for compliance.

I had been warned not to play with milkweed, as the liquid inside the stems was poisonous. I remember wanting to see what the inside looked like, so I broke the stem and white milky fluid ran out. No way would have I put any in my mouth knowing it was poisonous, but I knew I wasn't supposed to be playing with it, and there was probably consternation about whether I had. When Dad found me, I received due reckoning. Also, he whipped a person's bottom.

The other time was when Babe and Martha were visiting with Charles, who was about three, and Margaret, about one. I had recently learned to read and was quite proud of the feat. Unfortunately, I didn't yet know the concept of reading silently. Everyone was watching Margaret try walking, so perhaps there was a bit of jealousy there, but when Daddy told me to "read to yourself," I should have noticed the tone of his voice. I ignored him and kept reading aloud. Punishment was swift and sure. I remember Mama was upset about it. When the whipping was over, she took me to the bedroom and put me to bed, meaning to comfort me, I'm sure. But in the dark away from the fun and without the possibility of showing off my reading skill? What kind of comfort is that?

Pearl Allen Andree

Another incident happened when Babe and Martha's family was there. This must have been when Charles was about two. He and I were playing in the front yard. I don't remember that we were fighting, but he picked up a rock and threw it at me. A sharp point of it struck my forehead and the blood started flowing profusely. He was scared to death and started running blindly around the house. He stumbled on the cement form around the well and hurt himself. Everyone decided he didn't need to be punished—he'd had enough.

Mom's discipline, while not as stern, was just as sure and swift. Any child or grandchild of mine who's stubborn comes by it naturally.

While such discipline may have seemed too strict or stern, I have observed in life that children who have been taught obedience and disciplined strongly enough to make it stick have usually been the adults who adapt and have more self-discipline.

Stover Elementary School

I DON'T know how old that Stover School was, but it was well-built. The rural community supported a three-room school with a large auditorium and a duplex house for the principal's family and two teachers. It may have been that I first smelled greasepaint in that auditorium. My grown brothers and their friends performed Little Theater-type plays there. At least once a week, a program was performed at a morning assembly.

Margie and Mary Sue Cook were my playmates. Margie was three years older and Mary Sue was one year older. The year I was five, Mary Sue was starting school and I would be without playmates, so Mama asked permission from the school to let me start. I did know my ABCs and could count to 100. They must have thought that was good because they let me start. I was delighted. I finished the Primer by Thanksgiving. Miss Johnson was my teacher and, apparently, she and my brother Ornan had dated some. Maybe I had preferential treatment, but I fell heir to an 8" x 10" framed picture of her, which I discarded only a few years ago.

She found out I could memorize well, so she had me perform small things in the Monday morning assemblies in the auditorium at that three-room country schoolhouse. She wrote out "Little Orphan Annie" by James Whitcomb Riley in a composition book so Mama could read it to me and I could memorize it. It was the first monologue I ever performed and it set a precedent for my interest in acting.

Miss Johnson also gave me my first starring role, as the princess in "Sleeping Beauty." We performed it as three acts for a

Pearl Allen Andree

PTA meeting. I was married with children before I realized PTA meetings were for business and not for children to entertain their parents. I remember when the prince and I were talking to each other, she had us count to 100 to make it look like we were talking to each other.

As I mentioned before, my grown brothers and sister, Alma, and their friends got together and put on plays in the auditorium of that country schoolhouse for the community. One play was "The Haunted Rocking Chair." It was a murder mystery and I thought I was old enough to sit up front by myself, away from my mama. The third act opened with Leo's friend Mac Maize hanging in the window with blue lighting all around. I ran to find my mama. Pete and Dorothy were in that play. He was her son and they were made up in blackface. Since segregation was a fact of life in that time and place, no one thought it was derogatory.

Race

I DOUBT any place was more racist than Oklahoma during the Depression years. Marlow did not allow a colored person overnight. I heard stories that there had been a lynching at the Allen Hotel (no relation). A bit self-righteous for a town named after a family of outlaws! The school football team even called itself "the Outlaws."

In contrast, the main kinds of readings that I was given by my teachers to present for entertainment were Negro-dialect types. In addition, in those early grade-school years I took private expression lessons and many of those readings and monologues I was given to learn were in various dialects, including Black.

I know conventional wisdom says Blacks resent this and believe they are being ridiculed. I personally don't think that was true. When a comic imitates a well-known person we say, "Imitation is the sincerest form of flattery."

That may not be always true, but for me, those readings made me more aware of Black culture and more sensitive to the feelings of others. Most importantly, it gave me understanding and respect. Years later when I lived in Australia for a few years, one of the things I missed most was the musical artistry and other cultural contributions of Blacks that we may take for granted.

Actually, I never saw a black person until I was six and Daddy took Mama and me to Chickasha and we drove through the part of town where Blacks lived. My mother was such a kind person she could sit down and visit with anybody. Mama never met a stranger. It would never have surprised me to see her get acquainted and be friends with anyone, no matter their ethnic origin.

Pearl Allen Andree

One thing I remember about her is that when anyone told a joke about a Black person, she always remonstrated, "Now don't forget, it was a Black person that helped Jeremiah out of the miry pit." Mama taught me that all others were just as good as we were.

Birthday Party

I HAD two birthday parties growing up. One was my sixth, on the farm, and the other was my fifteenth, in Arizona.

For my sixth, several children came. We played winkum and other parlor games. The principal's son, my heartthrob at the time, gave me a "pearl" necklace. Refreshments were great. Mom baked a chocolate cake and Mrs. Cook made an angel food (in those days, from scratch), my favorite, with coconut all over it. Unfortunately, I never had a taste. It was eaten before I had a chance at it. At any rate, it was a memorable party.

The Sugar Bowl

A SUGAR bowl exists in my memory.

On that twenty-acre farm of my childhood, in that shack of a house with a pioneer-like kitchen, there was Dad's homemade dining table. The Blue Willow sugar bowl on it was one bright spot in that kitchen. Like most children, I liked sugar, and Mama used it without worrying about the consequences as we do today. More than that, the sugar bowl was a mystery—an object that held memories for everyone but me.

For Christmas of 1926, my brother Ira had given my mother a complete set of Blue Willow English dishes. On January 21, 1927, he was killed. I was born two months later. I guess the whole trauma nearly killed Mama.

In my memory, the only dish left of the set was the sugar bowl. I don't remember our having dishes, cups, or flatware that matched. Sometimes tin plates, dime store plates, flatware of all sorts, and fruit jars for beverages were used by all. But once, I've been told, my mother had white bedspreads and tablecloths and pretty dishes.

Many times, I've wondered how Mama felt every time a piece of the Blue Willow was broken.

I don't know what happened to that sugar bowl, but through the years I always wanted to replace it. I could have later in my life in Australia, but I kept postponing it, so never did. Back stateside, there was a shop with imports from England. Again, I kept putting it off, so never did buy it.

Maud and Pearl

Thanks to supermarket promotions, I finally acquired a Blue Willow sugar and creamer set. I think Mom's was larger, but many times things from childhood seemed bigger back then.

A Christmas Story

(Warning: Do not tell or read this story in the presence of children who have not learned the true meaning of Santa Claus.)

As a child on an Oklahoma farm, and my folks being members of the Church of Christ, I had never witnessed a church play at Christmas time. Our neighbors the Cooks, however, were members of the Presbyterian church. They invited me to go into Marlow with them on Christmas Eve for such an event.

I was six years old and had heard rumors at school about skepticism of Santa Claus. Surely they were wrong, I reasoned, because Christmas morning was always magical: a fresh orange and apple in my stocking—such beauties were not a regular bill of fare at our place. Always a new doll, but here I hit a snag. Every year I requested a stand-up doll, like a Shirley Temple doll, but invariably I received another baby doll. Another point bothered me: If you could request anything you wanted, why didn't you get it? And why did rich kids get what they requested? The old man with the beard was definitely a believer in class distinction, but I was too young to sort that out.

The Cooks lived on a hill in a big, beautiful, white house with columns about a city block from us. Dorothy Cook married my brother Pete Allen, and my playmates were Margie and Mary Sue Cook.

Christmas Eve became magical when I went with the Cooks to town in their car at night! It was the first time I had gone for a car ride in the evening and the first time I was not going with my parents. We saw a Christmas play in a church setting that included

Maud and Pearl

a decorated Christmas tree! All the children received little bags of goodies, a special treat for me. Naturally it was late (11:00 p.m.) when they brought me home. I was surprised to find Mama and Daddy still up; as farmers with milking cows, they normally retired about 9:00.

My stocking was hanging on my bed, which was in a corner of the kitchen, the warmest room in the house. Mama and Daddy were anxious to get me to bed "before Santa comes." I was so excited all I wanted to do was tell them about the play I'd seen. Sleepy, I wasn't.

Mama rushed me into bed. I was an accomplished "possum-player" (pretending to be asleep) and closed my eyes accordingly. It wasn't long before I heard activity near me. Peeking from the covers, I watched Mama filling my stocking.

Disappointed? Yes, but my reaction was to giggle!

Naturally she was aggravated—and probably a little relieved.

Do You Know Where Your Shoes Are?

WHEN I think about keeping things neatly where they can be found, it reminds me of my mother.

On the farm, that old weather-beaten house had no running water, bathroom, or electricity. The toilet was a privy out back, so I never wanted to walk out there in the night. (Mom put a slop pail under the bed, and it was emptied the next morning.)

When I went to bed at night, she insisted I place my shoes and socks (I only had one pair, except in summer when I had Sunday shoes) side by side under the bed, close to the head end. Always she would say, "Put them where you can find them and put them on in the dark if you have to." Since there were no lights to turn on, we used coal-oil lamps, and it was easier most of the time to do things in the dark.

When I asked her about ghosts, she assured me there was no such thing.

Sometimes I have trouble sleeping if there's too much light, but I'm not afraid of the dark and I always know where my shoes are.

The Porch on a Summer Afternoon

THE afternoon sun caused the house shadow to fall east, where the back porch was located. This made it the best place to take my nap on a warm summer afternoon. Cool breezes came through the screen to play around my perspiring hairline and sweaty brow. As I lay on the rugged homemade patchwork quilt made by Mama from old jeans, my hands moved across the designs, feeling the different textures. The wool was like little prickly hairs sticking up, but other patches felt smooth and soft, the old corduroy and velvets smooth when my hand stroked in one direction, rough and prickly when I stroked the opposite way. I traced a star with my finger and thought of the real stars that filled the nighttime sky. My mind drifted into a pleasant summer sleep.

I slowly awoke with a hazy feeling, gradually realizing I was sweaty at my hairline and where my body had lain next to the heavy quilt. I sat up, put my bare feet on the cool wood floor, and spied the canvas curtain across the room that covered the window cooler. This necessary appendage had been crudely built by my mother and provided a cooling respite in the hot summertime. Canvas around the framework was kept wet by soaking up cool, fresh, well water from the two- to three-inch depth in the tray below.

When I pulled back the canvas, a delightful coolness wafted on my senses. Dairy products were kept here fresh and sweet for the family table: delicate eggs piled high in their container; big gallon jars of sweet milk, some with cream, others skimmed, and the cream used to make butter; yellow butter already made, beautifully patted by hand into round bowls; buttermilk, that

Pearl Allen Andree

lovely liquid left from having churned the butter, with teeny bits of butter lumps still in it; clabber, thick and white with little rivers from one side of the bowl to the other, waiting for the time when it would be made into cottage cheese; and some cottage cheese itself with its little curds like so many minute snowballs in one place snuggling together.

I poked my finger into the thick cream and made a little ditch, bringing up a lump for the end of my tongue to savor. It was cool and sweet and made little chill bumps go up my back as I swallowed. I let the curtain fall back into place, realizing I smelled delicious aromas from the kitchen.

Mom must be baking bread; the yeasty scent could transport me to the make-believe world of hot cross buns and Simple Simon's pies. I could identify what we would have for dinner; there was the tantalizing smell of roast meat, the mingling aromas of vegetables—potatoes, green beans, and corn; and— mmm-mmm—the delicious fruity smell of my favorite dessert, cherry cobbler.

Surely there was no better place to be at this time.

Relaxation and Drama

I THINK Daddy was able to play any instrument he picked up. Pete sang and I loved it. I requested one song repeatedly: "When the Work's All Done This Fall." I always cried but asked for it again.

Years later while listening to the radio, Babe told me that Daddy once told him that the Grand Ole Opry musician Uncle Dave Macon was "one kind of a cousin or another."

Zeke Boy sang a silly song, but I took it seriously. I cried and said, "I don't want Zeke Boy to go out in the garden and eat worms and die." I definitely received a legacy watching Zeke do dramatic readings like "The Face on the Bar-Room Floor" and similar ones.

It wasn't easy for my brothers to dress up. A little mirror propped up in that front hall was the only spot for shaving, but the white shirts Mom and Alma had ironed with flat irons made them the handsomest of men. In many ways we were a family of hams, as surely as the professional theater families, except we didn't have to worry about bookings.

A Pet of My Own

I'll bet most people want to live on a farm so they can have a pet. With all those animals around, surely one could have lots of pets.

It doesn't necessarily work that way. If there's a pet on the farm, that pet has to pay its way. That pet has to work for what it eats, the same as most of the people who live on a farm do. The dog, for instance, helps bring the cows home evenings, and he goes hunting with the men when they go out to shoot rabbits to have fresh meat on the table. He chases varmints away from the house that shouldn't get in. I don't think I've ever known a farmer's wife who had a French poodle. The dog stays outside.

Now, a cat is different. A cat can come into the house because one of the things a cat does is catch mice. And if you live in an old house with cracks in the walls like the one we lived in, the cat had to come in because there were mice to catch. But the cats were not those green-eyed Persian and Siamese beauties people have today for pets. These were cats like, well, like the cat that was in the kitchen the day my mother said, "Get that cat out of this kitchen!"

I reached down, put both my hands underneath that cat's tummy, and started to pick him up, and he came with me—except his feet stayed on the floor. My mother said, "That's no way to pick up a cat," and she showed me. "Put your hands on the nape of the neck and pick him up." She put him back down and said, "Now, you do it, and get that cat out of this kitchen."

I reached down and I put my hands on the nape of his neck, and I pulled up. His head came with me, but his feet stayed on the floor.

To this day, people ask me, "Why don't you like cats?"

Maud and Pearl

My answer is, "I don't like to see cats hurt any more than anyone else does. I just don't like to touch them because of the way their skin slides over their bones."

I really did want a pet of my own.

I let it be known that I thought it would be a good idea for me to have a pony. My daddy promised me I'd get a pony on my sixth birthday. I want you to notice, he *promised*.

Of course, he promised me that when I was four years old, and my mother kept telling me, "You're not going to get a pony on your birthday. Your daddy can't afford to buy you a pony."

But I believed. This is the same man who said, "When I shake hands on a deal, it's a deal. A man's word is his bond. A man has to be trusted." So I believed.

But my sixth birthday came and went, and I still didn't have a pony. I never did get a pony, so my mother was right. But I did find out one thing. There is a lot of difference between a grown man shaking the hand of another grown man and telling him he'll sell a cow for $30 and that same grown man promising a child he's going to get her a pony.

One cold, dark night in the winter, my daddy went out of the house to check on the old sow in the pig pen because she was expecting a litter of pigs. She was having them when he went out so he stayed and helped. That litter of pigs must have had ten or twelve piggies in it.

After a while he came back in with a little pig in his hand. I was sitting in a chair with the oven door down (you know, one of these old wood ranges with the oven door that comes down). I was sitting there with my feet up on that oven door trying to keep warm, and he took this baby pig and put it down in my lap and said, "This is for you."

I didn't know what to do. I didn't know how to treat a pet pig. This one was a tiny little thing; in fact, he was the runt. Daddy showed me how to use a dropper with milk in it to feed him, because he was such a runt that he couldn't elbow his brothers and sisters out of the way so he could get some food from his mama. I worried about how I would treat that pet pig.

Pearl Allen Andree

Should I get a collar for him and lead him around? Would he follow me to school like Mary's little lamb? I didn't have to worry about things like that, because within two or three weeks, that baby pig was healthy and went right back into the pig pen with his brothers and sisters, healthy enough to fight his way to the dinner table. Within a few weeks, I couldn't tell my piggy from the others.

I liked baby chicks, but of course they grew up to be fried chicken. I understand that once I loved a baby chick so much, I squeezed it to death.

My favorite animal was a cottontail rabbit. My favorite book was about Peter Rabbit. We had a berry patch and I knew all about briar patches. So I really liked rabbits. One day, Mama, Daddy, and I got in the wagon. He'd hitched up the mules and we went over to visit the Harrisons. They lived about ten miles away, and that man raised bunny rabbits. He gave me a bunny rabbit of my own. I was thrilled. We took that bunny home, and Daddy built him a hutch up off the ground and warned me that I must keep the door of the hutch latched very well because if I didn't, the bunny would get out of the crate and run away and join the rabbits out in the wild.

I loved that bunny rabbit. I went out and talked to him practically all day. I took him pieces of lettuce, carrot tops, and pieces of carrot—any kind of food my mother gave me to feed him. I even learned to wiggle my nose.

Finally, the new wore off and I didn't spend as much time with him. I went down to check on him one day and the door was unlatched. He was gone! I was broken-hearted and could hardly believe I had left his latch undone. I just couldn't believe it.

After a few days, Daddy said he'd seen my rabbit down by the creek, and he must have eaten some poison weeds or something because he was dead. I felt guilty about that. I felt I didn't deserve to have a pet because I had left the latch undone and he'd gotten away.

But there's a scene that keeps coming back to me through the years. Every once in a while, I think about it, and then I forget it. This is the scene: the whole family is sitting around the great

Maud and Pearl

big square dining table my daddy built. We sat on benches around it, my older brothers, Dad, a teenage sister, my mother, and I. For some reason, there wasn't much talking going on, and since I never had a chance to talk ("children should be seen and not heard" was the way they figured it), I was talking like mad about what a good dinner Mama had fixed. We were having fried rabbit, mashed potatoes and gravy, biscuits, and peas, and we were going to have berries and cream afterward.

I was going on and on, and I thought it was kind of funny that my brothers didn't have much to say, but my sister Alma was having an awful time. She was acting like she couldn't eat her food; she acted like she had a stomach ache; she acted like she had a headache and like she wanted to cry. She was having a terrible time, and finally my father got disgusted. He looked at her and said, "If you can't eat your food at this table like the rest of us, you can just get up and leave." And she did! She left the table and went out of the room and didn't eat.

I was really worried about her, and I asked Mama, "Why doesn't Alma want to eat?"

All my mother said was, "Well, she just doesn't like rabbit."

All my life, I thought my sister didn't like rabbit. If she came to visit me, even if I'd wanted to, I wouldn't have served her rabbit because she didn't like it.

She's gone on to her reward now, but a few years ago, my son Pat was reminiscing about the summers of childhood when he visited his Uncle Lee and Aunt Alma on their Texas ranch. He said, "You know, Uncle Lee and I used to go rabbit hunting and we'd bring those rabbits back and Aunt Alma would fix 'em up and fry them. They were just like fried chicken, and she'd make mashed potatoes and gravy and biscuits. Boy! She really made a good meal out of that fried rabbit."

I said, "That was really nice of your Aunt Alma, seeing as how she didn't like rabbit, to fix it for you."

And he said, "What do you mean, she didn't like rabbit? She always ate it when I was there."

The Ol' Fire and Wasp Story

Pete and Leo had permission from ol' man Cook, who lived near their home, to take the dead blackjack sticks. One day, they were on their way there to gather firewood for Maud. They had the mules hitched and while Pete drove, Leo tossed the wood into the wagon. Leo was helping Maud and also might have been keeping an eye on young Pete with more than just a mite of interest, as Pete had a hankerin' for young Dorothy Cook. They'd done this quite often of late and thought they knew this stand of woods pretty well.

Leo was behind the wagon and had dropped back to tug down a good stick. Pete saw this and pulled up on the mules to wait.

Pete noticed a snag of wood had come up and crooked into the wheel spoke, so he commenced to back off. Suddenly, the mules started prancing in an unusual cadence with their heads high and backing into their collars in an effort to back the wagon. When Pete looked down at the hooves, he saw wasps burning the air and those hooves with their stings.

He yelled back to Leo, "What should I do?"

Leo hollered, "Pull the pin," as the horses were sure to bolt in misery. As Leo spoke, he ran up, beating Pete to the pin, and gave it a tug. As soon as he touched the pin, though, the swarm of hornets jumped all over him. He never had a chance to pull the pin free before the swarm hit him. Leo ran over a short way and began rolling on the ground in an effort to dislodge the hornets.

Pete hit the ground running to aid his brother in whatever way he might. This turned out to be by grabbing a stick and

Maud and Pearl

scraping the hornets from his skin. Poor Leo's eyes were already swelling shut from the poison. Pete had one thing to do before he helped Leo home: pull the pin. This was necessary in order to free the mules to find their way home.

The next morning, their brother Ornan lit out with the mules to fetch the wagon back. He also carried a surprise for those wasps. When he got close enough to see the wagon, yet a safe distance away, he tethered the mules and went to work. His surprise for the wasps was kerosene, which he poured down the wasp hole and lit, throwing just enough wood on the fire to keep it going but not to burn the wagon. He never said, but he was paying back the wasps that had severely wounded his older brother Leo and harmed the younger Pete.

While Ornan was busying himself with wasp eradication techniques, another bit of drama was playing out back at the farm. Leo had been set outside under a tree by the road to rest from his afflictions, quite possibly with a poultice of some sort made by Maud. Along came another brother, Zeke Jr, to visit Maud and help at the farm. He looked at the stranger by the road loafing under the tree and marveled at how truly ugly the good Lord had made this man, with a head the size and shape of a watermelon.

With this thought fresh on his mind as he came inside to say hello, he asked Maud and Pete straight off, "Who is that fat-headed stranger by the road?" He was quite surprised but went to help Ornan. Together, they freed the wagon from its spot and hitched it up to the mules for the trip home. Later in life, they wondered if that charred hole was still there.

I (Pearl) was a child when this story happened. We were truly scared for Leo's life when he arrived back at the house that day. The sight of his swollen face and arms was frightening. Since we used coal oil in our lamps, chances are it was coal oil that Ornan used to burn out the ground hornets.

Decades later my son, Patrick, wrote this story out after hearing it from his uncles.

A Class just Below God

I WENT through the second-grade work in half the year and was promoted to the third grade. I was not a fighter as a child—actually, I had an inferiority complex—but in the third grade, I found I could get quite angry.

One day it was raining so the teacher let us play in the room. The bigger kids never let me play ball (outside) because I was so scrawny, so I played on the swings or slide or other things. On this rainy day, we were playing hide and seek. I had found a corner for myself when a bigger girl literally pulled me out of it. I started fighting her, and her arm was in front of my face, so I bit her! I was not a biter, but I felt threatened. Now, my mama considered teachers to be in a class just below God (she had three sisters who were teachers), but when the teacher decided to punish me by not allowing me recess outside for the rest of the year (about three months), she was very upset. I was sickly and she felt I needed fresh air. She proceeded to plan for me to go to Marlow for fourth grade, paid the tuition, and received permission for me to ride the senior high school bus into town. I walked a half-mile to get the bus, but was used to walking a mile to school each day.

Cyclone

ONE afternoon, Daddy announced that a cyclone was coming and we should all go up to the Cooks' to share their good cement cellar (our cellar was dirt-walled and starting to cave in). The storm hit as soon as we got down there. The men wanted to play cards, but no one had remembered to bring a lantern. Walter Cook and Leo were appointed to go to the smokehouse and get one. When the door was opened, the storm started taking Leo up and the others had to hold on to him. The lantern was obtained and the card games ensued, but I was worried the wind would carry Leo away.

Other scenes in the dirt-walled cellar at our place made an impression. Of course, there was a wooden structure of poles and beams that contained the packed dirt. Shelves held Mama's canned goods, and a bench serviced as a couch. One night we were waiting out a storm and I saw a snake in the structure as I lay on that bench. No way could I nap after that!

Most snakes were harmless to humans, but Mom was lethal with them as they endangered her chickens. Sometimes she found one in the house, and once she killed one in a tree when we were walking across the creek.

In my adult life, I have adopted the attitude that God knew what He was doing when He put enmity between the female and the snake, and I'm not about to question His wisdom. Furthermore, I have never, of my own free will, lived in a cyclonic belt.

The discovery of the library was my biggest thrill in the fourth grade. Wonder of wonders! I thought I'd died and gone to heaven the first time we "had to" spend some time there. We

Pearl Allen Andree

were allowed to go and read books there sometimes, but I don't remember if they let us check them out to bring home. Anyway, I had so much studying to do, there wasn't much time for reading. Incidentally, on the farm at that time, all nighttime reading was done by the light of coal oil lamps.

In fourth grade, I started riding the school bus into town for school. Fourth grade was a great awakening. My teacher was Miss Mattie Kincannon, and she had taught Pete and Alma. She had taught for fifty years, and she was about age 75! She could take care of rambunctious kids, though, with the aid of the principal, Mr. Shrock. He was a tall Native American and very good-looking. He and my Uncle Lem were my first crushes. If Miss Mattie had to leave the room, I saw the principal's eyes watching us through the little slit windows in the hall doors. Boys who misbehaved would be called to the principal's office later.

The Marlow grammar school was a three-floor red brick building with big, round cylinders going up to the third floor on the outside as fire escapes. Sometimes we crawled up the insides of these metal cylinders and slid back down. On the same property were a junior high (seventh, eighth, and ninth grades), tennis courts, and a senior high building for tenth, eleventh, and twelfth grades.

The summer of 1935 was eventful, with the marriages of both Ornan and Pete. Mama had taught me to use the Singer treadle sewing machine and how to hand-sew. The latter became handy when doing embroidery. Once a week we got the *Kansas City Star* newspaper, and once in a while she would send for a pattern. That's how I was able to make a set of seven tea towels (from white flour sacks) for their wedding gifts, embroidered with each weekday activity. Since I only had one set, I had to give three to one and four to the other. I don't remember who was the winner!

Sickness

I HAD whooping cough when I was two, too young to remember. The result was an annual bout of some kind with flu and/or bronchitis. Now we know living in a house full of second-hand smoke didn't help much.

In second grade one morning—Election Day (it must have been the school board election since the year was '33) —I announced that I had a headache. Mama didn't believe me, probably thinking I was echoing a grown-up. Later in the day at school, the teacher recognized I was sick and told me to go see if I could find my parents among all the people there to vote. I couldn't find them, but I found the Cooks' car, laid down in the back seat, and went to sleep. The measles had struck, and never again did I have trouble convincing Mama I was sick.

Since Mom had lost her first child as a baby to measles and pneumonia, she was very particular in my treatment. For two weeks I was kept in bed with the windows shaded (this was to protect my eyes). I don't remember if we had the doctor.

In fourth grade, I walked a half-mile to get the high school bus into Marlow School. In fifth grade, the route changed, and I had to walk a mile and a half. That year, I was self-conscious about the long stockings and/or long underwear Mom made me wear to keep warm. Her expression if my legs were exposed was, "The wind'll go right up ya." On the way to the bus, I changed into anklets to be more like the other girls at school. Of course, I got sick. We didn't have miracle drugs, and I nearly died. I missed four weeks of school and the two weeks of Christmas vacation before I was well.

Pearl Allen Andree

Dr. Tally, a country doctor, came out to see me, and at the same time he went to Cooks', as their girl Thelma had pneumonia. For each of us, our illnesses were spoken of in whispers—how the doctor said to keep a window open and that the only thing left to do was pray. Dr. Tally said I needed cod liver oil, a whole tablespoon three times a day. Turned out I liked it! I reminded Mama to get my dose if she forgot it. We both recovered, but the cough medicine I took was awful-tasting liquid, yucky black herbal stuff that probably contained alcohol. That's when I learned that if your system needs something badly enough, you can like, or at least tolerate, it. When I grew old enough to taste alcoholic drinks, I hated them because they tasted like that medicine. One time Ornan walked at least three miles to buy a package of gum because it was good to take away the taste. I slept on the dufold in the front room where the heating stove was so I'd be warmer. Nobody connected the fact that when the men gathered round the stove in the evenings and smoked, my temperature always rose.

When we moved to Arizona, I never missed another day of school due to flu or bronchitis.

Summer of 1936

The summer of 1936 was notable. Pete and Dorothy were expecting a baby and Mama wanted to take me to stay with them to help for a while. While there, I was one sad sack story after another. Daddy was robbing the beehives one day and I was curious. I managed to let a bee sting me on my palm and it became infected. Then I went exploring along a creek and acquired a bad case of poison ivy. Mama gave me soda baths, and decided I could pull weeds out of the garden early in the mornings. But I got a rash doing that, too. More soda baths. Then one day Mama was ironing and I put my hand on the ironing board when she wasn't watching, and she put the point of the iron down on the back of my left hand. That bad burn took the rest of the summer to heal.

Every day, Dorothy walked over to see her mother. The round trip was about five miles. A baby girl was born on June 30th, named Dawn Marie. I thought she was so beautiful, but no one would let me hold her (which was probably wise). We stayed about two or three weeks before going back to the farm.

Before school started, Mama, Daddy, and I moved into Marlow. We lived in an apartment above the grocery store, and I was delighted to live in a place with a bathroom! It was only about a half-block to the schoolhouse, and the movie theatre was in the same block where we lived. I was allowed to go to a lot of movies, especially on Saturdays for the series type. I had never seen a movie until I was seven. When Babe heard about that, he personally saw to it that I got to see one on a Saturday. It was a cops-and-robbers story with lots of car chases.

Pearl Allen Andree

Another popular excitement of that time was "Bank Night" at the movies, when someone was announced as having won some money. It usually happened on Wednesday night, but I don't remember knowing anyone who won. When living in town, I could really enjoy going. I saw the first movie where I cried—and fell in love with Spencer Tracy. It was *Captains Courageous*, and when I went back to the apartment, I told it to Mama and Daddy and cried when I told it. Acting out the movie when I told about it must have started then. I was still doing it in high school for Mama and Leo.

I was in Mr. Shrock's classroom, and Mom had his wife give me expression lessons once a week. I went to her house, a short way from home. I started getting scheduled to give monologues at a number of events, mainly in the auditorium in the junior high school. Most of them were comedy, and I liked it when the audience laughed. This seemed to be the kind of reading I gave from then on.

This was a time when stores gave little gifts called premiums based on how much one bought. Daddy acquired things and usually he gave them to me as a gift. One of those gifts was a beautiful chrome platter (Pat has it now). That's also how I got my roller skates. There was plenty of cement around, so I proceeded to learn. A traveling rink came to town and set up across the street on a vacant lot. Alma took me one afternoon, and some bozo made the mistake of saying to me, "Why don't you learn to skate before you go skating?"

It was one of the few times I saw Alma angry. She countered, "How's she going to learn if she doesn't try?"

Vignettes

THE first Allen grandchild was Charles Walter, Martha and Babe Robertson's son. In the next six years, only granddaughters were born. I thought my nieces were the cutest, smartest, and prettiest little girls in the world. In my opinion, they're still world-class.

Saturday night baths were taken in a galvanized wash tub. It was placed on the kitchen floor, and water heated on the stove was poured into it. Being the youngest, I was allowed to bathe first. Apparently, Jenny Lee had witnessed Mom's difficulty with squeezing into the tub. When Dad bought a new gray 1936 Chevrolet sedan, he took us for a ride to Lawton. When we passed Lake Lawtonka, Jenny excitedly called from the back seat, "O-o-o Mamaw, take a bath!"

Rita, at age two, said, "Aunt Pearl, you wanna come play house with me, huh, why don'cha? Please, huh, why don'cha come play house with me?" until I agreed, which usually didn't take long.

Margaret (Totsy) repeated her Uncle Leo's remarks when she took a bath. Afterwards, you could hear her running around the house announcing, "I'm as naked as a jaybird and twice as cute." She looked exactly like Shirley Temple, I thought, including the double dimples.

I loved climbing trees, and so did my friend Mary Sue Cook. Our favorites were the two cherry trees, especially when the fruit was ripe. One day, she fell through the tree, from high up to the bottom branches. We had a conference and decided we must not tell our mothers.

Pearl Allen Andree

She and I learned to sew on the machine together. One day, at her machine, she ran the needle through her finger. Her grown brother Walter said, "I feel sorry for whoever marries either of you 'cause he'll have his hands full." One time, he spanked me—or so I thought—and I ran home yelling. He had actually clapped his hands behind me with a loud noise.

A most precious memory as a teenager was when I was 16 and took six nieces on the bus to Phoenix. We went to the Fox Theater to see *Snow White and the 7 Dwarfs*. Carol Lou was scared enough of the witch to hide her head in my lap.

The Encyclopedia

As I said before, when I was a little girl, I owned two books. One, the big book of Mother Goose, I knew by heart, all the rhymes. The other book, a small one about Peter Rabbit, was given to me by a friend of my father's. The Bible was read a lot in our house, plus *The Kansas City Star* weekly newspaper, which came to the mailbox on the farm. Once in a while, my older grown brothers brought home a Sunday paper with colored funnies. That was the sum total of our home library.

I became proficient at wandering through the stores looking at everything. A furniture store was my favorite haunt. It was thrilling to me to wander around this beautiful place exploring the latest appliances and sitting on the plush sofas. Strangely, the salespeople never minded. They seemed to accept my presence as if I might go home and tell my parents to come back and buy. Many times in my adult life, I have remembered how kind they were to allow me to spend so much of my time, especially in the hot summer, engaged in my pastime.

The five and dime store was farther down Main. I didn't go in there as much, but one day I saw a book! I told Mom about it, and she went with me to look. Priced at 49¢, I was sure it would make me the smartest student in school. A one-volume encyclopedia, it was like a dictionary, except there was a paragraph of encyclopedic description on topics.

Apparently, Mom thought it a good idea for me to have it, so she took me in hand and we visited my father in his real estate office, a nondescript room he rented from the local town hotel., My father rarely had any money, but if he did and you caught him

Pearl Allen Andree

at the right time, he could be generous. That is, as far as things like nickel ice cream cones and other small items were concerned. On this occasion, Mom asked for 50¢ for this book for Pearl, and he reached into his pocket, brought out the two quarters, and handed them over. This would have been in the year 1936.

Naturally, I was thrilled. The book was precious to me, and I used it throughout school. Even through high school, it was a fount of information for reports and themes, sometimes copied verbatim. I had never heard of plagiarism. Indeed, the teachers didn't comment and I made many an A with my method.

In December 1937, my mother and I moved to Arizona. I was in the seventh grade (and had made two book reports). She packed our things in a wardrobe trunk. It opened up so it could be stood on end. On the right side were drawers (like a chest of drawers). On the left was a place to hang things on hangars if you wanted, and at the bottom was a box similar to a briefcase. The latter space is where Mom placed all her precious family snapshots and photographs. Placed in the wardrobe trunk somewhere was my encyclopedia.

Cameo Shot Memories

THE time we went to Chickasha, Mom and Dad bought me a new coat. It was green and had a chinchilla collar and ties. I didn't know for years that the fur was fake. I felt fancily dressed anyway. I really thought that coat was special.

I would have liked to learn to ride horses. The one time my brothers put me on a horse and I was riding around the front yard, Mom ran to the front stoop and yelled something. When I turned around to see her, I did what she was trying to prevent: I rode into the clothesline, right at my neck. I wasn't going fast enough for it to even make a mark, and it wouldn't have happened if she hadn't yelled, but my riding days were over right then.

I was barely old enough to remember the wreck in the truck. We were in Marlow, and Daddy was driving a big truck (bigger than a pickup). I was sitting between him and Mom. Daddy made a right turn and some man in a car, driving on the wrong side of the road, collided with us head-on. The windshield shattered and Mom bent over to shield my eyes. Her forehead was severely cut. She had to have stitches on the wound.

Daddy always said, "You have to drive as if everyone else on the road is crazy."

The hoboes found our farmhouse rather easily. Mom always gave them something to eat. If Daddy was home, he asked them to chop wood or some other task. Sometimes they needed to stay overnight. One such was a man from Arkansas, and he ate dinner with us. It may have only been Mama, Dad, and me. He sat there and told stories that kept everyone laughing. He stuttered, and I couldn't keep myself from giggling. Mom tried to stop me but it

Pearl Allen Andree

was hopeless. Every time he started talking, I started giggling. She was so embarrassed. They wondered later if he was the one who wrote a popular book, *Arkansas Traveler*. He seemed well educated.

One of my favorite memories of Grandma Hall was when she was about 75. She went for a ride on a motorcycle with Luther Hall, a nephew of hers. Off she went on those old rutty country roads. She looked almost identical to the Granny on *The Beverly Hillbillies*.

I can't tell how you make sorghum molasses out of the cane, but I remember going to McCaulay's farm when almost everyone in the community came to do it. It was like a festival for the kids. We had sorghum cane sticks to chew on, and there were good things to eat, like a potluck. We took our sorghum home, probably about a year's supply, and that's where the enchantment ended for me. Never could I understand the rapturous delight the rest of the family seemed to enjoy from sorghum on biscuits. I liked honey (still do) and other molasses, but sorghum leaves me unenthusiastic.

Mama had a quote for almost every situation. If someone told her I was pretty in my presence, she always reminded me later, "Just remember, pretty is as pretty does." If she thought I might be too impressed with an accomplishment, she would quote, "Pride goeth before destruction; a haughty spirit before a fall." Another goody, which has been used repeatedly in the family since the homestead days of Ira's PTA performance: "If a string is in a knot, patience will untie it. Patience can do many things; did you ever try it?"

Box and pie suppers were exciting. Women (or girls) would prepare a box with a good meal in it, or a pie, and decorate the package in grand style. Supposedly, her male partner did not see this art vision so he would bid on others too. An auctioneer handled the bidding war and sometimes they ran up the bids. The man had to eat with the girl whose meal or pie he purchased.

It was while we lived in Marlow that Aunt Effie died, and one day we heard that Jean Harlow died. I was dumbfounded she could die at such a young age. The radio was a new plus in my world. I listened to *Little Orphan Annie*. I also read the comic strip about her, and there were ads in magazines for Ovaltine using a

Maud and Pearl

comic strip of her. When I was younger, I told Mom I wouldn't cry so much if she bought Ovaltine for me.

Since the grammar school was only a block away, I went there to play. I loved to climb the insides of the fire escape, that huge round metal cylinder that went all the way to the third floor. It made a wonderful slide. We had to be careful in summer, though, as it could get really hot.

I enjoyed going to school there. In fourth grade I had Miss Mattie Kincannon, as I had said before. I don't remember my fifth-grade teacher's name, but she may have been the unenlightened woman from Boston who taught English. I have a vivid memory of her humiliating Morgan Barker, who had a speech impediment. She got him in front of the class and grilled him on pronouncing "the" and other basic words. I felt so sorry for him.

In sixth grade, I hit the jackpot. The principal, Mr. Shrock, was my homeroom teacher. His wife was my expression teacher. Did I mention he was over six feet tall? I could never understand why the mean boys weren't smart enough to realize that Mr. Shrock had expectations and wasn't going to let them get away with bad behavior.

Just as I started seventh grade, in the summer of 1937, we moved out to the golf course. Doesn't that sound ritzy? Not true. It was a shack with no electricity, so it was back to coal-oil lamps. I had much more studying to do, usually not getting to bed until ten or eleven. I brought home a large stack of books every night. This was junior high. Seventh grade brought the opportunity to do book reports (one every six weeks). That meant I had to read a book, and I loved that idea. I believe *Katrinka*, about a little Russian peasant girl, was the first novel I read. In the mornings, I was one of the last picked up by the bus; and in the afternoon, the last to get off. I can remember walking through a great field of grass, about waist high, and sometimes Mom came to meet me. As the days grew shorter, it was nearly dark by that time. It was during this period that Mom decided to move to Arizona when Babe and Martha decided to see if they liked it.

Babe had bought a new pickup and fixed the back for carrying things, and put a mattress in so the children could ride

Pearl Allen Andree

comfortably. I was too young to understand the marital relationship of my parents, but I know my mama had been hoping Daddy would take us to Arizona. I think he may have occasionally implied that he might, and I know she was desperate to get me there for my health. She talked Babe and Martha into taking her and me with them. She packed up her wardrobe trunk (which would be with her for many years to come) and we rode in the back of the pickup with two of the children. The third child rode in the cab with Martha and Babe, of course taking turns.

We arrived in Tolleson, Arizona on December 16, 1937. The three older of us children entered nearby Union Grammar School in January. We lived about three miles south of Tolleson.

Beginning Arizona

The Arizona climate and sunshine improved my health. I never missed another day of school because of being sick. No more bronchitis and flu. I grew six inches and gained 20 pounds in the first six months. I was destined never again to be a runt. I felt better, even though within months I would be practically living in ditches with irrigation pumps in the summer heat. In my child's mind, I began to think that Oklahoma had the lousiest weather in the country. Mama saw me healthier, and while she didn't say it, I believed she was determined not to go back to Oklahoma.

I knew families that lived in tents. Sometimes there were two tents separated by a breezeway. They may have lived there long enough to have flowering vines growing over the breezeway, making it their outdoor living room, fairly cool in the hot Arizona summer. Castor bean trees furnished fast-growing shade, but small children had to be watched so they didn't eat the beans. The tents had wood floors and wood came up about three feet on walls.

One family had brought a huge tent with them from the east, and the father was prepared to move if he needed to for work. He even had the flooring movable. The family of parents and four children lived there, and the mother kept it beautifully clean. Even the children worked hard picking cotton when they weren't in school. In the evenings, outside in the cool, they entertained us with singing accompanied by the oldest boy's mandolin and the father's harmonica. I often think of that family as indicative of the indomitable spirit of the people coming to Arizona to start new lives.

Pearl Allen Andree

Very few people had evaporative coolers, and no one had refrigeration. In a big house, windows were closed early in the day to seal in the cool night air. Curtains were pulled or shades drawn to keep out the sun's rays. Some more affluent homeowners had adobe houses. Our Mexican settlers had devised these adobe bricks based on Native American methods. The walls of the adobe houses were 12" thick and sometimes more. The insides of those homes were *cool*. Modern architects are beginning to use adobe bricks again.

The Arrowhead and the Quarter

WHEN I was a little girl, Mama had an arrowhead plus a little China doll's head. She said the doll's head was about a hundred years old then, which would make it over 150 years old now. As the years went by, the doll's head was misplaced and lost, but I still have the arrowhead. I don't know how she came to have it. Did she acquire it as a child in rural Oklahoma? Or did Dad or one of my brothers find it on the homestead in northwestern Oklahoma? ¿Quién sabe?

When Mom and I came to Arizona in December 1937, these items were included in a few treasures she brought in her wardrobe trunk, which I enjoyed being allowed to look through occasionally. In the crummy places she and I lived, the wardrobe trunk was, I think, her link to sanity. She allowed me the top small drawer for my private toiletry drawer, and the plush-covered half-lid hinged back to become the only vanity shelf I knew until Leo bought the bedroom set when we moved into the house on the high school campus my junior year. Even then, the wardrobe trunk never lost its mystique for me. My last high school semester, after Leo joined the Navy and Alma and her family joined us in a crowded situation again, it reverted to my only private spot. Mama kept that trunk well into the 1950s.

A closed packet contained, besides the arrowhead, a quarter that Mama kept for posterity. A note with it in her handwriting, which was beautiful, explained how the quarter was acquired. For the record, in this missive, I will repeat that explanation.

I was in the seventh grade in my first semester at Union Grammar, a rural three-room schoolhouse. The tall, red-headed

Pearl Allen Andree

principal, Mr. Maben (a Baptist preacher in Glendale on weekends), decided to have a talent contest. I did a dramatic reading, "De Cushville Hop," which had a bit of a little dance step to it. I'm certain Mr. Maben used whatever change he possessed for the prize money. Mine was a quarter for first place, while second place was a dime.

About 30 years later, one time when visiting with Tempe friends Howell and Betty Hood, I happened to mention the latter circumstance in my life. In unison, they said, "Maben? Not Jack Maben?" He had performed Howell and Betty's wedding ceremony, and Howell coincidentally met up with Jack Maben in the South Pacific during World War II. Small world.

A little drawstring bag holds the packet. It was what men in those days used to buy tobacco in, to roll their own cigarettes. Mom kept the doll's head and the bag and packet for all those years. So that is the rest of the story.

Union Grammar School

I CAME to Arizona at the age of ten and started in the seventh grade at Union Grammar, south of Tolleson on 91st Avenue, one of the eight grammar schools feeding into the Tolleson Union High School district.

Many people ridiculed and made fun of Okies, and I found this out before I entered school. I learned also that an Arizonan would say "you guys" rather than "y'all" (a contraction of "you all" meaning "all of you"). Immediately I adapted to "you guys" so no one would call me an "Okie." Sometimes it worked. I was also good at mimicking others' speech and that helped.

The three teachers were Mr. Jack Maben, the principal and sixth-, seventh-, and eighth-grade teacher; Mrs. Blue for third, fourth, and fifth grades; and Miss Jones, first and second grades and music. That January, it snowed in Phoenix and Mrs. Blue had snow on her car roof. How startled I was to see children take on so about snow. Some had never seen it before.

Mr. Maben read to us. He was tall and red-haired, and I had a crush on him. His reading introduced me to the world of classical literature: *Don Quixote* and Shakespearean plays like *Romeo and Juliet* and *Merchant of Venice*.

I was expected to play ball and this was a new thing for me. In Oklahoma, I had been relegated to the swings and see-saws because of my small size. It turned out that I couldn't throw a softball properly and everyone laughed when I tried. It was a nice kind of laughter, though, and they tried to show me the right way. Track was similar; I was a total dud. Volleyball became my game. After a year and a half, I was actually allowed to play on the

Pearl Allen Andree

team in a tournament. A group of five boys were good basketball players, and four year later, in high school, they took our small high school to state competitions. They didn't have divisions in those days.

We were poor in Oklahoma, and I never was invited to birthday parties of the more well-to-do children; but in Arizona, the first week, I was invited to the birthday party of a girl whose father was on the school board. I felt accepted and it did a lot for my morale.

In May 1938, Babe and Martha decided Arizona was not for them and returned to Oklahoma, but Mama and I stayed. We were alone and by ourselves. I had just turned 11. Of course, at the time I didn't fully understand my parents' relationship with each other. I have speculated that Mama truly thought that if she stayed in Arizona, Dad would come out eventually. Early on, I was aware of her fear that if she and I returned to Oklahoma, I would get sick again.

We found a cabin next door to the schoolhouse for $6 a month. The landlady was a widow with five kids ranging in ages from high school seniors down to sixth grade. One girl, called Tootsie, was about my same year in school. The cabin was like a salt box—it had no cooling, not even an evaporative cooler, and became intensely hot in the extremely hot Arizona summers. There was no public pool, but there was an irrigation pump nearby with stalls where the water gushed out of the ground and ran down a curved ditch someone had lined with cement. Pete's Dorothy gave me her bathing suit, which fit, and I practically lived in the water all summer. I learned to swim by using those stalls to practice strokes. A mile south was another irrigation pump where the dairy farmers had hollowed out enough dirt on each side of the ditch to make a swimming hole. People in Tolleson called it the "three-mile pump." It was a great day in August when I first swam across that pool without having to put my feet on the bottom.

Mama loved the water but had never learned to swim. However, she made sure all of her children learned. The landlady loaned her a bathing suit, and she sat in that curved ditch so the water rolled over her, almost like rapids. Somewhere she had found

Maud and Pearl

an army cot, which she put on the east side of the cabin, and as soon as the shade on that side progressed enough, we could use it to take a nap.

Money was a problem. My father almost never sent us any. My mother couldn't apply for welfare because she wasn't divorced. If it hadn't been for my brothers, it would have been worse. Ornan was out of work. For this reason, he could sign up for welfare commodities (groceries) and claim Mom and me as dependents. Mom stewed prunes and put some in a dish, and I poured canned milk over them. Sometimes she gave me a nickel and a quart-size bucket to go to the neighboring dairy farm and get it filled with fresh milk. I know there were times she went hungry so I could eat. Mom kept me in the loop as to what we had and didn't have, so I learned how to "squeeze the nickel till the buffalo hollered."

Eighth grade saw me trying to be athletic without having any talent at it whatsoever. Arizona kids were very good at playing sports. Mrs. Blue also had a small group of 4H girls and taught us sewing. I made an apron, but I didn't know how we could get material so I could make a dress. Then one day, in the mail, a package came. Aunt Emma in Oklahoma sent a piece of fabric big enough to make a straight, plain dress. It was a pretty red, white, and blue print, but I grew out of it rather quickly.

I said readings and monologues from time to time, and we gave a little play once.

It might have been around Christmas that Daddy sent me an enormous peppermint stick, about five inches in diameter. Some of it was cracked into little pieces, but it could be eaten. I don't know if he sent any money, though.

Eighth-grade graduation loomed. There were seven of us and I was valedictorian. I envisioned being able to wear a long dress but had no idea how I would get one. Wiser heads prevailed and it was decided short dresses would be better. One girl's father was on the school board, which probably had a lot to do with the plans.

Instead of presenting the valedictorian and salutatorian, we had a Parade of Arizona History. The year was 1939, the 400th anniversary of the first European to arrive in Arizona. That was

Pearl Allen Andree

Marcos de Niza, one of the Spanish priests in the exploration and occupation period. I was the first speaker so I narrated his story.

But I had to have a dress. Somehow Mama found $5, and the landlady drove us into Phoenix to a department store that had a basement with low-cost items. We bought a pink one with pleats in the skirt, and it was almost as good as that long dress of my dreams. It was the only good dress I had for several months.

About three weeks before school was out, Mama and I moved to Tolleson into a cabin that probably Pete or Zeke had paid for before they traveled to California for the summer fruit and melon season. To get home from Union, my boyfriend, George Kelly, who had ridden his bike to school, gave me a ride on his handlebar for a half-mile to where he had to turn off to go to his farm home for chores. I walked the remaining one-and-a-half miles to Tolleson. Of course, the next morning I walked the two miles to school. George was two grades behind me but no one teased us, and I think I began to lose some of my shyness during that completely innocent friendship. Years later, as a senior in high school, I once dated his older brother Bob when he was home on leave from the military. I must have been attracted to the Irish at an early time in life!

Moving to Tolleson

TOLLESON was considered rough for that day and time. The roads were all unpaved, except for Main Street which was two lanes through town. When it rained, people's cars got stuck in their own driveways, and the streets were quagmires. My mother was probably more strict with me than other mothers were with their daughters, but she allowed me to go to school basketball games and dances even though I had to walk home at least six blocks afterward. The population was 95% Latino. There were no streetlights, but the only thing I feared were dogs that might bark. I walked down the middle of the road because there was no leash law.

I was fascinated with the Mexican people with whom I became acquainted. My foreign language study was Spanish, and we had a Spanish Club. The Hispanic mothers were great cooks and I learned about traditional Mexican food, for which I still have a passion.

That small-town high school had been opened in 1929, at the beginning of the Depression, and it was an extremely complete facility. Tolleson Union High School had an auditorium that seated at least 500, with fixed seating, a good stage with good lighting, and a large green room behind the stage. The latter served as dressing, makeup, band, and chorus rooms. A large gymnasium (a separate building) occupied a favored spot on campus.

It was the summer of '39, and I would be entering high school in September. Mama found a cabin for us in Tolleson that was cheap, and we moved into that. The good news was, this was a building with bathroom facilities, including indoor plumbing

Pearl Allen Andree

with a shower as well as a toilet. The cabin had screening on two opposite walls, so if there was a breeze at all, it was not as hot as we'd had.

I liked the older couple who owned the cabin court. The man worked at the meat department in the only big grocery store in town, which was owned by the mayor, Mr. Van Landingham. There was a nice, small house next door to the landlord's, and the couple renting it knew my brothers. Their names were Clyde and Pauline Doss, and they had a little boy named Jake Tony. Clyde was a barber, so they didn't leave during the summer.

I had never heard bad language from anyone, so it was a big shock to hear such a young boy curse like a drunken sailor. I was to find out his mother was where he'd learned it! However, Pauline was a really sweet person and I don't remember her ever being angry. Mama came to love her as if she were a daughter. Pauline was a chain smoker (and Mama was against women smoking) but kept her house spotless and kept her husband in beautifully laundered and ironed white shirts. Sometimes he changed into one when he came home for lunch, especially in the hot Arizona summer. Otherwise Pauline often lazed around while listening to the soaps. Mama visited her and listened to the programs with her (and sometimes I joined them).

Years later, after they had moved into Phoenix, Mama sometimes went on the bus to visit Pauline. In 1983, when Zeke and Ellen were celebrating their fiftieth anniversary, we tried to get in touch, but she had died of lung cancer at 69. Clyde had taken his own life before she passed away, and it was said he chose to do it in an outside workshop so as not to soil the indoors.

I found Jake Tony in the phone book and had a good conversation with him. He had graduated from the University in Tucson and worked as a civil engineer in Phoenix. During our conversation I didn't hear any bad language. He reminisced about his dad and my brothers' friendship, including the time they plucked feathers out of a live chicken and it ran around the yard. Good grief! Grown men acting like kids. I can't imagine how that happened!

Maud and Pearl

I met two girlfriends who went with me to the Baptist church. My best friend at Union Grammar School had been Jolene Golightly, and her mother took me with her and her family to church in Tolleson on Sundays. They had a Vacation Bible School for two weeks, in the mornings, so my two new friends and I went. On the final Friday, they made the invitation for all the children to accept Jesus as their personal savior. In previous services, they asked, "All who are Christians, hold up your hands." I never did because I didn't consider myself a Christian since I hadn't been baptized. So, that Friday day of reckoning, I didn't respond to their invitation. Children as young as three and four were going up, and I didn't feel that was right. My two friends and I were the only three in the room who didn't respond. The good women were weeping and begging us, and "Just As I Am" was sung over about 15 times, but we refused. Afterward, we all went down to the three-mile pump and the other children were all baptized. When I went home, I told Mama I wanted to be baptized!

Mama and I had been too isolated to go to a Phoenix congregation of the Church of Christ, but living in Tolleson we could go if we could afford the bus fare. Thus far, we hadn't had the money. The postmistress was a member of the same congregation, but her husband only had a coupe, which meant there wasn't room for anyone else. However, Mama was on a mission to get me baptized. She asked (begged?) Eva if we could scrunch into their car, and that's what we did. I sat on Mama's lap—and I wasn't a 60-pound weakling anymore. I was baptized by an elder, a Mr. Black, as the minister was out of town on his vacation, after my confession that I truly believed Jesus was the Son of God.

The fact that I was entering high school and had no clothes that fit me was getting critical. It was another low point of poverty that Mama and I had in our lives. Mama was writing people with whom she had little acquaintance, asking if they had any dresses they could give us. One day a box came, but the only dress I could wear made me look like a woman from the early 30s. The only thing I could use was an artificial rose.

But then another box came with five newly made dresses that exactly fit! I didn't know who sent them, but I speculated. Ornan's

Pearl Allen Andree

Dorothy's mother sewed for people during the Depression and she was still in Oklahoma. I suspected Dorothy wrote someone (Dad? Leo?), and they bought material and she made the dresses. Mama laundered, starched, and ironed those dresses, and I could get three days' wear out of each one.

The mystery of the five new, hand-sewn dresses that I received in time to start high school with adequate clothing was never solved. Who could it have been? It very well may have been Dorothy's mother, Mrs. Brown, who sewed the dresses. But who else could have afforded them? It surely could have been Leo, who became a second father and a protector to me.

Or it might have been Dad. It would have been like him to come up with money and tell the seamstress, "Here, buy some material and make and send the dresses she needs. Don't say it was me." After all, he was the one who'd sent me the big peppermint stick the Christmas before.

Divorce

Mama and Dad wrote back and forth after we left Oklahoma, although not often. I know there was no arguing in those letters because Mama let me read all the letters that Dad sent us. She never said anything negative about Dad, either. Occasionally, he sent us things that he had gotten free at the grocery; I think the peppermint stick was an example.

Shortly after I received the mysterious dresses, Dad sent papers suing Mama for divorce. I don't remember Mama saying anything when she got the news. Someone suggested she return to Oklahoma and try to get some kind of settlement, but she just signed the papers and sent them back. She later said, "I don't want to go back to Oklahoma, even in a box." I think I'm the only person she told that to, though.

Clearly, as would universally be the case, the idea of my parents divorcing overwhelmed me at first. One turning point was that Leo, who had been giving Dad money to send to Mama, found out that he had not sent it, and he and Leo had angry words. So later, in 1939, Leo came to Arizona to help Mama and me. Mama's brother, John, was darkly humorous when he said, "What did EZ sue Maud for, desertion or non-support?"

I was so upset. I was afraid of how people would react to us and treat us. At that time, of course, divorce was generally taboo, and it might be viewed even more critically at church. Mama never complained about its effect on herself; she was busy comforting me. She saw how I felt and said to me, "Those (divorce) papers don't mean anything to God; we're still married in the sight of God." That gave me wondrous relief.

Pearl Allen Andree

While Mama had been silent once getting the papers, what she did has stood out in my memory. Always religious, and religiously tolerant, from the homestead days she and the children went to any church that was available. It happened that a Pentecostal Church was around the corner from the cabin. For Mama, that church became a source of relaxation and a refuge for her heart. She left me alone in the cabin, put a padlock on the outside of the door (of course, if I needed to, I could escape through a screen), and went to the Pentecostal service nightly!

It was also a turning point for me. I began to think about what my relationships would be like in my future. I decided I would date but be determined not to get serious about anybody until my 20s or 30s. After high school, I would get two years of pre-engineering at Arizona State Teacher's College (it became Arizona State College in 1945 and Arizona State University in 1958). I was going to be a petroleum engineer, as Leo encouraged me to do, and have a career. But that phase of life was later.

Allen's Alley

It's been referred to obliquely so far, but in the late 1930s, when my brothers began spending time in Tolleson, which had two lettuce seasons each year, and returning there every year, they began considering putting down roots. After all, they had wives and young children who had stayed behind in Oklahoma tolerating cold and snow, and the central Arizona weather was ideal for most of the school year. With money carefully saved, they bought or built houses next to or near each other. All the homes were on Madison or Jefferson, streets that backed up to each other (in the mid-1940s, Alma and Lee built a house on Washington, north of Jefferson). The group included Leo, Ornan, Ornan's Dorothy's parents (the Browns, who had moved to Tolleson from Oklahoma), Zeke, and Pete. Leo re-enlisted and joined the Navy Seabees in early 1943. During World War II, the three remaining brothers worked at the Goodyear Aircraft plant. In 1945–1946, at the end of the war, the family began to migrate. Zeke and Ellen moved back to Oklahoma, and in the late '40s and early '50s, Leo (back from the war) and Pete moved away.

In the years that Leo, Ornan, Zeke, Pete, and Alma lived with their families at various times together in Tolleson, the close-knit Allen family did, indeed, live close by each other. There was fun within the family despite the lingering Great Depression conditions, with the little cousins playing together daily, the families hosting visitors and having get-togethers, and, of course, singing, praying, and going to church together.

My niece, Rita Jo, told this story:

Pearl Allen Andree

There was that big vacant lot between my house and Dawn Marie's house. She and I were close, and a lot of the time we took care of the little girls, my sister, Carol Lou, and hers, Charlotte.

Mrs. Tolby, who lived on the other side of the vacant lot from Dawn Marie, had the only phone in the neighborhood. We had read somewhere, or gotten the idea somehow, that with two tin cans and a wire, we could set up a phone line that would carry our voices. It would be our special private line. So, we strung it across the vacant lot, having put holes in the tin cans and strung the wire through each bottom. Our Dads didn't know what was going on, because we didn't ask them to help. We knew everything then! I remember us going outside and yelling at each other. We never thought it was not working. Little did we know that the string or wire had to be taut for sound waves to be conducted by it. We probably grew out of it.

We made mud pies and all kinds of things, and we had so much fun. We had the best upbringing, and we were so blessed, surrounded by our grandmother and aunts and uncles who were such good people, strongly religious, never swore, and got along with each other and with others.

With the cousins, of course, there was mischief and misdeed—like the time Lanier shot neighbor girl Janean Combess with his BB gun. In the forehead! She wasn't harmed, fortunately, but it caused quite a stir in the entire neighborhood. And the time Lanier and Earl caught and killed a neighbor's chicken, but while plucking it in a pan of cold water, they were caught red-handed! That also caused quite a ruckus, and the boys had to apologize to the aggrieved neighbor. Earl later said mischievously, "That chicken shouldn't have been in Lanier's yard! Lanier told me, 'Well, it's in our yard, we might as well eat it.' But we couldn't get its head off!"

Maud and Pearl

In my niece Charlotte's view, her brother Lanier looked like he hated his forced apology worse than brushing his teeth. Charlotte said, "Those were the days of getting chased on a bike by Blacky Ferris, the neighbor's dog, staying indoors to escape the summer heat blast, and listening to baseball on the radio, because radio was king."

My brothers became known to the neighborhood kids for their fun-loving nature, their kindness, and their helpfulness. Pete was Mr. Fix-it for bicycle repair. Charlotte later told me of a boy knocking on the door, asking, "Can Pete come out and play?" Pete and my other brothers set up baseball diamonds, jumping pits, horseshoe pits, and other sporty venues. The alley was the setting for the homemade butter incident that happened when I was in college (and will be told about in a later chapter). Later, my nieces came to stay with me and help me with my first pregnancy and Danny's infancy. Ornan and Dorothy and the Browns stayed. After Jimmy and I married, Mama went to stay first with Alma and Lee, then with Leo when he moved to farm in Somerton. Later after that, she stayed in a small house behind Ornan's.

Tolleson Union High School

SCHOOL was enjoyable for me. In classes we were seated alphabetically and I became friends with twins Doris and Dorothy Broadston. Around November, a girl named Topsy (a nickname for Margaret) entered her freshman year. By this time, Leo had arrived and we lived in a nice one-room cabin. I went home for lunch, and on Topsy's first day, I realized she also went home for lunch, and in the same direction as I did. I literally chased her to get acquainted. She was extremely shy and from Texarkana, Arkansas. We four girls were fast friends through the four years of high school.

Girls' League was the social organization for all girls and they held events. In October, there was the father-daughter banquet. My brothers filled in for that vacancy in my life; Zeke went with me to the banquet. The principal was giving a speech about the school when the back door of the gym opened and a big cat came in that some boys had put "Hi-Life" on and was causing a tremendous commotion. Men ran all around trying to catch it. Of course, afterward, the town policeman managed to locate the perpetrators, who were properly dealt with—the same boys who usually turned over privies on Halloween (the town had no sewer system yet). They were senior boys and one was the son of the woman whose father had founded the town and who now owned all the town that hadn't been sold to private citizens.

Leo, both working on a ranch and driving a school bus, became well known by all the students and was popular with them. In later years, at reunions I was always asked, "How's Leo?" He furnished me with good advice about boys, like "Don't slap a

Maud and Pearl

boy if he tries to get fresh; it will just make him more aggressive," and "Don't go on a date without having some money to make a phone call."

It was important to date the right boy, too! One basic rule was to never exit the house to meet a boy who honked the horn. That showed very bad manners by the boy, plus disrespect for the girl. I never was treated badly by any of those farm boys—maybe because they knew Leo would make them pay!

My life was much better after Leo came—beginning with Christmas '39. He gave me a Shaeffer pen and pencil set with my name on them, plus a blue satin housecoat. I kept them for years. I even had the housecoat in college, where I slept in it. Leo slept on a cot in the cabin, and Mom and I had a double bed. We put a curtain arrangement around the bed for me to use as a dressing room. In March 1940, Alma came out with the three children, and Mary was just a tiny baby. Mom, Alma, and I slept across the head end of the bed, and Dick and Jenny slept wedged in at the foot of the bed. Mary had a separate little bed, but she didn't take up much room. Later in life, when John Denver recorded a song about the bed that "would hold eight kids and four hound dogs and a piggy we stole from the shed," I could identify.

Alma French-braided my hair and I gradually learned to do it for myself. The spring formal at school was coming up, and as it was a Girls' League event, the girls were to ask a boy. Perhaps the farm boys wouldn't have come otherwise. I asked Bobby Hintz, who I thought looked like my brother Zeke. I didn't know he and my girlfriend Edis Higgins had just started liking each other, but he accepted my invitation, and she came by herself and helped serve at the refreshment table. When he picked me up, his friend Johnny Welch was in the car. Going with two boys was a no-no, but everything was done properly and with no repercussions. Bobby was already 16, and like many of the boys, he had to quit school sometimes in the fall to work. Edis was probably near that age, and they became serious about each other, even planning to marry the next year or so. But the next summer Bobby was working for the summer in California, and Edis was working there in town, and she eloped with the guy for whom she was working so she didn't stay around. Bobby stayed in school, graduated with our class, and entered the military.

I finally got to wear a long dress to that spring formal. The big question was, where would I get it? My sister-in-law, Pete's Dorothy, of course. I think it had been her high school graduation dress and it was blue taffeta. Alma helped with my hair and Dorothy and Ellen both came down to see how I looked. No one took pictures, though. However, the Sunday *Arizona Republic* had a picture on the society page, and there I was! Along with several others, of course.

Mrs. Hutchison, the Girls' League sponsor, started a Monday night dance class. I told her my mother probably wouldn't allow me to take dancing lessons, so she wrote a note to Mama explaining that school dances were very properly supervised and that if anyone disobeyed the rules, they were not allowed to come into the gym. So Mom let me go to the classes. We learned simple steps, like the waltz and basic foxtrot, but also round dances like the Virginia Reel and the schottische. Some of us girls would practice during lunch hour in the front of the auditorium while Virginia Wells played piano for us.

The Cedar Chest

I'VE had a feeling for cedar chests as long as I can remember.
It was the one beautiful piece of furniture my mother owned. In it she kept beautiful linens and other items she rarely, if ever, used. Once in a while, for a special treat, she allowed me to open the cedar chest and sit there feeling and looking. She told me what a hope chest was and I tried to put things in there for my hope chest—things like dishes from oatmeal boxes, flour sack tea towels on which I learned to embroider, and potholders I made on the old Singer treadle sewing machine when I learned to use it at age five. Once, one of my brothers sent me a perfume atomizer from Arizona. It was beautiful blue glass. I didn't have perfume to put in it, but it was precious to me, so I put it in there. It may have come from a dime store and atomizers like that usually don't work well—a fact I proved with that one later, I think. At the time, however, it was my most prized possession.

There had not been many precious items in my young life, and when we came to Arizona, there would be fewer for a few years. I was a typical girl, probably, when it came to liking boys, not wanting to admit an attraction, or embarrassed by it. There was a boy who helped me through that transition.

When I entered high school in Tolleson, several rural communities fed into Tolleson Union High School, and I met many new students. My best girlfriends, Doris and Dorothy, told me one day that they had heard "Bill Wells likes you." Do girls still find out that way? I hardly knew who he was because his name started with "W," mine with "A," and seating was alphabetical.

Pearl Allen Andree

Halloween was approaching. We didn't go trick-or-treating. It was nothing special, except for the ornery boys who tried to push over outhouses. One day Bill Wells walked up to me and handed me an invitation to a Halloween party at his house. He had a sister one year older and she was having the party, but he'd been allowed to invite a girl.

In that agricultural community, not many farmers were well off. The Wells family was an exception. I am now convinced that was because it was a matriarchal household. Mrs. Wells ruled with an iron fist, but she was ambitious, clean, hardworking, and (I think) tried to do the right thing. The home was a mansion compared to other homes I had seen. It sat back from the road with a long driveway passing citrus trees, around which flocks of peacocks showed their brilliant tails. The daughter Virginia's room was all white: carpet, bedspreads (twin beds), and curtains. There was a garage, kitchen, large living room (in which stood a grand piano for Virginia, who was planning on becoming a concert pianist—or maybe her mother planned on it), dining room, and three bedrooms with baths. A basement served as the party room, and that had been decorated accordingly. We played party games on the front lawn, then went to the basement for refreshments.

Transportation was never easy to arrange, but somehow it happened, and I was delighted.

Bill invited me as his date to class parties and FFA (Future Farmers of America) parties (clubs and classes had one each semester). I never went steady with anyone, so I dated other boys, but he and I were special friends. Since he wasn't old enough to drive, we never went on dates alone. Like other teens, we went to school-related parties by bus. World War II years meant gas rationing.

Christmas Eve of my sophomore year, a big, beautiful car drove up to our place. Bill got out and brought me a present. He didn't stay long. We lived in a two-room house and my sister and her family were living with us. The present was a small cedar chest. Never had I received such a beautiful present. It had a little lock and key, which have been lost through the years.

Maud and Pearl

The following Easter Sunday, Bill showed up unexpectedly (we didn't have a phone) with a stuffed rabbit and a box of chocolates. I had never owned a stuffed animal. He had walked a few blocks on muddy streets, because his father didn't want to take a chance on driving them. Bill invited me to go with the family up Apache Trail to Roosevelt Dam. It was the first time for me to go up there. We stopped alongside the road and Mrs. Wells fried chicken over a fire even though it was raining intermittently. That was the first time I tasted black olives. I remember her saying, "Oh, you must have ripe olives with fried chicken."

This budding romance came to a halt when I turned down his invitation to the FFA swim party because I had "the curse" and didn't want to go if I couldn't swim, as I would stand out like a sore thumb. Swimming at that time of the month was verboten by my mother's rules, and I wouldn't have been caught dead telling him the real reason.

His mother sometimes drove me to her house to entertain her bridge club with monologues. Years later, I put a few thoughts together and realized she was grooming me to become her daughter-in-law. So she wasn't too uppity—she knew how poor we were but thought I had merit.

What she and all the farm boys in that community didn't know was, wild horses couldn't have dragged me to the altar to marry a farmer, even if he were the richest one around.

As with all the boys I knew in high school, Bill and I are not embarrassed at reunions. They were good friends and there's no reason to be ashamed of our associations. He went to NAU and married a girl from Chino Valley, and they ranched there. I learned that she was quite a horsewoman.

The stuffed rabbit was eventually confiscated by nieces and nephews, but I've used the cedar chest for keeping special possessions, such as medals I received in high school. I gave it to my granddaughter, Brigitte, for safekeeping.

High School Years

MY FRESHMAN year, 1939-1940, was the year Tolleson High started student body government. Elections were held shortly after the start of school. Truman Anderson was our first student body president. It wasn't until 1944 that I heard of a man named Harry Truman. I was to find out later that Jim Anderson, a local dairy farmer, had served in WWI and came home vowing he would name his first son after the officer under whom he had served, Harry Truman. Truman Anderson graduated from high school in 1940, joined the Navy, and was killed in WWII. The Tolleson VFW Post was named after him.

In the spring semester, we had a Constitutional Oratorical Speech Contest. I took second place to Bobby McCreight's first place. Nine had entered. The contest was repeated the next year and the next, and I always took second to Bobby. He graduated in 1942, and my senior year the contest was canceled due to the war in progress. My junior year speech was entitled "In God We Trust."

Freshman year we could only take four solids and only general math, so I took English, math, civics (taught by Mrs. Hutchison), and home economics, plus my electives, P.E., band, and glee club. In home ec, the first semester was cooking and the second was sewing. I had read *Gone With the Wind* and ordered material from Sears that was green with wheat sheaves on it like Scarlett wore to the barbecue at the beginning of that book. My dress had a sweetheart neckline and an eight-gore skirt. I loved wearing it and did so for years.

Maud and Pearl

Mom discovered a clarinet for sale for $20. She managed to buy it to fulfill her purpose of helping me learn to sing by reading and hearing music better. Mama had always felt that singing was most important for religious expression. She had encouraged each of her children to sing and play music. It worked with most of her children. I loved singing, but unfortunately, I couldn't carry a tune. I blame that on Alma, who informed me of that fact when I was five and the teacher wanted me to sing "Springtime in the Rockies" for a program. I took glee club, too, but that didn't help, either. Mama sang beautifully, as did Daddy, and I think Mama must have agonized over my efforts.

At the end of the school year, we moved into Pete and Dorothy's house since they had gone to California for summer work. That enabled Leo to remodel the cabin so we had two rooms. He bought Mama a new range and refrigerator as we had Bu-gas. He also fixed up the 9' x 12' adobe hut on the back of the lot for a private room for himself. It had a dirt floor, but Mama put the bed legs in little dishes with repellent in them to control ants and other bugs. Leo hadn't started driving the school bus yet. After his heat stroke at the ranch, his boss, Norm, saw to it that he started working at the high school during my sophomore year.

Leo's Masonic friends included Mrs. Hutchison's husband, Sam. Bobby McCreight was her son. His dad had died about the time Bobby had been born. His mother told about wheeling him around the college campus as a baby while getting her teaching credentials. Bobby was in DeMolays and I was in Rainbow Girls, the teen groups for dependents of the Masonic Lodge. Once, before he took me to one of their formal dances, we had to be inspected (or was it just me?) by his paternal grandmother before going to the dance. I think that family may have had some state-level political prestige in the past. Bobby played tennis and, like Bill Wells, was active in Future Farmers. They had speech contests in that, too. He was valedictorian when he graduated, and he went to the University of Arizona in Tucson.

I started going to the First Christian Church when I couldn't get the bus into Phoenix. The preacher and his wife offered me the opportunity to go to summer Bible camp in Prescott—and

Pearl Allen Andree

they would pay for it! I accepted before they could change their minds, and it was the only Bible camp I was ever able to go to. It was many years before Churches of Christ had property for that. I met students from Phoenix, and while I didn't continue the friendships, I remember that week as a highlight of my summer. One boy, whose last name was Koontz, went to Phoenix Union High. I read in the paper that when he was a junior, he developed strep throat and only lived 36 hours. I had met his older sister, and she was my private drama coach a couple of summers later.

My grades were good enough to take five solids after the first year. I took algebra—I loved math—and American history, and added first-year Spanish. The first six weeks of the latter, I was sure I would never get it. Mama worried over my concern—I would almost get hysterical. But after the first six weeks I made an A, so then I relaxed. We had a Spanish club, and once a semester we had a party. At one dinner, a girl's mother did the hat dance in a beautiful red flamenco gown.

In the spring of 1941 I invited a boy I liked, named Wayne I think, to the formal dance. Alma sent me a formal gown from California that she thought I would look good in. He stood me up! That was a once-in-a-lifetime occurrence. He never apologized and I was never going to say anything to him. He was very good looking but he faded into the past. I always wondered if maybe Leo knew him well and informed him not to show up.

I call the summer of 1941 "fried chicken summer." Mom exercised her intent of teaching me womanly skills. That summer I was supposed to learn how to catch, kill, dress out, cut up, and fry a chicken. We had fried chicken every other day, but I never did learn to even catch, much less kill, a chicken. Leo showed me a better way than wringing its neck (I'd seen Mama do that many times back on the farm). He tied the feet together and hung it on a clothesline post, cut the jugular vein, and let it bleed out.

I did learn how to cut it up and fry it, and never got tired of eating it. I later taught my kids how to properly cut up a chicken so there was a wishbone. And when I was a mother of three, in a restaurant in Laredo, Texas, a maître d' said to me, "Lady, I've been a waiter for 25 years and I have never seen anyone enjoy their chicken as you do." I have never decided if that was a compliment or not.

On Sunday, December 7, 1941, I went to church at the First Christian Church in Tolleson. When I returned home, Leo was listening to the radio. It was, of course, the day that would live in infamy. Pearl Harbor would shape lives for years into the future. The next morning, Monday the 8th, we had a special assembly at school. They were able to set up a radio with sound system, so we heard President Roosevelt speak to Congress and ask them to declare war, which they did.

My junior year, a new boy came to school. His name was Leith Plunkett and he was from New England. He had gone to a boys' prep school in Massachusetts and his parents had moved west for his dad's health, but he was healthy enough to farm. Leith caused a sensation with the girls and the teachers because of his good manners. He had a good personality and made friends quickly. I took drama and he was in that class, too; we had a new English teacher, and he enrolled in that although he was a senior. He sat in front of me, so we got acquainted.

Mr. Cardon assigned us a project of writing our autobiography in short essay form. Leith's was a fanciful tale about a stork delivering him somewhere, almost like a Greek myth. When his paper was returned, Mr. Cardon had given him an A and in red had written, "Leith, you have talent. Why in Heaven's name don't you use it?"

By this time, Leo's job had entitled him to move Mama and me into the house on campus provided for the janitor and family. Leith asked for a date, and we dated through that year. Then he graduated and joined the Navy. We corresponded, but I knew he was more serious than I was so I never signed my letters "Love." I found out later that many in the community, even the English teacher, thought we would marry, but I had my sights set on a career that would require a college degree.

Farewell to Dad

IN MARCH of my junior year, I was planning the second birthday party of my life when, the week before, we received a phone call from Oklahoma. My dad was in the hospital with pneumonia delirium, and not expected to live. Since my brothers didn't have phones, it was my job to walk to their houses and tell them. I did not feel any emotion until I had to verbalize the message. I remember telling Pete, and then I cried. I asked Mom if I should cancel my party and she said she didn't think that necessary. My brothers took up a collection and sent Ornan to represent the family. Daddy had married again six months after the divorce was final. His new wife had already buried three husbands. Ornan told us that when he entered the hospital room, Dad said, "Come on over here, I've known you for more than 40 years." The only person he'd known that long was Mama. He also told Ornan that his present wife thought she'd get some money, "but all she'll get is a dirty shirt." In our home, Mama cried into the night. Dad died the next week.

The summer before my senior year, I obtained a job staying with a family in Phoenix that had a small boy. I babysat him when needed and helped with the housework. In the mornings I walked downtown and took courses at Gregg Business School. I had taken typing the previous year, but took more, plus filing and a class on the comptometer (a forerunner of the calculator). On Saturday mornings I went to a private drama coach to further my acting skills and improve my knowledge of the construction and delivery of monologues.

Finishing High School

WHEN I registered for senior classes, I signed up for senior English—it would be English literature. I wanted to study some Shakespeare. Unfortunately, I was the only senior who signed up for it. The principal, Mr. Harless, called me into his office and explained, "We can't give a course just for one student. Why don't you take shorthand? That would help you get a job in college." That made sense, so I went with it. In addition, I took my second year of typing, advanced algebra and trigonometry, chemistry, and modern problems. I had been elected Student Body Social Chairman, which meant I had to plan the weekly Friday assemblies.

It wasn't far into the semester before the principal called me in again. Mrs. Lucy T. Wyman needed to hire someone to work for her on weekdays after school and half a day on Saturday. I took the job for $3 a week and learned a lot. The "T." stood for Tolleson, as she was the daughter of the town's founder. (Yes, the mother of that ornery son who had since joined the Navy.) She had sold the town lots to people who built their houses there and then came into the office to pay their monthly payments. My brothers were in that group. I worked for her until I graduated and obtained a civil service job at Luke Air Force Base the summer before entering college.

Leo was influencing me about my future and he was wise in his approach. He wanted me to go to University of Oklahoma and become a petroleum engineer. He also knew I might want to act. I knew the money situation, and at that time the acting profession would require going to New York City and Actors Studio. I knew we couldn't afford that. He never told me I didn't have the talent, but he pointed out that a thousand girls would go there when I did, and 100 would have the necessary talent, and of that 100 maybe five would actually make it. I had enough sense to know he was telling the truth. Besides, he reminded me, I could always act in local productions. Added to this, I liked the idea of going on to college.

The Navy finally accepted Leo, so he rejoined in January 1943, the year I graduated. Mom and I moved back into the two-room house when he left for boot camp in the east. After his two-week leave in April and spending memorable time with myself and Mama, my senior class and my friends, Leo went to Port Hueneme, and from there he went off to war.

Leo hadn't been in the Navy but a few weeks when Lee and Alma came back to Arizona. They and their kids moved in with Mama and me. The adobe hut became Lee and Alma's room and we made do.

There was an honors assembly before the end of the year. In my junior year I had received the drama award—a year's membership in Phoenix Little Theatre, which I hadn't been able to utilize except to go to a couple of plays. My senior year I was valedictorian, and I received the Bausch & Lomb award for being most likely to further the sciences. I thought my classmate Georgia Combs should have had that as she wanted to be a doctor. I did study two years of pre-engineering, and eventually produced a medical doctor and a computer engineer, plus other children very productive in their chosen fields, as well as grandchildren who have contributed to the field of science in their own ways.

In the summer before college, I qualified for civil service "steno" rating and made $125 a month over the three summer months. The day I first went to the air base to get a job, I had to go to Headquarters to be passed by the Intelligence Office. The officer in charge asked me for a date! His name was Robert Wessling and he was a blond, good looking lieutenant. I was flattered and took a chance on saying yes. Wasn't I headed for college and adult enough to make my own decisions? What I didn't even consider strange was that he was, as I was to find out, 24, and of course I was only 16. But wasn't that all right?

Maud and Pearl

Of course, he picked me up at home and saw I lived low on the economic scale. He took me to a bar and bought me a mixed drink, which I recognized immediately as having alcohol in it. I had never tasted one but I figured it out so I just let it sit there. I think he thought he would take me to a motel overnight but that didn't work out for him either. On the next date, he took me to meet a married couple with whom he was friends. They were nice. We had dinner with them. At one point in this romance he implied that he would like me to go to his next posting, which he was scheduled for soon, to New Mexico, I think.

I made it clear I didn't plan on traveling anywhere but the college nearby and I wasn't going to get distracted from my goal. I think that must have been when he gave up. He must have thought I was dumb, and maybe I had been naive, but I knew what I wanted in life, and I wasn't veering off from it at 16! I know others in my situation would have been enamored of him, but in my thoughts and feelings I was determined. I wanted things: education, career, and a Christian husband. I was also religiously committed to not having sex before marriage. And I have been eternally grateful for the angel that must have been sitting on my shoulder.

College in Tempe

MAMA let me save all the money I made over the summer and I had enough to spend about $50 on clothes for college. My chemistry and math teacher and his wife helped me decide on going to Arizona State Teachers College in Tempe. He suggested I could use the Oklahoma University catalog and take the same classes as they proscribed for pre-engineering. In addition, he arranged for me to get a freshman scholarship of $300 from Phelps Dodge (a copper mining company) as well as a half-time job in the Dean's office. Room and board would be $35.00 and the job would pay half of that.

Leo sent me $35 so I had $17.50 for other expenses. I usually was able to put $5 of that in my savings account. I was about 20 miles from home, but it took three hours one way to get there: from Tempe to Phoenix on one bus, walk six blocks to the other bus station, and get another bus for Tolleson. The first part of September was Freshman Orientation Week. The only embarrassment I remember is when Mama visited me the first time and met the Dean of Women (not my employer, Dean Grimes). Mama said to her, "Pearl's my baby and this is the first time she's ever been away from home."

Freshman Orientation Week was enlightening, what with registering for classes and learning procedures and so forth. At the end of the week there was a military ball! I dragged out a long dress and prepared to meet a cadet. I had met a girl who would be a close friend. Her name was Jane Holloway, and she had stayed out of school and worked for three years before going to college. Her mother was an executive secretary for a prominent company.

Maud and Pearl

Jane had been a majorette in Phoenix Union High School and was a good dancer.

She met a cadet who was really good looking and also a good dancer who invited her to go with him to his military ball, which would be in November. He said he was an actor and even showed her his Screen Actors' Guild card. Ironically, she never heard from him again until about a week before his ball! She didn't date as she was absorbed in her studies. She was a 4-point (A) student, so we were very curious whether he would show up or not. Well, he did, corsage in hand. His name was John Forsythe. As far as I know she never saw him again.

Jane became a best friend. She had obtained a private room to avoid distractions, but we did many things together. We pledged the same sorority and, in the future, she was my maid of honor and when I had a daughter, I added a *t* to Jane for her name.

I registered for classes in chemistry, English, algebra and trigonometry, and engineering drawing. In addition, I took classes in physical education, modern dance, and tennis. A Tolleson high school athletic friend had a part-time job teaching tennis. Zada had graduated a year ahead of me. Although I wasn't an athlete, tennis appealed to me—and it only cost $5 to buy a racket! We couldn't wear slacks or Levi's to classes, but could wear shorts to P.E. if appropriate.

The theater was one of the three original Normal School buildings built in 1885. It had the structure of an opera house, with a balcony and footlights at the front of the stage. Its capacity was 1500. The original gym had been in the basement. The building had already been condemned by the fire department, but since it was war time it was still being used.

The drama professor was a Tallulah Bankhead-type woman named Galloway ("Galley" for short) who was a chain smoker. Her students were supposed to alert her if Dr. Gammage was in the area so she could staunch her cigarette. One day I decided to see her and tell her I would like to audition for any plays she was planning on staging. She was the type of director with the rule that you had to be either dead or dying if you missed rehearsals, but she took my name in case anyone left the cast. Since there were

Pearl Allen Andree

practically no males available her choices were scarce. A couple weeks later she contacted me and told me I could take a girl's place in the current play. It was *Trojan Women* by Euripides and had a lot of choral reading and modern dance movements in it.

My roommate was Connie DeRuhlach, another Tolleson girl who had graduated in '41. She and her brother had graduated together but had to take turns going to college. It was her turn (as a sophomore) and her mother had found out I was going and a few weeks before school started visited Mom and me to see if Connie and I could room together. I was delighted. Connie was beautiful with a peaches and cream complexion. My first thought was maybe I could find out her secret. She had a younger sister about my age still in high school named Jean who was also very beautiful, with more of an olive complexion.

A few years later, in 1949, Jean became a Miss Arizona finalist, and when I married Jimmy Goggin she came to our wedding. He teased me for years that I kept him from meeting her until I married him! When I got around to finding out Connie's secret, she told me she and Jean had tried lots of things, but one thing was honey. I went right out and bought some honey to add to my bare necessity cosmetic items. I don't know if it worked, but I used it as a mask. It washed off easily with cold water. After all, bacteria won't grow in honey.

When I entered Arizona State Teachers College in the fall of 1943, the total registration numbered 525. My half-time job was in Dean Grimes' office, so I knew. There were only 14 of the male gender, but the good news was, 2000 cadets were enrolled in the College Training Detachment preparing to become future pilots in the Army Air Corps. Each Wednesday evening we had a social hour from 7:00-8:00 p.m. in the Moeur Building. That enabled us to get acquainted and possibly line up a date for the weekend.

In November I met Jesse. He was from Texas. In December I heard other girls talking about inviting boys to their homes for Christmas dinner. No way was I going to do that. I was from Tolleson, which had no sewer system. Consequently, my home consisted of two rooms (plus a little adobe shanty on the back of

Maud and Pearl

the lot) with no indoor plumbing and a privy. In addition, my sister and her husband and three children shared this dwelling.

In December Jess started hinting. He would say, "What are you going to do Christmas?" and I would answer vaguely. Finally, I suggested we meet in Phoenix and have dinner at the Flame Restaurant. I guess he figured that would be it, so he agreed. On Christmas Eve Alma and Lee had some shopping to do so they took me into Phoenix.

After dinner Jesse walked me to the parking lot where I was to meet them and of course I introduced him. Lee, also from Texas, shook hands and said, "Hello, Jesse, come on home with us."

And Jesse replied, "Thanks, I will."

I could have cheerfully killed Lee. All the way home I kept wondering what I was going to do with Jesse. I decided to take him to my brother's house, which was bigger. Before the evening was over my brother had invited him back for Christmas dinner.

Homemade Butter

We may not have had nice houses but the table groaned from the amount of food. My mother made the best yeast rolls in the country, besides all the other good stuff. My brother's sister-in-law lived with them and worked at Goodyear Aircraft, and was especially talented at changing the pound of lard-looking oleo into a delicious-looking dish of yellow margarine: get it warm and, with the hands, squish it up, mix it good, and pat it out in a bowl.

Jesse was happy as could be. There must have been about fourteen around the table. We were all loading up our plates when the oleo got to Jesse. His eyes bugged out and he joyfully said, "Homemade butter!" We were stunned and nobody uttered a word. My mother wouldn't lie if you put her on a rack, but she didn't say a thing. A nephew started to say something, but I think his mother kicked him. Before the day was over my brother had invited him back for New Year's Eve and Jesse and I joined him and his wife for a movie in Phoenix.

After the movie we went to the Central Drive-In for hamburgers and then dropped Jesse off at the bus station to return to campus. I found out later he was late and was restricted for a month, at which time it was time for him to leave for Santa Ana and Pre-Flight School. I never saw Jesse again, but we corresponded for a time. I never forgot Jesse, especially since every time my brother and I shared a meal he would invariably ask, "How about passing me some of that homemade butter?"

Jimmy Goggin

During the month that Jesse was on restriction, on January 8, 1944, I met a cadet that I later fell in love with and married. The first week of January was also the start of more classes at Arizona State. I had pledged a sorority, Kappa Kappa Alpha, and we pledges were told we had to go to the first dance on Saturday, January 8, and dance every dance, even if we had to ask a boy. There were a lot more cadets than girls, even though many cadets just stood around and watched, so I didn't figure this would be a problem. I was standing in a large foyer crowded with cadets when two boys came in the door. It was their first liberty since arriving a month before, and they had been to the nearby watering hole. I overheard one say, "I'm going to ask that girl in the pink dress to dance." I looked around and noticed I was the only one wearing a pink dress.

Chuck Gionnini was his name, and we spent the rest of the evening together. At one point he introduced me to his roommate, Joe McGuire. When my girlfriends and I were talking about the evening I said, "I met a guy, and he has the cutest roommate. His name is Joe McGuire." Chuck and I dated for about three weeks, going into Phoenix on the bus to a movie. He was very nice. If we were crossing the street he might hold my hand, but that was it, and that was fine with me. I always figured most of the boys had girls back home anyway. About three weeks later he didn't show up at the mid-week social hour in the activity building, so his roommate must have agreed to keep me occupied. Joe McGuire and I were dancing and I noticed his name tag. It was not Joe McGuire!

Pearl Allen Andree

I said, "Your name is Jimmy Goggin?"

He stopped short, right still, looked startled, and said, "That's the first time anyone has pronounced my name right the first time they saw it." It turned out that "McGuire" was just a name the guys called each other. "Joe" may have come from the movie *A Guy Named Joe*, starring Spencer Tracy and Van Johnson. Goggin could generate more mis-pronunciations than any name. It's why I acquired the habit of automatically spelling it for everyone I met. I also figured the reason he got interested in me was that I pronounced his name right the first time I saw it.

There was the monthly military ball the end of January and I was going with Chuck. They asked me to get a girl to go with Jimmy. I arranged for my friend Vera Jo Hendrix to accompany Jimmy. When the night came, Jimmy and I were on my program for the next-to-the-last dance. When it concluded, he wasn't very interested in finding Chuck and Vera Jo. I was nervous about it because it just wasn't done not to have the last dance with the boy one came with, but that's what happened. As they walked us back to the dorm, conversation was almost non-existent. I guess that's when I started dating Jimmy instead of Chuck.

Jimmy had trouble getting to a first date. He hadn't finished high school and had trouble with the studies. Some of the cadets had already graduated from college. He couldn't have time off on the weekend if he didn't pass the week's studies. The popular remark was, "If you dropped your pencil you missed six weeks of work!" If they were restricted for the weekend they had to march gigs in front of the girls' dorm—one hour was one gig—with a broom over their shoulder like a gun.

The week finally came when he told me, "I'm going to have Sunday off. Could we do something?"

I said, "Well, I go to church and you are welcome to go with me, but if not, we could meet for lunch and then do something in the afternoon." He went to the Church of Christ in Tempe with me. I found out later it was the first time since he was 12 years old that he had gone. We had a Mexican food lunch and climbed the A butte next to the campus.

Maud and Pearl

One of our first dates was to the opera! A girl in the dorm gave me a couple of tickets she didn't want. I didn't know at the time how tight money was for him (he only received $6 a month) and neither of us had ever been to an opera. Traveling shows were presented at Phoenix Union High auditorium and our tickets were in the nosebleed section. It was *The Barber of Seville* and when he returned to his dorm all the guys sang "Figaro" to him.

A few weeks later I took him to Tolleson for Sunday dinner and meeting Alma and Lee and their kids. Since Christmas, Lee had managed to build a couple more rooms onto the original building, and we had a dining table for a regular Sunday dinner. At one point, Jimmy looked around at the seven of us and asked, "Does everyone in this family have blue eyes?" No one had been talking about eye color!

There was no question that I had fallen hard for Jimmy Goggin. But there were many unanswered questions. How did he feel? I knew he liked me but was I just another girl? How would I handle my life plan? The first part of May he would be leaving for Santa Ana for Pre-Flight school; would I ever see him again? Along with some of the other girls, I went to the train station to see him off, and the next Sunday I met Mom in Phoenix for church and she came back to the dorm with me. We had gone to a movie, and it was one of those flying ones. At the dorm we went into the restroom and Mom heard me crying in the stall. When I came out, she hugged me and said, "You're in love with him, aren't you?" I didn't know how to answer that, but I knew somehow, I wanted to know him better and what the future might hold.

May became rather active in our dorm room. Connie left school, having completed her classes, to marry her fiancé in the military. A girl in another dorm was caught sneaking back in at 3:00 in the morning. My boss, Dean Grimes, disciplined her by moving her in with me until school ended! I would, of course, be spending the summer at home in Tolleson.

I looked for a job for the summer. I discovered there was an office for the Geodetic Survey in Phoenix and thought I might try there to learn something toward my petroleum engineering

Pearl Allen Andree

interest. I could tell they thought I was nuts—I was only 17 with no experience, and they hadn't advertised for help.

As previously mentioned, during this summer our family helped to start a congregation of the church in Tolleson. Mama's two lady friends from area dairy farms who attended were Mrs. Turner and "Tinny" Anderson. Tinny was a good musician and had a sister living across the street from Pete. The sister had a piano and Tinny helped Pete learn how to get the pitch and other rudimentary things about singing.

The congregation was important to me, too, because if the relationship with Jimmy were to continue, I was determined to get Jimmy interested in the church. No way was I going to marry out of the church ("don't be unequally yoked"), so I wanted a path open to a conversion process.

As things turned out, I didn't get a job that summer. Jane's mother gave us tickets to a fund-raising dinner held at noon and Jane fainted. She was exhausted from the year of school, and instead of working in an office for the summer, she obtained a position with the Campfire Girls at a summer camp in the cool pines of Prescott, an ideal place to spend a summer.

I did a lot of sewing, as did Alma. I wrote to Jimmy almost daily. We had a post office box and I walked to the post office every day to get the mail. I didn't hear from Jimmy every day, and I didn't expect to. I had no idea if he would get sent to one of the Arizona bases for training after Santa Ana, but of course I hoped. I got a letter from him about once a week, but sometimes it stretched to two weeks. I walked to the post office thinking, "If I don't hear from him today, I'm going to forget him and continue with my goal of a career"—and I would get a letter!

On an afternoon in August there was a knock on the door and when I opened it, there he stood! I was ecstatic. He visited every weekend. I started back to college in September. He was baptized in October. It was about this time that the Air Force began to believe they might be turning out more pilots than needed and they extended his primary phase training by five weeks by sending him to Hemet, California. One of the popular songs was "A Small Hotel" and he went to the town of Riverside and found

Maud and Pearl

the Mission Hotel. He wrote to me about it and two years later we were able to stay overnight there.

When he was sent back to Arizona it was to Marana Army Air Corps base near Tucson. He had to hitchhike up to Tempe and we would go to Tolleson for Sunday. One Saturday he didn't arrive. We couldn't phone each other so I thought he hadn't been able to get a ride, or maybe they had restricted passes for some reason. I went on to Tolleson, and I didn't hear anything all day Sunday.

That night, back in my dorm room, the radio was on. The news had an item about an accident on the highway from Tucson. "A flatbed truck was hit head on by a drunk driver. Six cadets were sitting in a circle on the truck bed and were thrown out into the desert. One of them was killed and the other five were taken to the Marana Base hospital." I had to wait till morning to get on the phone and call there for information. Jimmy was one of the five. He had a skull fracture and his left leg was broken in two places. I had to wait till the next weekend to go see him.

My friend Vera Jo lived in Casa Grande so I caught the bus to Tucson from there. It stopped at the base and I walked the half-mile into the base to the hospital. I went down every week if I could, and especially on Thanksgiving. Coming back, I had to wait at the bus stop on the highway where the military waited when hitchhiking. There was nothing else around, no stores or phones. One time I was late and the bus had already gone by. There were no more buses that night.

A coupe with two men in it stopped and offered me a ride, and I accepted. I was nervous but tried not to show it. I sat in the middle and was a veritable chatterbox. This made me say, later in life, "If I have a home invasion I could probably talk 'em to death." Fortunately, they were nice and took me right to my dorm. I reckon that angel was sitting on my shoulder again.

Jimmy was released from the hospital after the first of the year and was given a leave of a few weeks to go home to see his mom. He was evaluated because of the head injury and the doctor testified he had not been unconscious a full two hours, which was the determining time.

Pearl Allen Andree

While at home in Santa Rosa, California, Jimmy used some of the money he had sent home to Mother Goggin from his boot camp days (apparently he played cards well enough to win, and instead of spending it she had saved it) to buy a lovely diamond engagement ring for me. When he returned to Arizona and got back into the program, he was able to resume coming to see me in Tempe and Tolleson. On my birthday in March we took a picnic lunch to Papago Park and climbed the Hole in the Rock, where he gave me the ring. For many weeks I was distracted in physics class because the ring was so beautiful to look at under the bright ceiling lights.

With my engineering curriculum I was scheduled to take organic chemistry that semester, but since I planned to marry a pilot, I had decided to take a new four-hour course called ground maintenance instead. It included seven hours instruction in a Piper Cub airplane at Sky Harbor Airport and was the first such class for women in that area. Some students later got together to discuss the class and the others talked about their parachutes.

I said, "You wear parachutes?"

They responded, "Yes, don't you? We're supposed to."

My instructor was a bush pilot with about 25,000 hours and at the next opportunity I asked him, "Are we supposed to have parachutes?"

He answered, "Well, yeah, but if anything happened, we could glide down."

I was also making my wedding dress. I had to borrow a sewing machine in the home economics department. Fortunately, my roommate, Lula, was minoring in that so she was my go-between. Lula was able to live in the house for home economics majors for six weeks of the semester. Her major was actually education, and she would be graduating in May—the same week I was getting married. Lula lived at home until that last semester. I knew her from church and our mothers were close friends. My roommate Georgia from the first semester had arranged her schedule so she could commute from her family's home in Avondale.

Georgia had been a classmate all four years of high school and was hoping to become a doctor. She was a tomboy who wore

Maud and Pearl

tailored skirts and plain white blouses most of the time. Her mother had a beauty shop in her home and her dad was principal at Avondale Elementary. She always went deer hunting with her father in the fall and always got her deer. She went to Flagstaff State College her freshman year and had contacted me to see if we could room together.

There wasn't room for one more in West Hall where I had roomed so I changed dorms. Instead of a large sleeping porch, we had two rooms with two girls each and a connecting sleeping porch with four cots. She showed me pictures of her roommate, a beautiful blonde, and told me how they had gone deer hunting the previous fall. They obtained two licenses, but Georgia admitted she had shot both deer! The roommate was living with her parents in Avondale so that was probably why Georgia commuted her second semester. She had been a good friend when Jimmy had that accident.

The wedding was on Friday, May 18, 1945. It cost me $20, and that included the material for my dress and the necessary fresh flowers. Alma decorated the auditorium with flowers from friends. There had been some speculation that Jimmy might be transferred to Colorado. If so, we'd have to be married in Colorado. My friend Jane had told me she had a dress for being maid of honor and would go to Colorado if we had to. Jimmy had written Chuck to see if he could be best man but hadn't heard back, so he had a red-headed buddy named Tom Dooley stand with him.

When Jimmy had asked a panel for permission to leave for the week-end he had to tell them why. When he told them he would be getting married, one officer on the panel remonstrated, "Gig that man!" He wasn't serious of course, but when Jimmy arrived in Phoenix it was getting close to the 7:00 p.m. wedding time. He got a taxi and told the driver 9th Street & Madison. There was no church building there and the taxi driver realized he must have meant Avenue, so he got him to the church on time. Had I known then what I learned later, it would have been a red flag. Jimmy Goggin, when not in an airplane, was directionally challenged!

Pearl Allen Andree

His mother and sister Vona came from Santa Rosa. Mother Goggin thought she had arrived in hell, it was so hot. The wedding was in the church house where each of us had been baptized, a Spanish-looking building. I phoned the newspaper and asked if a photographer could come and take pictures. He showed up and, low and behold, it was on the society page on Sunday! We had good quality photos from him.

We had a little reception at home in Tolleson, but many guests couldn't come because of transportation. Alma's friend Catherine Cochran made a cake with the obligatory coin, ring, and thimble embedded in it. Someone took us back to Phoenix where we stayed in a nice motel for the weekend.

Marriage and a Humorous Man

I BEGAN to share life, and later family, with Jimmy. I have to say something about his incredible and natural sense of humor. Even though he'd survived a lot of hurt in his upbringing due to his father's alcoholism and his parents' discord, he still always was a crack-up funny person. In everyday life he did not take himself seriously, and he could find humor in anything. He was winsome. Later, when home from the South Pacific, Leo had no trouble getting well-acquainted with his new brother-in-law. Years later when a pregnant Dorothy and Pete found out they were both Rh-negative, Jimmy told them, "I'm glad to know you're compatible." He gave me a healthy sense of humor that I've always kept.

Surviving the hardships of his youth gave Jimmy an inner confidence in doing the things he knew he was good at. He had always loved the idea of flying, and having become a flyer, he exuded that he would always fly. Early on, he also loved the motor and anything that motors powered. Working for a local trucking company as a teenager, he earned the nickname Leadfoot by dependably making deliveries.

When he began visiting me in Tolleson, he was unpretentious and put everyone at ease. My nieces soon idolized him. When Lanier was sad that his toy airplane broke, Jimmy explained that it wouldn't be a problem at all to fix it, which he helped Lanier to do. Several of my nephews followed his example by going into military service, and Ornan's son, Jim, transitioned his Air Force mechanic training into a civilian career. My family saw in Jimmy his unforgettable qualities.

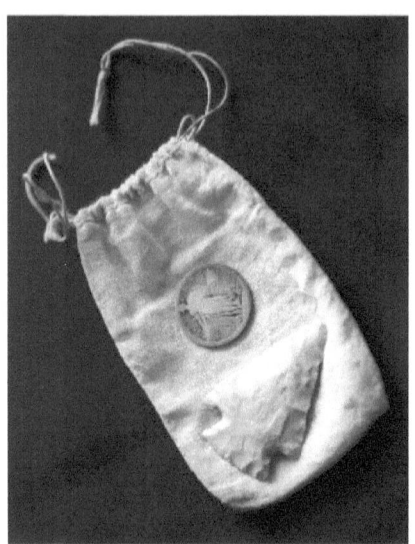

The collection that Maud Allen kept on the trail of many places: arrowhead, Leo's tobacco pouch, and Pearl's prize quarter (1916-1917), together April 1938
© 2024 Amanda Coleman

Jimmy Goggin as teenager in work uniform
Santa Rosa, California
About 1939

Leo Allen, front right, WWII Pacific Theater
Seabees 82nd Construction Battalion, Co. D-3, 1943 – 1945

Jimmy Goggin
Primary phase training

He wrote on back of photo:

"The cause for that silly grin on my pan is due to the ride I gave my instructor—I almost lost him—he forgot to fasten his safety belt! For a minute up there I thought I was going to solo before my time! … Say how's the world? I haven't had a chance to read a paper or hear a radio since I left Santa Ana."

Hemet, California
1944

"Getting to know you, getting to know all about you. Getting to like you, getting to hope you like me."

Jimmy and Pearl
probably in Tolleson
1944-1945

Lyrics ©1951
Rodgers and Hammerstein

Pearl and Leo Allen
Tolleson, Arizona, probably 1946
Leo returned from the South Pacific in 1945

Jimmy and Pearl
The Steak House Restaurant, Phoenix, Arizona, November 1946

Pearl and Jimmy's wedding
Westside Church of Christ
Phoenix, Arizona
May 18, 1945

Allen Family Reunion

in front of Zeke and Ellen's house
photo by Ed Spencer, Ellen's brother

Front L to R: Carol Lou Allen, Jenny Lee Curtis, Martha Anne (Tanny) Robertson, Dickie Curtis, Terrell Wayne Allen, Dawn Marie Allen, Mary Curtis, Jimmie Allen, Charlotte Allen, Lanier Allen

Middle L to R: Ellen Allen, Billy Allen, Dorothy B. Allen, Alma Curtis, Maud Allen, Rita Jo Allen, Pearl Goggin, Margaret (Totsy) Robertson, Martha Robertson, Dorothy C. Allen

Back L to R: Ornan Allen, Lee Curtis, Leo Allen, Pete Allen, Charles Walter Robertson, Babe Robertson, Jimmy Goggin, Zeke Allen, Earl Allen

Tolleson, Arizona
December 1946

Three Cousins and a Friend
L to R: Dawn Marie, Lanier, Carol Sue Lauer, and Carol Lou
Tolleson Church of Christ
Arizona, 1947
Sketch by Louis Daniel

Margaret (Totsy) Robertson Scott,
Age 15
Expression recital playing movie star
Jeanne Crain on stage at Marlow
High School
Oklahoma, 1947-1948

Jimmy Goggin
in civilian clothes
Goodyear, Arizona
between 1946 and 1951

Jimmy, Danny, Pearl
Goodyear, Arizona
1949-1950

Tanny, Martha, and Totsy
Fuqua Park,
Duncan, Oklahoma
1947

Zeke Jr. and Ellen Allen
and family
L to R, front row: Rita Jo,
Earl, and Carol Lou
Tolleson, Arizona,
1945-1946

Pat and Danny Goggin
with Santa Claus
Williams AFB, Arizona
1951

Jimmy's jet trainer
accident picture
Laredo AFB
March 1953

Instructor and trainer jets flying in
formation with weapon load
Photo by Jimmy Goggin
Laredo AFB, 1953

Jimmy Goggin
Tiger Lovers squadron insignia on helmet
and wearing squadron canary yellow scarf
Laredo AFB, 1954

The Goggin family
Pat in Jimmy's lap, Danny, Janet, and Pearl
Del Rio, Texas, 1954

The Devine Family in Sunday Best
"Okay, everybody, line up."
L-R: Mike with Mini Mike and Mark; Denise, Dawn, Judy
Clairemont Ave, Oakland CA, springtime 1961

Martha and Babe Robertson
Marlow, Oklahoma
1968

Alma Curtis
Dumas, Texas,
early 1960s

Allen Grandchildren Collage

Allen grandchildren, 1950s, 1960s, and earlier

Dickie Curtis in his early 20s
Canyon, Texas, about 1960

Vergin and Leo Allen
Dome Valley or Yuma, Arizona
early 1960s

Pete and Dorothy Allen house, 50 years later. Garage that Pete built on right. Madison St., Tolleson, Arizona. Photo taken by family, 1988.

Part II: Pearl's Life

Jimmy and Pearl, 1944–1955
Widowhood, 1955–1957
Pearl and Bill, 1957–1977+

Jimmy and Pearl

ON SUNDAY afternoon Jimmy hitchhiked back to the Marana Air Force Base and I rode the bus to Tucson to the Pioneer Hotel for the remaining two nights before his graduation from the middle phase of his flight training. Afterward we returned to Luke Air Force Base, where he went through advanced flight training and got his wings in August.

I had no trouble getting a job on the base, and there was a building across the road from the base with rooms for single women who worked on the base. I happened to be the only one there. Jimmy still had to live in the barracks but could go off base on Saturday nights. After about three weeks, an enlisted man came into the barracks wanting to know if anyone wanted to rent his off-base apartment (but considered "on-base government property") while he and his wife went on leave, and Jimmy snapped it up. We even shared it when they came back, until we had to move out because officers couldn't live on the base.

I worked in the Publications office, where all the paperwork forms were kept. Other departments had to requisition forms for their work. I shopped at the commissary for groceries. Some things were hard for the military to get and those items were saved for certain people like the CO. One day I was in the produce area looking for bananas because I smelled them. I said, "Where are the bananas?" to a worker.

He responded, "Lady, if you can smell them, you deserve to have some." He went into the back and brought out some for me!

I bought some tomato juice in a gallon tin because they didn't have bottles or small cans. I had a glass with my dinner. I

Maud and Pearl

knew to put the rest in glass, but we didn't have a glass container and I thought it would be all right just overnight in the fridge. I had a glass the next morning and threw the rest down the drain. Soon after arriving at work I was sick at my stomach so badly someone had to take me to the base hospital. Of course, because I was newly married, they all thought I was pregnant. Not true—it was the bad tomato juice.

Jimmy and I met in the evenings and went to a movie on base or just spent time together. On Sundays our friends Gerald and Mildred Lauer picked us up to go to church, and brought us home afterward.

I was a strict budgeter so we saved about $250 from my salary, and the time came when we had to prepare where we would live after he got his wings as we would not be allowed to remain on the base. There was a big shortage of places to rent. One place was an apartment with terrible linoleum, a terrible bed, an old kerosene stove in the kitchen—and a shared bathroom down the hall! Gerald and Mildred in Goodyear suggested we talk to their neighbor, who wanted to sell and move to Virginia. Her father was very ill and she felt the urgency.

Jimmy received $300 to buy new uniforms and Valley Bank (where our savings account was) loaned us $300 as a personal loan. We told the owners we could pay $500 down on their $3000 equity and pay $100 a month plus interest. They took the offer and we owned a house! They left us a bedroom set, a dining table with chairs, a 9' x 12' rug in the living room, a mangle (an ironing appliance), a washing machine, a stove, and a refrigerator. The house was a two-bedroom stucco frame with an evaporative cooler, a gas furnace, and an enclosed garage. It was in Del Webb's first subdivision and we took over a mortgage of a little over $8000, with monthly payments of $32. We felt very blessed.

Jimmy graduated on August 5th and received his wings as well as the rank of Flight Officer. Harry Stanford Anthony, one of his friends, had no one to pin his wings on so Jimmy asked if I could get Jean DeRouhlac to do so, and she did. She hadn't yet become a beauty pageant finalist, but she was beautiful.

Pearl Allen Andree

Jimmy had a two-week leave so we went to Santa Rosa. We traveled by train and were side-railed in Cadiz, California for eight hours. Cadiz consisted of a telegraph pole and a train car serving as a café in the middle of the southern California desert. When we stopped later in Barstow we had enough of a lay-over to get a motel room to shower and change clothes. I had been wearing a white summer wool dress that had gotten quite smoky.

The rest of the trip was nice on the Sunset Limited going north along the coast to San Francisco. I nearly froze in my unlined corduroy jacket. We stayed with Mother Goggin and Vona. I also met Jimmy's father, James, a carpenter who had and would continue to struggle for years with alcohol and keeping steady work, neither of which Mother Goggin tolerated. He treated me with pleasantness and gentleness. I knew that deep down Jimmy loved his father.

We enjoyed a day at the beach where I froze again, bundled up in a coat from Vona while she and her brother frolicked on the sand and water. I also met Peg and Ed Millerick, for whom Jimmy had worked, and Jimmy took me to see gardens he had worked on as a teenager. One excursion was to the Russian River, where there was an Italian restaurant he remembered, and I had my first family-style Italian dinner. I was full after the first course of soup.

On the return train trip back to Arizona, we read the newspaper account of dropping the A-bomb on Hiroshima. I remembered the chemistry professor telling what could happen with atoms.

The military realized they had too many pilots so they started letting them out, but Jimmy didn't want out. We could have been transferred to Alaska as some were doing. I didn't want to go there; I wanted us to go to college. He was able to get assigned to an auxiliary field in Ajo that was still attached to Luke Air Force Base. They were not set up for spouses yet so he went there and I continued in the house, working on the base. We rented the house to my boss, who was married with a small boy, and I took the extra bedroom.

During the spring of 1946, the Ajo base had a hangar remodeled to a few rooms with private baths, so I quit my job

Maud and Pearl

and moved there. We had acquired a little white dog from Alma and named him Ike. We gave him to my former boss, thinking he would take Ike for the sake of their little boy when he left the service and took his family back to their home state. They didn't, and we didn't find out about it until much later and poor little Ike was on his own. He became a neighborhood scrounger. A car hit him and injured his leg, which healed twisted and caused a painful limp and other health problems. It broke Jimmy's heart to have to kill him, but we couldn't afford a veterinarian and in those days most people had to take such things into their own hands.

Not long after I moved to Ajo, I obtained a job at the Phelps Dodge copper mine, as Ajo was a company town. I needed transportation to work, about seven miles, and Jimmy found someone selling a Model A Ford for $375. Cars had not been built during the war. My job was in the personnel office. Sometime in June we found an apartment in town so I could walk to work. Around this time, I realized I was probably pregnant. It wasn't a good idea to drive the Model A up to the Valley (Phoenix, the "Valley of the Sun"), so we went with someone else for the Fourth of July weekend. While there, I saw our family doctor and he confirmed the pregnancy.

Back in Ajo there was a bad fire in a section of town where the houses must have been tinder boxes. We wanted to see the damage so on Saturday evening we drove through the rough ruts, bouncing in the Model A. I was skeptical about whether it would cause me to lose the baby, but I told myself, "Think of all the women who came west in wagons and had babies on the way." We went back to the apartment, had dinner, and went to bed.

Jimmy had gone to sleep but I hadn't. Soon I started having cramps. I was about seven weeks along, and staying in the bathroom all night, I knew I had lost the baby but didn't know what to do about it or how serious it could be. I never saw an embryo, just a tube-like bit. I stayed in bed all day Sunday instead of going to church with Jimmy. One of the elders and his wife came to see me in the afternoon. I felt well enough to go to work the next day.

Two weeks later we went up to the Valley again and I saw the doctor. He was quite perturbed with me for not having gone

Pearl Allen Andree

to the company hospital. He told me to take two weeks off and just be lazy—go to the beauty shop and such. I complied. My hair was fairly long and bleached blonde by the Arizona sun. Underneath the top layer it was a medium brown. A very good beautician had a shop in Ajo, so she bleached the dark to match the light. I had to touch up the roots every three weeks, a several-hour task. I bled for a month, but I didn't know that was unusual.

In November Jimmy got out of the service and we moved back to our house in Goodyear. One of the personnel directors had explained unemployment to me, so I applied to the unemployment office in Phoenix. Every job involved long bus rides or some such. Finally, they found one that was perfect and I went to work for Wingfoot Homes.

The housing shortage was still acute. P. W. Litchfield, a prominent man with Goodyear Tire and Rubber, had built an estate and founded the small town of Litchfield Park just south of Luke Air Force Base. Someone in the company had designed a small house, about the size of a trailer house, and they had erected a hangar in which to build them. The company had put the sales and accounting departments in an end space and walled off the building area. The Wingfoot Home was the forerunner of the prefab.

My job was in the accounting department. Jimmy got a job in the building section.. This is when I found out how badly Jimmy's hay fever could affect him at times. Not only did he have a problem from mowing the lawn, but the sawdust in the factory caused him to have to lie down on the floor for about two hours when he got home.

The sales department found out he liked, and was good at, building model airplanes. They had him build the model homes they used for sales promotion. I also modeled, sitting in the kitchen for a picture they used. One day the Goodyear blimp showed up. The pilot came in and asked if anyone wanted a ride. Of course, several of us did. It held about ten of us. We went up and observed the Valley of the Sun from the air. As I write this, I am over 90, and I have never met anyone else that had a ride in the Goodyear blimp.

Maud and Pearl

The doctor was right. I developed secondary anemia. He wanted me to come in three days a week for liver shots for $5 each. I told him I couldn't afford that, plus it was too big of an inconvenience. We had sold the Model A shortly after the miscarriage and replaced it with a '37 Ford, which we sold when Jimmy got out of the Air Corps. He had stayed in the Reserve and went to the base one weekend of each month. The doctor said I better eat a lot of liver so I did. Jimmy didn't like it, but I did and had learned from Mama how to fix liver 'n onions. I stayed thin, though, getting down to about 111 pounds.

Hank's Thingamajig and Swooning Aunt Mandy

In the summer of '47, Lee and Alma convinced us to go to the wheat harvest with them. Lee took a combine and Jimmy followed them up the plains states to hopefully make some money. Alma and the kids stayed with them to cook and I visited in Oklahoma. They put me on a bus at their starting place in southern Colorado and I went to Paducah, Texas, where I stayed with Aunt Dona and Uncle Lem for a few days before going to where Martha and her family lived in southern Oklahoma. I saw cousins Neil and L. B. while at Aunt Dona's. At Martha's, I had a great time with Charley, Totsy, and Tanny, who were all still in their teens.

Charley, one of the most notable Allen pranksters, had played a trick on me. He tried to get his friend Bob Alexander to get friendly with me at one of the area teenager parties that I went to with him and the girls. When Bob realized I was married, what a shock for both of us! And that nephew had a hearty laugh that made everyone else laugh along.

I don't know why neither Jimmy nor I thought of his hay fever, but the wheat nearly killed him. I had been at Martha's about three weeks when he had to come get me so we could go back to Arizona.

Jimmy and I loved that shower that Babe had made, playing in it and enjoying it. Jimmy was so impressed with Babe's thingamajig that thereafter, he gave Babe a special nickname, "Hank." Babe chuckled and smiled at his novel new name.

Maud and Pearl

Jimmy recovered in Marlow after leaving the harvest, but before we took a bus home to Arizona, something hilarious happened. Martha took Jimmy and me to get acquainted with Grandma Hall at her home, and we all sat out on her front porch together, along with Aunt Eula. It was the same home Mama had walked me to as a toddler, a few miles south on the country road from the farm into Marlow. With dementia and being late in her life, Grandma didn't recognize me. Martha introduced me as "Maud's girl" and then introduced Jimmy.

Then things livened up. Jimmy was knockdown handsome; all of my nieces had become madly in love with him, and he caught Grandma's attention and interrupted her life story mantra. Besides, Jimmy never had trouble talking to people—he could talk to anybody. Grandma and Jimmy began a conversation, and she was listening and asking him questions!

Slyly, he asked, "Wouldn't you like to go out to Arizona and see Maud? It'd be good for the two of you to visit. I'm a pilot; I could pick you up in an airplane, and you could fly with me out to see Maud."

Grandma responded, "My! How far is it?"

Martha, knowing that she didn't have a clue about distances, spoke up and said, "A hundred and fifty miles."

Grandma replied, "Oh, that's too far!"

Since we couldn't access our bank savings, we had to borrow $50 from Babe to go home. We paid that back as quickly as possible after we returned home.

Back to Home, Work, Study and So On

AFTER getting home from Marlow, we prepared to go back to college. In Tempe, Mill Avenue curved into Apache Boulevard, and on the acreage there, Arizona State had put in Victory Village—house trailers for veterans and their spouses to rent while studying on the G. I. Bill. So many were going that we had to get on a waiting list. That meant the next year! In the meantime, Jimmy enrolled in college and we rented a room from a family nearby. Jimmy's sister Vona from California had decided to go back to high school and was living in our house, going to Tolleson High School, so we couldn't rent it out. Jimmy received a monthly stipend for going to college, and another for going to the base once a month and flying for the Reserve. I got a job as a professor's assistant that paid $90 a month.

The family we rented from had children still in high school. They went to the Friday night football games, and one Friday night a boy on the home team was killed while playing. When I had sons later in life, I didn't go to their games without getting nervous. We found a room closer to campus. A professor's parents had a room available. There was a little gas heater in the room and when it was on, the white paint with which it was painted smelled so we had to open the window. So we tried not to light it. For the first time in my life I got a flu shot—and I got the flu!

Around Thanksgiving, Alma brought Leo over one Sunday after he'd been in the VA hospital. He had a job on a farm and Mama moved in with him to cook and clean for her boy.

In December 1947, I began getting sick in the mornings and realized I was pregnant.

1948: On the Road to Parenthood

THE semester ended the latter part of January and we realized we couldn't continue on. We'd had to borrow $200 from Leo and the same from Mother Goggin. We moved back into the house in Goodyear. Vona would graduate from high school in May and move back to Los Angeles to marry Frank Amaya. That was the plan, anyway.

Jimmy and I had seen a newspaper or magazine ad for a place in Kansas selling white nylon parachutes and wooden propellers. I'm sure they sold other war surplus also, but these were what we ordered. I secretly made Vona a beautiful gown and negligee set in white nylon while she was at school. I knew from experience she was never happy with a garment in the formation stage. We bought a sewing machine, a necessary appliance in preparation for a coming birth. I made many baby clothes from the parachute. When our name came up at Singer, it was for a featherweight and I didn't want a light-weight one. We found a rebuilt one and saved money because Jimmy built a box to set it in and a cover for it, plus a cabinet with a fitted chair, later in 1950 in college industrial arts class.

Jimmy was qualified to do drafting and could have obtained a job at the Arizona Public Service electric utility doing that, but it would only pay $150 a month. He decided to take a job with the Highway Department doing road surveying. He had to travel during the week but was paid a per diem and we felt that might be better. The base pay was about the same.

Jimmy had job-searched the whole month of February so he went to work for the Arizona Highway Department in March.

Pearl Allen Andree

During his search time we had to be creative. For a few days he worked on a pipeline, which was extremely laborious. Ornan took him to pick cotton a few days. We even borrowed $20 from Ornan for groceries, and I was budgeting on $5 a week. We ate a lot of cream of tomato soup. I added two cans of water and a bouillon cube to a ten-cent can of soup and it served the three of us for a good first course. Once Jimmy teased Vona about the way she put so much jelly in the middle of her toast and ate around it. She responded that she ate the same amount he did—he just chose to spread it out!

One day Dorothy and Ornan showed up with their three boys, Terrell, Jimmie, and Billy. She came into the kitchen and proceeded to fix a meal for eight people. I can't remember if we had meat, but she fixed breaded canned tomatoes and I think made biscuits. I have never discovered how to make breaded tomatoes as tasty as hers. I didn't dream we could manage dessert, but I remember her statement, "I always like to fix a little dessert, if I don't have a very big meal." I had a large can of peaches in the cupboard, and she proceeded to make a most delicious shortcake. I learned a lot of things from my sisters-in-law.

Vona graduated and went back to Los Angeles to be near Frank. She got work at Bullocks Wilshire department store and he went to college at USC, like so many other vets. They lived together but there was always something Frank wanted to "wait until" to keep from going ahead with marriage. We liked Frank. He had been raised by two single aunts as a Baptist, somewhat unusual for a Hispanic, and we sat up late many times discussing the Bible. Sadly Vona and Frank never married.

I turned 21 that spring. Before that, Jimmy teased me with, "You're not even old enough to vote."

To which I responded, "But I didn't have to get my mama to sign so I could get married."

We always considered voting extremely important. We voted for Truman. I don't remember much else about the election, but it was a big day in my life when I went to the polls that first time, the next November, with Danny in his baby carriage, at Avondale Grammar School.

Maud and Pearl

When I visited Martha in 1947, a neighbor told her, "Your sister has such pretty hair, and for it to be so natural, too." Martha said she didn't have the heart to tell her about my chemistry set.

During my pregnancy in '48, I decided three hours every two weeks was too much, so I let my roots alone for awhile. I looked pretty funny, but when the darkness was about three or four inches long, I had Jenny Lee cut the blond off and give me a home perm. The following Friday evening Jimmy came home and I was sitting on the couch. He didn't recognize me—he thought I was Dawn, my niece!

Mom had pounded into me not to live with relatives so I never initiated her coming to stay awhile, but Jimmy did. He might perceive her excessive tiredness and say, "Mom, I think you ought to come over and visit us." She lived at Alma's because she was needed there. When she stayed with us she kept us fed scrumptiously, and Jimmy loved the way she ironed his uniforms. In the Reserves, he was now going one weekend a month to Williams Air Force Base for flight duty, for which he got paid. During this period of time, he began training to fly fighter planes with jet engines. He practiced gunnery, flew acrobatics, and simulated combat exercises. Mom slept a lot when she was at our house. I think she'd rest up for a week or so, then feel guilty and go back to Alma's where she was needed.

Our next door neighbors, the Lauers, always had kittens around. Vona loved having them around and would bring them in every once in a while when she was there. Everyone knew not to expect me to pick them up. I had a wringer washing machine and had to leave the back door open sometimes. If the five or six kittens crawled into my house I had to go get the eight-year-old Lauer girl to come get them. Sometimes Jimmy wore a flight suit while working in the yard and he'd come in, limping, on purpose. I would discover he had a little black kitten in a leg pocket. The flap would be snapped down and the kitten's head poking out.

One of the things I did that summer was go to a four-day cooking school in Phoenix. I rode the bus into Phoenix to the Shrine Auditorium at 15th Avenue and Washington. It was sponsored by the Meat Institute and I still have the recipe book

Pearl Allen Andree

they gave us, which I have used many times through the years to make prune apple pie, gingerbread and other mixes, cakes, and meatloaf.

Our family doctor at that time was a Dr. Philip Johnson. He was credited with saving Charlotte's life as a baby, was Carol Lou's doctor when she had to stay in bed her second-grade school year with TB, and had come for a dying man when his own doctor wouldn't. All this was during and after WWII. He took care of me after my miscarriage and the secondary anemia afterwards. He was seeing that I took vitamins and a nasty tasting blood builder during this pregnancy.

Apparently he had failed to report a lot of income he made during the war years. Doctors were scarce as most were in the service and he even made house calls. As a doctor he had good gas rations. Anyway, the IRS got him convicted and he was sent to Florence for six months. The preacher commented, "Whatever he did, he's still the best doctor I know." One thing I know, those prisoners had one good doctor while he was there. That was the first time I got a bad taste in my mouth about the IRS. As a result, though, I was transferred to Dr. Donald G. Carlson, an OB, when I was about five months pregnant.

When I went for my check-ups I had to ride the bus because the doctor's office was at 7th Street and McDowell. I went to a movie in the afternoon to get out of the heat before going back home. Mom came to stay with me. During July, I went every week. My due date was the 31st, and on the 23rd, a Friday, Dr. Carlson said he thought he'd see me at the hospital before the next appointment. However, Friday the 30th I was back, and he said I was dilating. "You won't be much longer." I was too tired that day to even go to a movie, so I went on home.

That night, Mom had fixed a lovely meal. Jimmy was expected home from his work week. However, that week the phone had gone out. Jimmy was trying to call me but it would register busy. He told the operator, "I know my wife doesn't talk that much." He was frantic. He wasn't home yet when I sat down to eat. Suddenly I realized I was sitting in a puddle of water.

Maud and Pearl

We managed to cross the street to the Westphal's phone to call the doctor. He said, "Your pains won't start for another five hours, so when they get about five or ten minutes apart, come in to the hospital." We're talking 20 miles from Goodyear to Phoenix, so we'd have to find someone to take us. The town's only employed policeman told us he'd take us.

While I was on the phone, Jimmy came home. We went back home and I told Mom I had sort of a menstrual cramp. She said, "That's a labor pain, so lie down." My first two pains were five minutes apart. Jimmy ate, took a shower, dressed up, shined his shoes, and then went to find the policeman, who he found was compelled to chaperone a teenage dance and couldn't take us!

Pete and Dorothy drove into the driveway, car fully packed with kids and stuff, on their way to California for the work season. Dorothy's parting words to Jimmy: "She'll have a seven-pound girl." He insisted we'd have a boy. Later, she told me she told him that because many men get it into their heads the first should be a boy so she was getting him prepared just in case.

Jimmy talked Rudy Westphal, a high school student, into taking us to the hospital before continuing his Friday night date (his girlfriend was already with him). Nobody warned anyone that women in labor may get sick to the stomach, so there wasn't anything to use when I did, lying on the back seat. Cleaning the car was another thing they had to do before the rest of that date. I always wondered if she married him.

When we reached the emergency room, Jimmy had to go to the administration office so Rudy took me back and went with me in the wheel chair in the elevator. He was asked twice if he was my husband. I sometimes wonder if he and his girlfriend remember that night as clearly as I do.

By the time I was wheeled into the delivery room it was nearly midnight. All of a sudden, Georgia, my roommate from college, was there! She was supervisor of nurses. They shot something into my left arm and I was out before they did the right arm. I was vaguely aware Dr. Carlson had come in. Daniel Anthony Goggin was born at 12:29 a.m. Later in life, I have wondered if that was the last time Danny was on time, because he grew up and has

Pearl Allen Andree

always favored thoroughness, concentration, and completion over punctuality.

When Danny was born, he already had a double chin, and five days in Good Samaritan Hospital gave him a heat rash on it to take home. It festered and we had to have the doctor call in a sulfa ointment for it. The hospital had evaporative cooling but not refrigeration. They had a rubber sheet on my bed and it was miserable. Ever since, I've been a nut about always having a quilted pad under the bed sheets.

Mother's Daughter's Mothering

WHEN I prepared to leave the hospital, the pediatrician I'd requested came to see me and gave me formula to use and so forth. I said, "What's this for? I'm going to nurse my baby."

He replied, "Oh, that's in case you break a leg or get shot or something." He instructed me to keep nothing on him but a diaper and keep the cooler going full. At home, however, Mom and Jimmy were concerned about the draft. They insisted on putting padding around his bed. We had a friend, Dr. Jim Cox, who was at the Goodyear Naval Base. He came by one day, saw all the padding, and started taking it off and opening the vents. After that Danny slept fine. He was a healthy baby.

Mama stayed with me for two weeks and then I started taking care of my baby all by myself. I wanted him to get a tan so the sun wouldn't be so harsh on him. I took him into the backyard, put him on a pallet in the sun, only shielding his eyes, for a minute, then turned him over for another minute. It worked; he had a nice tan after awhile.

I didn't have a dress I could fit into for going to church so Jimmy had to go buy one for me. It was green, his favorite color. Jimmy could only come home on weekends and he was so eager to see his son that he immediately went to the crib. If Danny was sleeping, Jimmy woke him up.

One of the most notable events of 1948 was Jimmy's first deer hunt. He really felt accepted by working colleagues when they invited him to go deer hunting. One even loaned him a gun. A party of eight went north of Congress Junction to Yarnell Hill

Pearl Allen Andree

and beyond. Two or three cars carried men and supplies. One man, Ralph, brought all the food supplies in the trunk of his car.

When they arrived at the campsite Ralph and another man went for a hike, ostensibly to look for tracks or signs. They didn't come back, even in the evening. That's when the others realized no one had a key to the trunk where the food was stashed. One man had a couple of packages of cookies, which they shared.

The next day the main group went hunting as planned. Ralph and his buddy didn't return until time to come home. They had found a cabin and stayed there and had food! Needless to say, the others were not too happy with them.

They did get one deer, which had been packed out on a litter about five miles. We had eight pounds of venison from it.

On the way home that night Jimmy sat near Ralph, who was driving. As they passed a river Jimmy remarked, "Any SOB should've known by which way that water's flowing which direction to go back to camp."

To which Ralph responded, "Are you calling me a SOB?" And they got into a fight right there, driving down Yarnell Hill. At one point Jimmy's foot got on the accelerator. The other passengers finally got them apart.

Jimmy arrived home about 2:00 a.m. His first remark was, "Do we have any steak?" and I saw why he asked.

He had a black eye, his shirt was torn to pieces, he had several days' growth of beard, and the soles of his new rugged work shoes were worn completely out. He determined to never, ever go hunting again with men he didn't know very well.

Ralph left the Highway Department not long after that and later became a TV photographer in Phoenix. He also worked for Arizona Highways and became fairly prominent in Phoenix. When my children were growing up, I sometimes heard his name and always thought, "I'll bet they don't know what I know about him."

Thanksgiving was the annual Allen family dinner, but I don't remember which house. Leo may have already moved to Yuma to start improving the homestead acreage he'd acquired via the VA lottery at the beginning of the year. I probably had

Maud and Pearl

something to do with the salad as that was what they always told me to bring. I think it was the only thing they figured I couldn't ruin. Pete's Dorothy's sister Margie never let me forget she had to make the gravy when she came to my house one time for dinner. Except for the first year of 1945, however, I could do a great turkey and stuffing. Each year we went to the Lion's Club carnival at Tolleson Grammar School around Thanksgiving and Jimmy won a live turkey at the turkey shoot. He penned it up in the backyard and fed it till Thanksgiving. I told him he'd have to kill and dress it if it was ever done, but I could cook it. It was standard procedure; he did the same for any game or fish he brought home.

Sometime that year or the next we started buying the *Book of Knowledge* and *Encyclopedia Britannica*. Our child was going to be introduced to books! At only a few months old, he already loved to look at books and be read to. I stressed "be good to the books and don't hurt them." (We didn't have cloth books.) He was visibly sad if he accidentally tore a page in his children's books. I still have the *Book of Knowledge* set. *Lands and People* came with that, too. In the latter was a picture of an Irishman Jimmy used to turn to, look at, and laugh at because it looked so much like his father. It did, too.

The Allen family drew names at Christmas and we had the Christmas Eve gathering at our house that year. Pete drew my name for the third year in a row and gave me a rocking chair. They all thought it was sinful I didn't have a chair in which to rock my baby. Our dining area was fixed like a stage with curtains pulled across and we had a pageant with all the children in it. I taught Charlotte "The Night Before Christmas," and she was dressed in a flannel nightgown with pink ribbons around her feet. She peeked out the curtain, poked one foot out, then the other, and said the whole thing. That may have been the night my nephew Jimmie Allen wrote on my dresser mirror with my lipstick.

Mother Goggin visited for Christmas. I gave Jimmy a 5-in-1 tool. A lathe was one of the tools. He made a little baseball bat and on New Year's we dressed Danny like a New Year Baby and put that bat in his hand and took his picture. His expression seemed to say, "What terrible indignities one is forced to endure when one can't do anything about it."

Early 1950s:
The Goggin Military Family

BY 1950 we had decided I would go back to work so Jimmy could return to school. In January he was still with the Highway Department, surveying Arizona roads. He and his work buddy, Don Welty, were assigned the Kingman, Arizona area and would be there for about three months. Don's wife happened to be a former sorority sister of mine, so we all decided to go to Kingman and get apartments there for the three months. As we were moving, I realized I was pregnant again as the morning-sickness phase began. The fourplex had a common duct system, and I could smell what everyone else was cooking.

We attended church in Kingman where the preacher was Bill Douhit. There I met June Trimble, whose parents lived there. She had just lost her husband from acute severe pancreatitis, and she had three children. The youngest was just enough older than Danny that she gave me his little suit. It was Danny's first and it just fit. June and I were friends for the rest of our lives.

My due date for my second baby was September 30 so we began planning. Jimmy started back to ASC that semester. We were finally able to buy a car, a brand new Crosley Hot Shot. It was a small convertible with only one seat, but a jump seat behind the front seat. Jimmy began teaching me to drive. We went to an empty parking lot to practice. This child was not in a hurry to leave the comfort of my womb until the early morning of October 9. The crystal in our bedside clock was broken so I felt the hands to know the time was about 4:05 a.m. My second pain was five

Maud and Pearl

minutes later. I woke Jimmy up and told him. He groaned and said, "What are we going to name this one?" He had decided we would have another boy. The conversation went like this:
Me: Dennis Leo.
Him: What do you think of Patrick?
Me: Patrick Leo Goggin?
Him: Yeah.
Me: I'm having pains five minutes apart. Am I going to have to wait until you shower before we go?

He shot right up and got busy. At a little after 7:00 a.m. in the hospital delivery room, we had Patrick Leo.

Sixteen babies were born that night in Good Samaritan Hospital. Some were on beds in the halls. I shared a room with another woman. A day or two later I remarked to a nurse who was very busy, "I wonder why so many were born on the same night. She (the other mother) was two weeks early; I was nine days late."

The nurse answered, "I don't know, but it must have been awfully cold in January!"

Mother Goggin come to stay with us and I returned to work about six weeks after the birth. Goodyear Aircraft was still nearby and a working engineering company. Mr. Pentecost, the man I had worked for at Wingfoot Homes, was head of accounting, so I thought I would be in his department. But the personnel manager saw I had worked in personnel at Phelps Dodge, so he put me in his office, along with another lady.

I lived close enough to walk to work, come home for lunch, and then nurse Pat. I bathed him at night, as that was a special time for loving him. I powdered and massaged his back, and he'd lie there as if he were grown and enjoy his massage.

When Pat was three and a half months old I started weaning him. He weighed 17½ pounds and I figured I needed the strength more than he did.

About that time, I thought I could go for a weekend without him and we had learned Vona was possibly having something like a nervous breakdown in LA. We drove there to check on her. She had, one day, found herself in the store, not remembering how or when she got there. She could call on her older half-sister Hazel,

Pearl Allen Andree

and Hazel's husband Dale was a doctor, so we visited the weekend and came back home. We felt she was in good hands, but marriage was still was not on Frank's agenda. He was still going to USC and now it was "when we get a new car," or "when we can get a house." He definitely had a problem with commitment.

On the way home, driving overnight, a few miles before Salome, the car conked out on us. It was about 2:00 a.m. and no one stopped to help. Finally, a Good Samaritan black family stopped. They had gone to Los Angeles for a respite; they felt going to their home area for recreation with their two boys was more enjoyable than their new home in Phoenix. He drove us to Salome where Jimmy stayed to get the mechanic to go get the car and fix it, and then they took me home. What a blessing that family was! He was the service department head at the Cadillac dealership in Phoenix. In later years we saw him as a local politician in the Phoenix area.

Later in January, the other girl in the office and I were reviewing applications to be filed. I remarked about one, "Here's a guy with no more college math than I had and he's applying for engineering technician."

A male voice nearby said, "How much college math have you had?"

I looked at him and saw a man who looked like Oscar Levant, the piano player. I told him my math studies. He was waiting for the personnel manager to get a girl to work in his office. This was pre-NASA and Goodyear had tried to hire him in Akron, but he told them he would only work for them if they would set him up in Arizona. His name was Carl Wiley and I guess he had an IQ of around 180. Yes, Goodyear had created a Basic Physical Research Lab for him. During WWII he was a swabbie in the Navy and spent time writing Sci-Fi stories, sending them back to get published in Sci-Fi magazines. I got the job. There were two engineers, a developing engineer, a lab technician, and me. He wrote space travels and I was able to write the mathematical formula since typewriters didn't have the symbols. There was an Ozalid machine (the forerunner of Xerox) in the regular engineering department where I made copies of these writings.

Maud and Pearl

In March of '51 Jimmy had the opportunity to be hired by Goodyear as a test pilot for their airplane, just like Chuck Yeager, whom he admired very much. At the same time, he was informed he could be recalled to active duty in the Air Force due to the Korean conflict. He thought it would be better for a family man, so he returned to active duty and was promoted to First Lieutenant. Since it meant leaving college, he would get credit for the courses he was taking. He would have to commute the 65 miles before base housing construction was completed.

I quit my job in July and we moved to Williams Air Force Base. Jimmy, who had been gunnery-tested and certified combat-ready for Korea, was assigned there as an F-84 flight instructor. Because of his drawing and model-building skills, he was also designated as the training aids officer and training materials curriculum specialist, and he made scaled demos for the student pilots. He later designed some flight logos, and his call sign became Lover.

We needed to get the house in Goodyear in shape to sell, which necessitated going there three days a week to check on painting and so forth. We had hardly moved when Jimmy had to go on temporary duty in Alabama, meaning I had to drive back and forth to the other house. But I didn't have my driver's license yet! He had realized in the spring that the Crosley's rod was about to blow, so we had traded it in for a Studebaker. Mother Goggin still lived with us and helped a lot.

Jimmy left on a Saturday, and on Monday I had to stop in Phoenix, get my driver's license, and go on to Goodyear. When I finished the written test and was to take the driving one, the man assigned to me knew Jimmy from his Highway Department days. He passed me, commenting, "You need more confidence, so stay out of congested areas till you get more." I went on to Goodyear, and coming home stopped in Tolleson to pick up my niece Dawn. I brought her home two days later, and when we entered the Phoenix city limits, the first sign I saw read Congested Area!

Six weeks later, on a Friday morning and with three-year-old Danny as my companion, I drove to Texas to meet Jimmy on Saturday night in Waco and on to Alabama. Coming back to

Pearl Allen Andree

Arizona, we visited Dad's sister Aunt Mary and her husband Ed Hinkson in Arkansas, and in Oklahoma, Martha and Babe and Zeke and Ellen.

Jimmy had been checked out in jets and after serving as training aids officer for a few months, he began instructing student pilots.

We had accessed medical services at the base hospital. I'd had a wisdom tooth pulled during my first pregnancy, but the dentist thought I should have the other three pulled and suggested all at once. The deed was done one Thursday in late fall. He gave me a pain pill and told me to go home, drink a milk shake, and nap. I slept for four hours. When I woke up my jaws were swollen and I was broken out with chicken pox! I hadn't had them as a child and Danny and Pat had just had them. The fun wasn't over yet. The next Monday morning I started having morning sickness with my third pregnancy!

Sometime around the end of the year we became concerned about Vona again, and Jimmy drove to LA and insisted on her coming home with him. She moved in with us, sharing Mother Goggin's room. She liked the night life and since she didn't have a job she stayed out late, then slept sometimes into the afternoon. She and Mother had never lived easily together. I got along with her fairly well, not confronting her on things but arbitrating between the three of us. Sometimes I felt I was acquiring the ability to join the diplomatic corps.

Around Easter, Frank came to visit and we took the kids and all but Mother Goggin went up to Canyon Lake and rented a boat. I had fallen and sprained my ankle. We had the feeling their relationship was getting rocky and sometimes we thought they were rethinking things. It didn't seem to be healthy for her. She had met Bill Mundy, an Air Force administrative officer, and we were pretty sure Frank was on the way out. It turned out to be Frank's last visit.

Things came to a head when I was about seven months pregnant. Danny and Pat were playing loudly at about 10:00 a.m. when they awakened Vona from her daily slumber. She came out of her room ready to slay dragons and headed toward them. I was

Maud and Pearl

in the bathroom and came into the hall, remarking, "They have a right to play in their own home." She turned her anger on me, actually hitting me and remarking something about thinking I was so smart because it was my house.

I decided the time had come to call Jimmy at the Flight Line. I never wanted to call him at his work place, but this was it. I told him we had a crisis: it was her-or-me time. He came home and we went into Phoenix and found her an apartment and a job at a furniture store within walking distance.

Jimmy's first six-month training period for a group of student pilots ended in June and we had them over for a steak dinner the night before the graduation when they received their wings. We went to the ceremony at the base theatre. Three of them were Scandinavian, two from Denmark, and one from Norway. The speaker was Barry Goldwater and it may have been the first speech of his first campaign for the US Senate the following fall. We were impressed. As we walked home, I remember saying, "That man should be president someday."

The foreign students were a part of NATO arrangements. The instructors had to report to a panel as to each individual pilot's competency. Jimmy felt that the Norwegian should not be flying, and said so. He predicted he would accidentally crash, killing himself and taking the plane with him. The panel kept him in the program anyway. These pilots would be returning to their home countries right away, and two weeks after returning to Norway, tragically, the Norwegian did exactly what Jimmy had predicted.

Fourth of July weekend was coming up. On Tuesday mornings in the two base hospitals, ob-gyn doctors saw about 90 pregnant women. When I saw the doctor, I asked him if it would be okay if we went to the mountains for the weekend. My due date was July 20. He said, "Yes, if you stay on the paved roads." We went on Friday, planning to meet with friends Jan and Bill Wright and Vona and Bill. Vona was back living in an apartment on the base and with a job at the hospital. We didn't have a tent and the Yellow Front store was sold out. We had a dining canopy, which we strung up to trees. A new Ford station wagon had replaced the Studebaker so there was some protection from the rain. Mother

Pearl Allen Andree

Goggin was with us and we had sleeping bags. It seemed everyone in the Valley of the Sun was in the White Mountains and near the White River. We never met with our friends. Jimmy had a pair of hip boots for going into the water, but the fish were not biting. Other fishermen told him, "Heard the fish are biting over in Cibecue Creek."

Saturday morning we packed up and started for Cibecue, a small Apache community. On the main highway we found the sign so turned off the main road. The sign said 14 miles and the road was paved—for a couple of miles. When we reached the little village a sign on a big building read "The doctor arrives Tuesday at 9:00."

About three miles further we came to a lovely meadow with a beautiful creek running by. We made camp and had a lovely, quiet holiday. Jimmy caught fish, Danny and Pat played, and we had lunch and dinner. We spread our sleeping bags out on the thick grass under a bright moonlit sky. I had just gotten comfortable when I realized I had a labor pain! Mother Goggin thought she was going to have to deliver that baby right there. Gradually I relaxed and the pains stopped.

The next morning we had breakfast, packed up, and started home. After going through the village we encountered three creeks that hadn't been there the day before. The mountain rains were filling the creeks. The third creek was like a raging river. Jimmy put on his hip boots and walked across to find the ruts to drive through. As he drove across, I looked out the right side and saw a little waterfall washing away the road. If we'd been 30 minutes later, we might have been marooned!

I continued to have labor pains from time to time, but not strong, especially if I relaxed and went to sleep. One night I had a hard labor pain, and Jimmy slept in his clothes, but that stopped too. On Tuesday, August 5, I was in clinic again. The doctor hadn't examined me for dilation before this. I said to him, "It is 16 days past my due date. I've been having small labor pains in the waiting room."

He examined me and said, "Go home and get your suitcase and meet me back at the maternity ward at 3:00."

Maud and Pearl

I did that and they gave me a spinal shot. At 4:00 I was in the delivery room and the shift changed. A ward boy sat with me, soothed my brow with a cool washcloth, and talked about his wife who was a nurse back home in Wisconsin while he was in the service. When the doctor came in, he cut the water bag and voilà, my daughter Janet arrived. That's all that was needed? That was one tough water bag.

She weighed nine pounds and they put her in an incubator. I asked later why they put a nine-pound baby in the incubator and they answered it was standard operating procedure. My Practical Nurse sister Alma said that if they hadn't forced the birth, she might not have made it.

Jimmy had taken a short flight but wasn't there until about an hour later. Vona saw him when he came and told him we had a girl, and a few minutes later when the doctor asked him what he thought we'd had, Jimmy wisecracked, "Well, she wanted a girl so I thought I'd let her have one."

I was in the hospital until the following Monday. Jimmy was scheduled for temporary duty at Air University in Montgomery, Alabama within a week. The doctor said I should wait and fly there with the kids in about three weeks, but we couldn't afford that.

And Now for My Next Magic Trick

JIMMY fixed up the new station wagon as a great ride. He lined all the windows except the two front ones with newspaper. The back area was a floor, with an air mattress for me, and he built a bassinet for Janet, with removable rockers so we could have a cradle. We had a new diaper pail into which he put a large block of ice to evaporate as we traveled in the heat of August. He went to Sears and bought an evaporative cooler to be attached to the front passenger window. The boys rode in front with him. We didn't have seat belts or child seats but we had found a child seat with a belt to go around the waist and curved pieces to go over the car seat back. This enabled Pat to sit up high enough to look out the window. Danny rode shotgun. We would be in Alabama for three months, so Mother Goggin went back to Santa Rosa. It would be a record trip with unforeseeable adventures.

The first night in a motel, Pat discovered how to turn a little handle on a gas wall heater. The next night we were in El Paso and Jimmy wanted to go across the border to see a border town. An hour later he returned to the motel room to find me asleep in a rocker holding Janet, the two boys asleep, and the gas stove in the kitchenette turned on, but no flame! Close call.

As we drove further east the roads got worse and it was irritating to drive on them sometimes. In Baton Rouge, Jimmy was irritated by a driver who did something stupid and he said, "You bastard." About two blocks further another driver did something that irked him but this time he didn't say anything.

Suddenly Danny piped up. "Why didn't you call him a bastard, Daddy?" Little ears are always listening.

Maud and Pearl

In Mississippi we were in a motel overnight and our room seemed a quarter mile from the highway. The next morning I was busy getting Janet ready and Jimmy was packing the car outside when Danny alerted him that Pat was going toward the road. By the time Jimmy got to him a big 18-wheeler had come to a screeching halt at the bottom of the hill. Patrick was standing on the road looking at him!

In Montgomery Jimmy found a house on the outskirts with a yard that would be good for the boys to play. Unfortunately, when we moved in, we found the house inside was filthy. Jimmy had to report to the base in a few days, but he got the camping gear out and set up the Coleman stove. I worked on cleaning the stove for three hours before I would cook anything on it. The refrigerator wouldn't work so the landlord sent a repairman. He had to drain Freon gas out of it and told us to stay in the house to avoid the gas that would permeate the outdoor area. I took Janet into the bedroom to nurse her but didn't think about the open window. As soon as she nursed, she upchucked all of it. Apparently gas was filtering in from outside.

Jimmy felt it wasn't a good idea to stay there so he found a duplex apartment not far from downtown. It was on a corner near a street intersection with a traffic light, but it was clean and spacious. The front porch was well built for the boys to play on, with concrete fixtures they liked climbing on. I sat on the porch with Janet as much as possible, but one day Danny came inside and told me Pat was in the street. I hurried outside and found our not-yet-two-year-old in the middle of the intersection directing traffic! Four lanes of cars were stopped.

Another time Danny asked me, "Mama, why don't we ever have ice cream beans?"

I said, "I've never heard of them. Where did you hear of them?" He told me there was a woman came by selling them. I said, "Well, next time you see her, let me know." A few days later he came in to get me.

A black woman with a basket on her head was walking past the house, singing, "Nice green beans... Nice green beans..."

Pearl Allen Andree

Maxwell Air Force Base was the Air University, considered to have been the forerunner of the Air Force Academy. We were there for three months. As often as the movies changed at the local drive-in, we put the kids in the car and went to the movies. It was relaxing for us and the kids often got lulled to sleep.

We had finally acquired a tent. When it was time to return to Arizona, we decided to use it—at least one night, and then drive straight through, since I could now help with the driving.

We decided to camp the first night in a roadside park outside of Selma, Alabama. The next morning we were getting the car packed and Danny and Pat were playing a little distance away when we noticed a tall Black man walking across a plowed field toward us. He was probably going toward the road. He had to cross over a fence near the boys and Jimmy walked toward them to talk to him. When he arrived at the spot where the man was, the Black man spoke first.

He said to Jimmy, "These boys don't even know I'm Black!" I was so proud of my boys. Several years later, in the 1960s, with all the strife in Selma, I often thought of that little scene. My children were colorblind.

We returned to Arizona before Mother Goggin had moved back to Santa Rosa. Vona was in a steady dating relationship with Bill Mundy. There was a major on the base who was unusual in not using bad language. He and a captain found out Jimmy had a tent, so they invited him to go elk hunting with them. Major Sellers' alarm word of choice was "mercy" and many of the officers copied him. On the Sunday of the hunting weekend, the newspaper headline, in the dramatic Second Coming font, read "1000 ELK HUNTERS MAROONED."

A heavy snowfall was the cause. Jimmy said there was a five-foot drift outside the door of their tent. They did hunt but no elk was harmed. When Jimmy came home, he wanted me to retrace the trip with him, to find the tent that had been lost on their way back. Mother Goggin hadn't left yet for California so I could go. I was still nursing Janet, but I would be back for her next feeding. We went to where they had camped and returned, but only found pieces of the tent blown out of the pickup.

Laredo AFB:
What Will Kids Say and Do Next?

IN THE New Year of 1953 Jimmy was transferred to Laredo Air Force Base in Texas. He had to find a place for us to live and it was March when the children and I went down there. Until finding a house to rent, we shared a large ranch house with Joe and Maudie Orell. They had two children. A caretaker for the property had a separate house nearby.

The first Sunday I went to church Jimmy stayed home with Pat and Janet, and Danny went with me. Between Sunday school and worship I was getting acquainted with a couple when Danny came up to me after his class. I said, "This is my son, Danny," and to him, "Did you enjoy your Sunday school class?"

He looked up at me and replied, "We didn't color a damn thing!"

The caretaker was a member of the church and had a swimming pool. They planned an evening pot-luck. "Mixed bathing" (meaning males and females together) was still taboo in some settings so the younger boys were the only ones who swam. Danny's bathing suit hadn't been unpacked yet so he wore his undershorts. During the preparation time I went out to the pool to see if he was okay, and he asked me why I didn't come in swimming. I said I didn't have my bathing suit. He piped up, "You could come in in your panties, like me." Wow—that would cause a mild consternation. The way I was raised early on was that women went in the water in their dresses, and I reckon that was much more revealing than a decent bathing suit. Apparently,

Pearl Allen Andree

Mama had agreed as she wanted all her children to learn to swim. Wet T-shirt contests came years later.

We found a two-bedroom house, wood frame, with a carport, in a neighborhood where the Orells found one, along with another family, the Arnolds. Jimmy had enjoyed the craft shop on Williams AFB and readily started doing things at the one in Laredo. We took *Popular Mechanics* magazine and he found he could order plans for building a boat. There was a lake at the local country club and he hoped to use it for our recreation.

The project took place in the carport. It was a 12' inboard and he was very qualified for the effort. One afternoon he had been working on the boat, with the boys watching of course, when he came into the kitchen quite perturbed. He said to me about Danny, "What's with this kid? He keeps asking me, 'What're you trying to do, Daddy?' I'm not *trying* to build a boat; I *am* building a boat!"

When it was finished, he found an ironworker in town to build a trailer for it. He even had the bright idea to present a plan to the town council to build several boats to rent at the lake, as there weren't many recreations for the military. They rejected his idea because he was military but the next week the newspaper headlines proclaimed the city would purchase some boats to have at the country club lake for rental!

Actually, there was a certain amount of animosity toward the military, which was odd since they contributed so much to the economy. One time a few of us wives went across the border to a fabric shop and on coming back, at the border, the lady driving was asked the standard, "Are you citizens?" When she answered in the affirmative, the border guard said, "It's nothing to brag about."

She angrily responded, "Well, it sure as hell is!" and put the pedal to the floor to speed away. Another time the local paper had an editorial that was derogatory toward the U.S. and the military, and half the base population canceled their subscriptions.

The summer of 1953, the Rio Grande went dry, and the city relied on it as their major water source. We kept five-gallon water cans full for those times when water would not come out of the taps. On weekends we went down to South Padre Island

Maud and Pearl

to the beach. The children loved watching the sand crabs. We didn't worry much about Janet as she wouldn't go near the water; however, she loved sitting under the lifeguard's high chair. One time we found her opening his shaving kit, which he kept lying there.

There was a pier where people went to deeper water to swim. Pat hadn't learned to swim yet and one time we saw him walking on the pier toward the end. When we called him and started running after him, as did the lifeguard, he started running. About halfway to the end, he turned and jumped into the water! We were there so no harm done, but I was not surprised years later when he became a champion swimmer.

Later in the year we moved into a three-bedroom townhouse apartment in Wherry housing closer to the base. Janet had her own room and we had an extra bed. Another officer's wife, Willie Arnold, and I hired a young woman from Mexico to help us with meals and housework. She stayed six nights a week at our house and worked with us Monday, Wednesday, and Friday and for the Arnolds Tuesday, Thursday, and Saturday. I picked her up at the border on Monday morning and Willie took her back on Saturday. She didn't speak English, so I got my high school Spanish books out and brushed up on it.

Vona had married Bill Mundy and he was stationed in Greenville, Mississippi. They visited us in Laredo and Mother Goggin came down for a visit.

Christmas of 1953 was a good time for us. Jimmy put together the bike with training wheels for Danny in the living room. I had found a good child-sized clarinet at a music store, and while Santa filled the stockings Jimmy practiced on the clarinet so he learned to play "Mary Had a Little Lamb." The next day we used the 8-mm Brownie to take movies of Pat playing with his football and Danny learning to ride his bike.

The spring of 1954 ushered in a new period of our lives. Around Easter time the officers' wives decided to have a fashion show of clothes they made for themselves. We had it on a Saturday night at the Officers Club, having a family night. I made a mother-daughter outfit and modeled it, as all the others did.

Pearl Allen Andree

Someone asked Danny which model he thought prettiest, and my sweet five-year-old said the name of our friend Polly. This woman was the mother of one of his friends. When Jimmy gave Polly's husband rides to work, sometimes he left Danny to stay at their house and play with their boy. Polly was not the conventional beauty as many of the wives were, but she had a loving sweet way about her, and Danny had experienced this. I realized I had produced a son who could discern an inner beauty in a woman and in later years this proved to be true.

Stardust Melody

JIMMY had long wanted an overseas assignment and found out it would happen. He was being transferred for three years to the United States Allied Forces in Europe (USAFE) 79th Fighter-Bomber Squadron, 20th Fighter-Bomber Wing, stationed at RAF Woodbridge, southeast England. His unit would fly specifically modified F-84Gs capable of carrying limited nuclear warheads on their wingtips. Units such as his would fly Cold War-related missions, sometimes secret, accompanying bombers across Europe, down to Africa, and to the outer limits of NATO airspace.

Alma came down from the Panhandle in May to stay with the kids while Jimmy and I flew to Mexico City for our ninth anniversary. She told how the boys were always on deck to watch her give Janet her bath. One time, she said, Danny announced, "She's the sweetest one of us." Years later when he was going through the "don't like girls" stage, I reminded him of that and he tried to deny it.

Jimmy and I saw the Floating Gardens and the pyramids and wondered why people thought they had to travel to other places on the planet to see antiquity. He had always wanted to see Florida so when June arrived, we saw to packing up the household goods to send to Arizona, then took the boat to go on a near-month-long camping trip to Florida.

The first night driving east through Texas, we camped in a roadside park and experienced mosquito biting, especially Danny—in the heat, the boys went bare chested. The next day we camped on a beach in Galveston. During the morning the

Pearl Allen Andree

children and I played on the beach while Jimmy took the boat into the gulf to do some fishing. He caught a hammerhead shark about two feet long. We never even considered eating it. We put up the dining canopy and a couple of folding cots and fixed some lunch. Jimmy pulled the boat onto the beach so it would stay put and laid down for a nap.

Danny and Pat were playing and after about 30 minutes Danny called to us, alerting us that the boat was slipping back into the water. Jimmy woke up quickly, jumped up, and ran to stop it. Unfortunately, the tide had already taken it off the sand and he had to swim to retrieve it. I was very worried as he had to go farther and farther. He reckoned he had to swim about a mile before he caught it. I asked him when he got back what he did and his answer was, "I held on to the side of the boat and tossed my cookies." Neither of us had a clue there was a medical school there that would turn our son, daughter-in-law, and two grandchildren into doctors in the future.

One night in Florida we camped near a motel, but the mosquitoes were so bad we had to get a motel room around midnight. They didn't seem to bite, just flew in swarms around us. Near Jacksonville we found a campground by a lake where we could stay for a week and go boating on the lake. We had to carry water to use at our campsite, and our home movies show Danny struggling to carry a bucket back to camp. Of course, Pat had to do his part so we gave him a pan with a handle. The home movie shows him blithely swinging it on his way. At his destination we see him tilting the pan and emptying a tiny stream of water onto the ground. Jimmy wasn't catching fish so he decided to take the boat out after midnight one night. He caught a weird-looking fish. Since I wasn't with him, he described it as having a head that looked like an alligator and a body that looked like a snake. He showed it to another man who was also fishing that night and the man said it was a gar fish and if it bit a person they would likely die before getting to a hospital. He showed Jimmy how to get rid of it without getting hurt.

We visited Cypress Gardens and saw the water shows before driving back west to Del Rio, Texas, where Jimmy would do one of two required periods of gunnery training. Again, we did not

Maud and Pearl

envision that in the future our Janet would live in Florida and raise two granddaughters.

As we drove through Alabama, we were passing a lovely pastoral scene where a field of green grass filled the view. About a half mile from the road was a pretty farm house. Suddenly Pat announced, "I used to live there."

I said, "Oh, is that right? When was that?"

He answered, "When I had that other mommy!" Good thing I don't believe in reincarnation.

Pat was the only one of my children who had an imaginary friend, a tiger. He had told his Grandmother Goggin that if she didn't do what he wanted, he would sic his tiger on her. He loved Danny's book, *A Child's Garden of Verses* by Robert Louis Stevenson, and that may have been where he met his tiger. I knew, even when he was only six months old and loved playing with plastic farm animals, that this child would need animals in his life.

In the summer of '54, the Rio Grande flooded. Across the river, Ciudad de Del Rio was nearly leveled. We found a duplex two-bedroom apartment to rent and, fortunately, there was a public swimming pool nearby. Years later I tried to find a snapshot of all five of us together and the only one I found was all of us sitting on a small concrete fence at that pool in our bathing suits.

We met with friends we knew from Arizona at church, Jim and Mary Lee Fry, and their two children. Another couple we knew in Laredo were Steve and June Szalay. They were from Ohio, and Steve had been in the National Guard. When he finished college, he was able to get into the Air Force program and was in the same flight as Jimmy. They had a girl aged four and had just had a baby boy on May 18. Steve took the same two gunnery sessions as Jimmy and then he went back to civilian life in Ohio and the National Guard. Later, the Szalays moved to Phoenix, Arizona.

For Danny's sixth birthday, we had the Szalays over to our very humble abode. We gave him a pair of roller skates, which he had to learn to use on the little strip of concrete in the front yard. Pat again got into our home movies by secretly getting behind his brother and pushing him forward. We sat on the front porch where there was a swing and a rocking chair. We surely resembled a page out of Erskine Caldwell's *God's Little Acre* and June, holding

Pearl Allen Andree

the baby in the rocking chair, remarked, "I just have to say this: 'Y'all kids git'."

Jimmy's favorite songs were "Stardust" and "Stranger in Paradise" and he loved doing slow rolls in his airplane while flying. One day he was taking a friend to work and those songs were on the car radio. He shared his favorite choices when flying and his friend, who, with his wife, were the jitterbug champions at the officers' club, remarked, "Sound like funeral dirges!" Guess not everyone liked slow dancing.

Soon it was time to go to Arizona. We found an apartment near Luke Air Force Base in Goodyear. Pat turned four while we were there and Mother Goggin came to visit. Mama was living nearby and we got to spend time with her again. We had the household goods with us and had to plan what things we needed to take care of before going to England. Jimmy would leave the first of November and the children and I would leave the first part of December. We knew we wouldn't have the household goods in time for Christmas, but we bought gifts at the PX for late holiday giving. Jimmy had been cutting the boys' hair with manual clippers and decided to treat himself for the future with a pair of electric clippers. After he left, I purchased a new automatic Bendix washing machine to take with us. It was my job to sell the boat and the car. Ornan had the four boys so I sold him the boat for $100. I knew they would use it for its intended use and enjoy every minute of it. After I sold the car, I took the kids on a bus to Yuma to see Leo on his farm.

It was not easy to buy winter clothing in Arizona so I went to New York a week early, where we stayed with my cousin Anita Florence in Brooklyn. She and her sister Hazel had worked in Washington, D.C. during the war. Anita had married an Italian from New York and Hazel had married a man from the D.C. area. Their mother was Aunt Eula, Mom's youngest sister. Anita took us on the subway to Macy's to get snow suits for the boys, as well as sweaters. On Sunday she and her husband took us to church in Steinway Hall, where the church was meeting at the time. It is now the Manhattan congregation and, of course, has its own building. Anita had a little girl Janet's age. While we were

Maud and Pearl

there, my nephew Charley showed up. He was en route back to Oklahoma and civilian life after being stationed in Germany. I never did find out how he knew we were there or how he found Anita's address.

It wasn't far to where we had to report for traveling to England on an ocean liner. I had never gone on an ocean voyage and had heard all about seasickness. I thought, with three children, I had better get some advice. I went to a drug store and asked the pharmacist. He sold me some Dramamine and said to take one 24 hours before leaving, which I did. I didn't get seasick but Danny did. A rumor was heard that many got sick from the orange juice at breakfast, but for him it may have been his inner ear. He did have earaches, and had had one at that camp in Florida. His dad had wrapped some salt in a cloth, warmed it in hot water, and put it on his ear to get rid of the pain. The ship was named the *Alexander Patch* and at one time it had been a cruise ship, but it had been given to the military in WWII. The dining room was great and I found out my daughter Janet loved green olives, which were always on the relish tray. The boys and I did not like them and could hardly stand to watch her wolf them down.

We arrived in Southampton on December 21, 1954, and Jimmy was there in our new VW bug. It had just been delivered to him two days before. We put the luggage on the luggage rack, the three kids in the back seat, I got in the front passenger seat, and he got in to drive. He handed me a map. I said, "What's this for? I've never been in this country."

He replied, "You've got to be better than me. I got lost coming down here."

We managed to skirt London, but we saw a lot of the English countryside. One sign pointed to Windsor Castle, about a half mile away. Another pointed west to Stratford-upon-Avon. We finally found a pub in a rural area where we stopped and had lunch. Eventually we arrived at our landlord's place, where we stayed until he finished getting our house ready to live in. Alderton was the village, and the family was the Oakleys—and yes, they did have a daughter named Annie. He was Bill and had survived the Battle of the Bulge in WWII. They had one boarder, and Mrs.

Pearl Allen Andree

Oakley fixed dinner every day for the workers in the area, like a café, in the dining room.

On the afternoon of the 23rd, Jimmy, Danny, and I went into Ipswich to get me a driver's license. The first place was the wrong one but they gave us the right address and we drove up to it about five minutes before closing time. We couldn't find a parking space, so Jimmy let me out, intending to find a place to park. I didn't see them for two hours! I was standing in a misty rain in my lined trench coat and an office worker in the garage across the street saw me. She came over and invited me to come into shelter and have a cup of tea. I didn't stay long as I wanted to be sure and see Jimmy and Danny when they showed up.

Finally, they came walking around a corner. Jimmy had parked the car about a mile away and we had trouble finding it! We would have been truly lost if it hadn't been for Danny helping us find our way. Ipswitch is laid out like the spokes of a wagon wheel and we had trouble finding our way out of town. We stopped and asked directions to Woodbridge and the Brit always answered, "Ah, you turn right that road ahead, then go straight ahead and you can't miss it." We'd miss it every time. We did finally get back to Alderton, but it wasn't easy.

On Saturday, New Year's Day, Jimmy went duck hunting with Bill, and the cold and wet caused him to get a cold with a bad sore throat. Early in the following week, Jimmy was notified that he would be promoted from First Lieutenant to Captain in three weeks. Naturally, he was excited and I was thrilled and proud of him. He was a flyers' flyer.

He was scheduled to go to Germany with some other pilots on Thursday for a test in an oxygen chamber. I drove him to the Bentwaters base, from which they would leave. The Lack of Oxygen test was on Friday afternoon. When I picked him up Saturday evening, he told me he had spent Thursday evening going around Munich in a taxi trying to find medicine for the sore throat. Then on Friday, when volunteers were requested for the test chamber, he felt a responsibility to do so, having been recently advanced. Afterward, he developed the most excruciating pain in his throat he'd ever experienced.

Maud and Pearl

On Sunday he found a book the Oakleys had that he had read as a child, *Wings*, and bundled up all day while reading. He stayed up long enough to finish it that Sunday evening. I was still awake when he came to bed. He talked about goals he had for the future: working on his college degree by correspondence with the University of Maryland, how we would do church with the kids, and so forth.

The next morning we were the only ones in the kitchen when I fixed our breakfast. He was still doctoring his sore throat. I mentioned that he ought to go to the infirmary instead of flying, but he rejected that idea. He was only worried about being late to work. If he was late, he would have to fix coffee for the guys the rest of the week. He left for the base about 9:30 a.m.

About 11:00 a.m. there was a knock on the front door. I was close so I opened it. Standing there were three uniformed officers: the base CO, a friend who would be the Summary Courts officer, and another officer. They informed me that Jimmy had disappeared during maneuvers over the North Sea near Brussels, Belgium. Given that he may have gone down, the standard procedure was to search for 72 hours before making a final decision.

He had been flying formation with another pilot at 15,000 feet when they dove down and leveled off at 3,000 feet. Jimmy was in the lead and when he started down, the other pilot, thinking he thought the ocean was another cloud layer, got on the radio and said, "Better watch your altimeter, Jim." Jimmy never responded with the expected "Roger."

News like that travels fast in the military and that afternoon Jim Fry, whom we hadn't seen since Del Rio and was at another base in England, showed up where the children and I were with his wife Mary Lee, and left her there to stay with me for three days. The searchers never even found an oil slick.

His life cut short, torn away from me, his family, and his friends were the many things he exemplified—his engaging personality, his right-on wit, his determination to do things as perfectly as he could, and his infectious love of flying.

The base had a memorial on Friday the 14th, which Jim Fry organized, with a full 21-gun salute and giving me a flag. I

Pearl Allen Andree

took Danny and Pat, but Janet stayed with the Oakleys. Sometime during those days I was interrogated with a few questions. Because of the Cold War and not finding anything from his crash, I guess they were exploring possibilities. They mentioned that someone had heard Jimmy say, "Communism is an ideal." I answered that he had heard that first at the classes he'd had at the Air University, then based in Montgomery, Alabama. I also told them the whole statement was "Communism is an ideal that *won't work*."

While in shock, I still had to face his loss and keep parenting. The following Monday they put the children and me on a cargo plane to Edinburgh, Scotland, then flew us back to the US. An escort officer was assigned to accompany us. His wife was gravely ill in Florida, so he was going there and we would go on to Santa Rosa, California, as that was the place where Jimmy entered the military. When Janet was grown, she asked me one day, "Mom, did we ever fly on a plane where we sat around in a circle instead of seats like in a passenger airplane?" She was only two but she remembered that cargo plane!

They put us on an Air Force passenger plane after going through customs. We were over the Atlantic when the pilot announced there was a problem with the radio, and we would be returning to Scotland. If anyone wanted their checked luggage, all the passengers would have to go back through customs! There I was with three kids, one still in diapers, and no way was I going to cause an upset! They put us in a Railway Hotel in Ayr, Scotland for two days. The escort officer was very helpful. He took care of the kids while I went to a beauty shop to get my hair done. He bought a little Scottish doll for Janet, and gave me a belt that had Scottish plaid links in it.

The children didn't understand what was happening. I think Danny understood he'd lost his daddy, but at one point he asked why the escort didn't sleep in the room with us! Fortunately, the officer wasn't around when he asked that. Janet even asked if he was her new daddy. Again, I was lucky it was a private question. The children and I went to a movie one afternoon. It was either *Holiday Inn* or *White Christmas* with Bing Crosby. I was in survival mode and heartbroken.

Sat. night
Jan 15, 1955

Dear Mother & Vona,

This is the most difficult letter I have ever written. By now you know why & I do hope you're feeling as well as possible under the circumstances. There is so much to be done here & I've had so much help & company that I haven't been alone very much. I know you're anxious to know what happened & I can explain more I guess when I see you. It was & is so unbelievable to me I didn't believe the Colonel when he first came & told me Jimmy was missing. They searched the North Sea for 72 hrs before they sent the death

RAF Station Woodbridge
Suffolk, Eng

Via Air Mail

Mrs Myrtle M Goggin
Box 33
Fulton, California

Letter to Mother Goggin

Screen Memories

I HAVE learned that the psychological definition of a screen memory is, the memory of a childhood experience that unconsciously serves the purpose of concealing, screening out, or conflating associated experiences of a significant and possibly traumatic nature.

My father was an experienced Air Force fighter pilot who was killed on active duty while doing acrobatic training over the North Sea when he was stationed at RAF Woodbridge station in southeastern England. His voluntary participation in pilot testing experiments and a severe head cold may or may not have been mitigating circumstances related to his death. I was nearly two and a half years old.

I have only two memories of that time. One day in the house where we were staying, I heard my mother crying out "Jimmy" loudly from the bedroom. I thought my father must be tickling her, because when he did my mother sounded like she was crying. When I ran to the door to open it and help, it was locked. The people in the house ushered me away from the door, put some kind of vest on me that smelled like Vicks VapoRub, and put me to bed.

Many years later when I was an adult, married, and living in Florida, I asked Mom if there had ever been a time when we had flown in a military plane over the Florida Keys. I remembered that I had been with her and my two brothers, and we were alone on the plane except for the pilot.

The pilot invited us to the cockpit and said, "Look down there; you can see the key." I felt confused, because my brothers swore that they could see the key far below but I could not, and I wondered

Maud and Pearl

how anybody possibly could. My mother was dumbfounded and amazed, because she knew what I was remembering. During the flight when the Air Force flew our family from Bentwaters to Scotland after my father's plane went down, the pilot tried to show us the quay along the coast, metal and stone structures jutting out for boats to attach to. And quay is pronounced the same as key. While I couldn't understand this as a toddler, when I moved to Florida I thought perhaps I was remembering that we had flown over the Florida Keys for some reason. The memory of this flight had always been very vivid in my mind.

Janet Goggin, Pearl and Jimmy's daughter, an Allen cousin

Postscript

WE FINALLY got on a plane to Goose Bay, Newfoundland, where we changed to the flight that would take us to San Francisco. Mother Goggin lived near Santa Rosa and Vona was there waiting to leave for Japan where she would join Bill for his tour of duty. I needed to be with my brother Pete and his family in Brentwood. We were with them for a month, and I let Danny go to school while there. I received many sympathy cards, amazed at how many military heard of Jimmy's passing and knew how to send a message. I answered each one personally, and collapsed with pneumonia. Dorothy put me to bed and someone else was sick at the same time. I teased her about her "hospital ward." Gradually we came out of our state of shock. Our children and I would keep Jimmy in a special place in our hearts forever.

Mother Goggin was living in a house trailer and I knew I needed to do something about her housing. Jimmy and I had added $10,000 life insurance to the $10,000 we originally had, and I knew $5,000 was for her. Vona still had her car so while we were at Pete's, she and Mother Goggin came down and picked Janet and me up (I left Pat and Danny at Pete's) to go south to visit Hazel and her husband, Dr. Dale Baskett, in Thousand Oaks. While there, Hazel actually put out feelers for adopting Janet. No way on God's green earth would I have even dreamed of allowing that! Years later I found out, as little as she was, Janet was afraid she might lose her mommy!

When Vona and Mother Goggin returned to Santa Rosa, Vona found a three-bedroom house she rented so the kids and I could join them after the month in Brentwood. Danny could go

Maud and Pearl

into first grade at the school a couple of blocks away after having been in school in Brentwood briefly. He had started in Avondale, Arizona, so this would be the third school for his first grade year. I found a nice two-bedroom wood frame house for Mother Goggin, paid down on it, and assumed the mortgage, which would only be $58 a month. I stayed there until the car shipped from England. Vona and I went to San Francisco a few times for shopping, and we usually went to a movie. On one trip she had to ship her car to Japan. When she received her orders, we borrowed Aunt Alice's pickup to take her to embark on the ship to leave for the Far East, to be with Bill stationed in Japan.

Danny started to school again in the first grade at a school a long block away from the house. They had an end-of-year skating party at a nearby rink and I volunteered to help chaperone. When the party was over and parents were coming to pick up their kids, I was standing in the foyer when a little girl came up and took hold of my hand. She looked up to me like I was a long-lost friend and I just kept holding her hand. She stayed with me for several minutes, until a woman came up to take her. She didn't want to let go of my hand, but she didn't resist. The woman who took her whispered in my ear, "I'm a foster parent. You look like her mother; in fact, I thought that's who you were when I first came in." It was a sobering moment to experience.

One day the doorbell rang and it was a preacher who had heard I was a widow with three kids. He offered me a job as his secretary. His name was Harland Dilbeck and I actually knew of his brother, Elton, who was a minister for a congregation in Phoenix. Harland was the minister with a new small congregation on the edge of town. Like most preachers, he had to have another job, so he sold insurance, as many others did. I explained I didn't need a job and would be going to Arizona when the car was delivered, but I decided to take the kids to the Vacation Bible School they were having for two weeks, and would help with that. He and his wife Florence had three boys, the youngest four years old, so they became good friends. The first day of VBS, at intermission there was a commotion—a fight! It happened between their

Pearl Allen Andree

four-year-old and another little boy. They were fighting over my Janet!

On the Fourth of July, the Dilbecks took us out to the Russian River for a picnic. After lunch I suggested buying all the kids snow-cones. When I started asking flavor choices, Harland said, "You're doing it wrong. Just go get the snow-cones, then when you come back, they can take what they get!" They didn't argue, so I guess that was good advice.

The Volkswagen was delivered in July and the four of us packed up and headed for Arizona, where I planned to raise my children. We stopped to see Pete and Dorothy, and because the summer weather was hot, I put a block of ice, about a 12" cube, in a small, insulated bag. The block was 12 pounds and I put it on the floor behind my seat. Pat and Janet were in the back seat and around Fresno I realized they had gone to sleep. I could see Pat but couldn't see Janet. I knew there was no way she could have disappeared since there were no back doors, so I stopped and parked to see if she was all right. She was sitting directly on the block of ice, sound asleep.

When he was growing up in Santa Rosa, Jimmy had been called another nickname, unflatteringly, because of his father's chronic problems. Even some in his extended family used this name. It was The Dead-End Kid. He was aware of it, and it hurt him. Over a half-century into the future, the Kid's final resting place was a memorial section in Arlington National Cemetery.

Beginning Life in Tempe

In Tempe I found that houses were being built near an elementary school as well as a middle school and only four blocks from the high school. I decided to buy a three-bedroom, two-bath house with a den, covered patio, and carport. It wouldn't be finished until the following March, so I found a two-bedroom furnished place and decided to leave the household things in storage until moving into the new home. The same Realtor had a small one-bedroom on a nice lot within walking distance from the church building for $2500 so I bought it for Mama. It was more spacious than where she was in Tolleson, and I would need her to help me with the children from time to time. I registered for classes at Arizona State, put Danny and Pat in Broadmor Elementary School, and we settled in to start the rest of our lives. There would be many rocks in the road, but it had to be done.

I changed my study focus to secondary education, majoring in English and minoring in drama. I went to some meetings at Phoenix Little Theatre but found things had changed since last I had participated there. Some professional actors had retired and moved to the Valley. I reconnected with a friend, Polly, whom I had known before, and she mentioned the formation of the Scottsdale Community Players, a much smaller group. They met once a week for a workshop. Their space had been a stagecoach stop in early days and the main building was the small Scottsdale Library. The original barn was our theatre space, with dirt floor and bleachers for seating. Someone had built a stage and we had a curtain that would only close half way. There were no dressing rooms, so we chose uncomplicated scripts.

Pearl Allen Andree

I loved being with my children and had a lot of fun with them, but I became very lonely. Widowed for nearly a year, with three small children, I was not prepared for that much loneliness, and I was having trouble with my emotions because of it. I read a lot. One story I read was *A Many-Splendored Thing* by Han Suyin, a love story. One song at the time had the lyrics, "You don't know lonely till your love is gone." I thought I would do something about it so I went to a holiday party at the officers' club at the base.

I met an Italian who was in the pilot training program for NATO nations. Aldo was four years younger than I, but I enjoyed being with him. He was a fantastic piano player and was invited to homes to play for their parties. He would have rather been a musician than a pilot, but his father had insisted on his going into the military. There was no question of my getting serious with Aldo, so I stopped seeing him shortly before he was to return to Italy, which was about the time we moved into the new house in the spring of '56. We got the household goods delivered, I made drapes for the living room and other rooms, and settled in… to live some of the worst six months of my life.

The Summer of 1956: Crisis

I HAD been taking Danny to horseback riding lessons weekly. Pat was too young for them to enroll him, and he watched Danny longingly. He wanted so much to get on a horse. I even took Danny with me for a weekend at a dude ranch in Wickenburg where we had a breakfast ride in the desert. I began to worry about Danny, the oldest, asking questions when I began to show. Also, I thought Danny could profit from a father figure, so I asked Pete and Dorothy if he could spend the summer with them. They consented.

Aldo and I had never considered getting married. He was here only while getting a pilot's education. He really liked music but he was four years younger and I never considered him marriage material. Despite Mom's appreciation of the Catholic faith, I wouldn't have wanted to marry him on religious grounds, having received the admonition previously in my life to avoid marrying outside one's faith, if possible.

But pregnancy happened, accidentally. I did consider keeping the child. At that time, I feared that, while Christians might not treat the child badly, some might act in a way which could become an emotional or even a spiritual strain on the other children. It was painful, but I felt it would be best to work out an adoption.

Instantly, life became extremely complicated. Through Steve Szalay's Air National Guard connections, I contacted a Wickenburg general practitioner and made arrangements to stay in Wickenburg the second half of the summer with the younger children.

Pearl Allen Andree

At the end of the school year I took all of us to Disneyland on our way to Santa Rosa. On our way West, we stayed the first night in a motel about 60 miles west of Wickenburg, where we knew the couple that ran it for the owner, another friend. We got up very early to get on the road before the heat of the day, but the night before there was bathtime before bedtime. The boys showered and got into bed, and I bathed Janet and put her in a clean bed before I showered. When I came out of the shower, my beautiful creative daughter had found the brown shoe polish and decorated the bed sheets with it! I had to get clean linens from my friend, and we remade the bed.

The next morning, we got on the road early and stopped in Blythe, California for breakfast in a coffee shop. We left there about 7:00 in the morning. Highway 60 (now I-10) was then a two-lane highway. We'd been on the road about 20 minutes—the kids had all gone back to sleep—when I woke up on the opposite side of the road, in the desert! I hadn't hit any cacti, and there was no traffic on the road. I just drove back onto the highway and continued driving. It was a grim portent of future sleep apnea. The children didn't wake up.

The night before our first day in Disneyland, Janet found the talcum powder and decorated the motel room. At least it wasn't as bad as brown shoe polish! We had a day at Knotts Berry Farm and another at Disneyland before traveling further north.

We went to visit Mother Goggin and stopped at Pete's on the way back to drop Danny off for the summer. Their son Jerry was Pat's age and would be a good companion. At Pete and Dorothy's, she and I were hanging clothes on the line when Pat came outside. I had bought a small bottle of child aspirin to use if he got tonsillitis and he had come to tell me, "Mommy, Janet ate that whole bottle of aspirin!" In the house, Lanier had found Janet lying listless and looked around, finding an open toiletry kit with the missing aspirin, and with Pat had run to get me. We rushed inside and grabbed her up, jumped in Dorothy's car, and drove to her doctor's office, about six blocks away. He pumped Janet's stomach and said if we hadn't known, within an hour she would have had convulsions and died. I credit Lanier with the lion's share

Maud and Pearl

of having saved Janet's life. I never bought child aspirin again until I was an old woman and needed a blood thinner.

Patrick, Janet, and I traveled back to Arizona, stopping in Wickenburg to rent an apartment where we hibernated for the rest of the summer. There were horses nearby that Pat could talk to, and Janet liked to do that, too. We celebrated Janet's birthday on August fifth and returned to Tempe the first part of September to start a new school year.

Of course, before that, I had arranged sitters for Pat and Janet. I went to the hospital and delivered on September 6 a baby girl. Tragically, the doctor told me she was stillborn. I felt so much hurt and pain and I was emotionally devastated. I was anemic as well. Experiencing shock at the news after all of my preparation efforts, in those moments I chose to accept what the doctor said as a profound personal loss. I was not asked to assist with arrangements.

Despite the immediacy of my physical condition, I arranged for Mama to stay with the younger children and flew to San Francisco to pick up Danny. Pete and Ornan brought him to the airport so I could just turn around and fly back.

Years passed, and my thinking changed. Because I knew the doctor was experienced with informal adoption, I began to doubt, and in fact not believe, that there had been a loss. Had my doctor been involved in something not informal but rather illegal? Were there surreptitious and monetary motives? I began to search for the true facts, but ran into a number of dead ends, and I was not successful. I can only hope that sharing this can be helpful to others.

The Mulberry Tree

GRANDMA Allen's house was cottage-like with a big front yard and a small backyard. In the middle of the backyard stood a tall mulberry tree, old and with many sturdy branches—an ideal tree for little kids to master climbing up, out, and down, and inventing tree games. Of course, what drew the Allen cousins to spend the night with Grandma, other than the yard and tree, was her fabulous food at every meal. At the time, I thought it was odd if not unnecessary that she ate my scraps rather than a full plate of her own great cooking. Of course, later I learned that even before the Great Depression she had fed her family first, before herself.

Then there was Grandma herself. Sweet. Kind. Religious. The only drawback to staying with her was that if I had misspelled one or more words in that week's spelling test, I had to write them correctly 25-50 times; and if the candy store I'd walk to was already closed, tough luck. A Saturday night stay meant visiting Mrs. Nell, the widow next door, talking religion, and watching Lawrence Welk. Sunday morning, I assisted her (she was in her mid-70s) to walk to church a few blocks away while practicing the memory verse I had to recite in Bible class. Of course, Grandma also asked me to explain what it meant. Not easy.

One day at Grandma's, I disobeyed her by doing something. I cannot remember what it was. Clearly, Grandma got upset and told me that I needed a spanking. Fearing that, I ran out the back door and climbed the mulberry tree as fast as I could, and then kept going until I got to the highest, broadest branch. My time in the mulberry tree began. My confidence grew about having made a successful escape from Grandma's wrath. After all, she clearly did

Maud and Pearl

not have a tree climber's build. She did come out and implore me to come down and come into the house. But in my mind the words from the fairy tale "The Gingerbread Man" kept repeating: "Run, run, fast as you can. You can't catch me; I'm the Gingerbread Man!"

After awhile, other things came to mind. What about my future? Food. Water. Dessert. School attendance was going to involve racing away from the tree and racing back to the tree many times each week. And how would I explain tree life to Mom? Once she got ahold of me, she would spank harder than Grandma.

I realized I had reached a moral dilemma, although I was too young to phrase it that way. Escaping discipline for wrongdoing was okay now, but it didn't seem that it would work for the long run. Then I thought about what I was going to grow up to be. A person who would do wrong and try to get away with it? Then and there, I decided I wouldn't be like that. Grandma was a good person. Patient. Fair. She had been right, and I had been wrong.

I climbed down out of the mulberry tree and went into the house. I told Grandma that I was sorry. I don't remember the spanking except that her swats were soft and she gave me only a few. I grew up and became a physician. I have never forgotten Grandma and the lesson of her mulberry tree.

Dan Goggin, Pearl and Jimmy's son, an Allen cousin

Meeting Bill Andree

LIFE was a blur awhile in the autumn of 1956. Eventually I started thinking about having the children take piano lessons, so I needed to get a piano. My next-door neighbor was the Baptist minister and his wife knew pianos, so I asked her to go with me to look at one advertised in the paper. I had heard an upright was best and that is what this one was. But it was painted black, and I wondered if it would harm the instrument to paint it another color.

I had met a man in the Scottsdale Theatre group whose house a group of us had gone to, and I knew he had a piano. He also had done some carpentry remodeling at his house. He was the advertising manager at the *Tempe Daily News*. I decided to ask his advice. I went to the paper's office and asked for Bill Andree. He was there and came up to the front desk to talk to me. I told him my query and at the end of the conversation he said, "Well, I don't know about the piano, but would you like to go with me to the Ladies Night at Toastmasters Friday night?"

I thought, why not, so I said, "Sure." I had no idea I was sealing my fate.

I discovered Toastmasters were nuts. They had to introduce their guests, and after Bill had introduced me, another man stood up and introduced his wife as "Bill Andree's first wife!" I didn't have a clue about Bill's background, just that he lived with his sister, who was a real estate agent in Scottsdale. He had apologized for the car he was driving, a Packard. He had ordered a new '56 Dodge from the Tempe dealer, with refrigeration, but it had come without installed refrigeration. His new car was with the dealer getting that problem fixed, and the Packard was one of the fleet

Maud and Pearl

he and his sister had in their previous business (dress shops) in Washington, D. C. His sister had one too. When we got back into the car he leaned over and kissed me—and then had trouble finding his way out of the parking lot!

In the ensuing weeks Bill would come to the house unexpectedly. I would be fixing dinner and he'd come walking around to the back of the house. Of course I invited him to share our dinner. I began to wonder about the old saying, "I may have to marry him to get rid of him!" Actually, by Christmas that's what was developing. He was coming to church with us and, yes, I liked him very much. I was thinking, oh dear, here we go again. I guessed his age at close to 45, but he had a birthday in October and declared he was 39, in spite of the old saw that 39 is a generic age.

My girlfriends visited—Mary Friend, whose husband had been killed about six months after Jimmy, and Evelyn Dyer, whose husband had been the Flight Commander and was now divorced. Evelyn was a talented artist and had painted a beautiful portrait of Jimmy. We went to San Francisco for a weekend. We went to Fisherman's Wharf, rode the cable cars, and reminisced.

Pat was growing big enough to tussle with Danny so they fought sometimes. Bill recalled his dad building a boxing ring in the home basement, where he and friends sparred. He gave the boys a set of boxing gloves at Christmas.

All my brothers descended on me for Christmas 1956, except Pete. They were against me marrying Bill for the same reasons I was skeptical. He was divorced, and my brothers and I had been raised with a different background than Bill. I didn't want to make church membership a condition for marriage, since that would be the wrong motive. I thought about how I didn't want to continue a revolving door of male friends for the children to deal with, and also my brothers hadn't walked a mile in my moccasins. Our conversation was intense, and at times I began to feel I was getting railroaded. Afterward, I made the decision to go ahead and marry Bill. I set the date of January 23.

We went to Las Vegas on our honeymoon and Mama stayed with the kids. Bill wasn't interested in gambling, but we did see the stage shows. I was amazed at how much alcohol he drank.

Pearl Allen Andree

That became a serious problem for most of the next decade, and an on-and-off problem at times in the years following that. At the time I wasn't alarmed as I knew his family background was German and they considered it part of their culture. It was the first time for me in Vegas and there were ghosts from the past that I couldn't share with Bill. Those memories from the past were because Jimmy had gone on cross countries there and told me of the trips. The pilots went together to see the shows, for fun. Frank Sinatra and Ava Gardner were together then, and one pilot got a lot of kidding when the others pronounced his wife Eva's name as "Ava."

One day he'd had a lot to drink and then was hostile toward me. He was mean, saying he'd go back to Arizona and leave me stuck. I realized it was the alcohol talking and left it at that.

When we returned home, I found out Pat had gone to the school nurse for a sore throat. She couldn't find anything wrong with his throat, so she started talking to him. She knew us as her husband was in Kiwanis with Bill. Pat told her his mama had gotten married and gone to Alaska on her honeymoon and wasn't ever coming back! My sweet boy must have been in agony.

The church attendance question hadn't been resolved, and I told Bill he didn't need to go with us if he felt uncomfortable. He felt the preacher was talking right to him. I discovered he was embarrassed for us to go without him. About three weeks after coming home he told Pat to do something, and Pat didn't do it right. For discipline Bill insisted on not letting Pat go to Wednesday night Bible study—Bill didn't go to that. The next day or two I hit the ceiling and informed Bill he would not keep a child home from church for any reason.

By Saturday morning he had his bags packed to leave and I was glad. I insisted he was to tell the kids, but they raised a furor, even Danny. They were all crying at losing another daddy. In later years when they complained about Bill, our marriage, and our family, I occasionally reminded them about this time when each was young, when they had expressed their feelings differently.

I kept the checkbook and paid the bills. In March we received a bill for the purchase of a baby blanket at the local children's

Maud and Pearl

store. I knew I hadn't bought one so I showed it to Bill to see how we should handle it, as all the merchants were his advertising clients. He told me he had bought the blanket to send his daughter Kathi for the baby boy she'd had in January! So, Kathi was not a 16-year-old; she was married and living in Albuquerque. I got excited. We could go and visit her as it was only an eight-hour drive. He quickly told me we would not do that and in a polite way told me it wasn't anything I needed to bother with. Okay...

On Friday of Mother's Day weekend, I was visiting with my friend June Szalay, who lived just a few blocks from where Bill's house was. I was telling her about the things he was doing carpentry-wise to the house and suggested we go to his house where I could show her the louvered wall he'd done there. We drove over there and his sister Louise's car wasn't in the driveway since she would be at work, but I rang the doorbell. If someone did happen to be there, I didn't want to alarm them by walking around outside. Lo and behold, an elderly woman came to the door. I introduced myself and she said she was Louise's mother! So, this was my mother-in-law? I was confused, to say the least.

That evening there was a come-to-Jesus conversation. As it turned out, Louise was not Bill's sister. She had been a family friend that seemed to have been associated in some way with him and his wife. I knew he had come to Tempe in 1951—at least, that's what I'd been told. The two of them had traveled from Washington, D.C. up to Canada, across to the west coast, down to southern California, and into Arizona in their two Packard cars. He swore it was completely platonic. Yeah, right. No wonder she hated me so. Everyone he knew considered her his sister—at work, the theater, everywhere. I didn't blow his cover, but I did wonder, what do I do now? It would not be the last time that I went to bed wondering, what was I going to do about this tomorrow? I felt like Scarlett O'Hara.

So Bill had lied to me throughout our courtship about many things. By the time I had figured out everything, I was already married. From then on I tried to be vigilant about his truthfulness or his lack of it, or his efforts to avoid the truth with an embellishment.

Pearl Allen Andree

On Sunday he was baptized. My thinking went something like this: I am a Christian; I married him for better or worse; I guess this is going to have to work. Now that he has obeyed the gospel—and I don't have a right to question his motive or look into his heart—I better try to make a go of it.

I really wanted to have another child so I stopped using birth control. Why? Had Bill only told me one big lie (Louise) and one small lie (Kathi)? Was I overly forgiving because he had been converted recently? While I considered these things, more importantly I wanted to have another child, and I was not by nature a doomsday person.

Bill had woven a spider's web of deception around me, so I began the effort of constructing the kind of person he actually was, what his values were, and who had molded him early in his life. This wasn't easy.

Origins

Over time, I was able to piece together some things while others remained missing threads. Bill grew up in Oak Park, Illinois. His father was a die maker and his paternal grandmother a grocery store owner and businesswoman whom he looked up to. He was taught to work for everything he received. Growing up he was a Boy Scout, musically talented, and athletic. He attended the University of Illinois Urbana-Champaign. On the college track team he had medaled, once finishing a race with his track shorts accidentally nearly torn off. When the markets crashed and the Depression began, he performed gigs in a band and played several instruments including piano, clarinet, sax, and banjo. After his first marriage in his early 20s, he worked for a period of time in Illinois and Minnesota. Family oral tradition is that during that time he may have taken more courses, some in architecture. Later, he and his family moved to Alexandria, Virginia. There he owned at least one women's fashion shop, honing skills in fashion design and advertising.

Later, his personal circumstances converged into his geographical exodus to Arizona. Fatefully, we began together. As time passed in our busy lives, surprisingly, he hardly ever picked up the banjo or sat down at the piano in the living room, although he let Danny and Lilly play his handcrafted clarinet. It was as if he kept an old chapter of his life closed. If he played, it meant he was in a good mood. He really liked playing "Stranger in Paradise" from Kismet. He seemed to get caught up in the lyrics while he sang them. And he played the piano beautifully.

The Coming of the Fonz

It was about this time that Bill told me he would like for his son, Herb, to come and live with us. I said, "Certainly." It never crossed my mind to say otherwise. I don't think they'd seen each other for six years or more.

Before Herb arrived in June Bill said, "He will call you Mom."

I immediately responded, "He will call me what he wants to call me." The kids loved him and he fell right into the habit they had of calling me Mom, so that went well. He was a delightful almost 15-year-old who spoiled me for future teenagers and maybe saved my marriage to his dad.

We decided to have a family vacation in the Dodge. We discovered, for the first time, its injured radiator—a worker at the dealership had taken it for a spin and hit a cow. We couldn't go sixty miles without overheating. We went to northern California and visited Mother Goggin and Pete's family. We tried camping on the desert between Las Vegas and Reno. The air mattresses had to be chased down as they became airborne. One night we stayed overnight in the open air beside a creek below Yosemite when ice was on top of the water. We drove into Yosemite and managed to have a rock knock a hole in the oil pan. The local garage in the park had a repairman that repaired it with fiberglass and we never had a problem with the oil pan again.

Getting home meant school was starting. Herb had his birth certificate and I noticed that his father was 31 when he was born. When I added 15 to 31, I got 46. Surprise, surprise. I never blew his cover until 35 years later. The kids found out but never said anything either. Bill was the only one who didn't know he was older than he really was.

Herb's grades were not the best but it wouldn't be the first time I tutored a high school student. He had an adult goal to be an NFL football player but he also applied himself to study and excelled in his grades. He did play football and, wow, was he popular with teachers as well as fellow students. He had those eastern manners, like standing when a lady came into the room, opening doors, and so on. We had a large number of girls at church and I started having them to the house one afternoon a week for a social. They could walk to the house from school easily and we discussed anything they felt like talking about. It was the time when girls started phoning boys, and girls not associated with the church called Herb. He joined the Circle K, a club for high school boys sponsored by Kiwanis Club. Bill and I were among the chaperones for a sock hop one time. Herb was active in student government and at the end of the year was elected Junior Class President. This was a big deal as there were 750 juniors and they put on the junior/senior prom. They had a budget enabling them to hire a large venue and a live band.

In October of '57 I found I was pregnant. The due date was the first part of June '58. That spring Bill began considering building apartments. He had a talent for talking to bankers and mortgagees. We started building the first 16. They were considered luxury and we had them for rent in August. Arizona State College became Arizona State University that year. Herb went back east that summer to visit his mother and brought a friend, Dick DeCosta, home with him for a two-week visit.

We had an opening of the one-bedroom apartments and they rented right away. Bill had designed them in a Polynesian style, landscaping and all. His interest in that style emerged from a family experience at a Polynesian restaurant named The Islands. Soon, menu items were fancied as apartment names, to be put on wooden name cards for each apartment. That same month, we had a birthday party for Herb and yes, the girls went bonkers over Dick DeCosta, too. The first two sets of eight apartments also had Polynesian names, Vali-Hi and Tahiti House.

Pearl Allen Andree

The most blessed happening that summer was on June 4, when Raymond Allen Andree joined our family. He weighed nine pounds, twelve ounces. The news made the front page of the *Tempe Daily News* and it spoke of his red hair. That would change to blond later. At first, we put him in the cradle Janet had as a baby in our bedroom, to make night feedings easier. One day I walked in and he was on his tummy, with one of his arms hanging out through the side dowel rods. I had the feeling he was thinking, Can't they find anything bigger to put me in? I still had the crib from the other three, so he soon graduated to that, and that was in Janet's room.

Bill was good to get up in the night and change him. Ray was off night feedings when one night Bill went in to take care of him. He had changed him and, he thought, made him comfortable. As he walked away, Ray kept fussing. Bill heard a little six-year-old voice from the Jenny Lind bed say, "He wants a drink of water." So Bill fetched a drink for him, and sure enough he quieted down. Bill asked Janet how she knew what he wanted and she replied, "Well, I can still talk baby talk." Even though she is a grandmother now, she still knows how to make a person happy.

Herb had never heard of the Church of Christ but went to church with us willingly. Toward the end of his sophomore year he started asking questions. The preacher preached against dancing and he was curious about that. We had discussions. He knew I liked dancing so I mentioned that he should think about, if that was the only thing holding him back then he had to reconcile how he himself considered it spiritually. He obeyed the Gospel that spring and began a life close to the Lord. He had study sessions with friends, and two of his friends plus one of their mothers obeyed the Gospel. I never knew about her health, but I visited her and she must have had something terminal, as she passed away about a year or two later.

One of Herb's friends was a paper carrier. He used a car and sometimes Herb went with him. As a result, we had a huge amount of rubber bands around the house. He taught the younger boys about spitballs. Everywhere I looked I found rubber bands. I used a dinner bell to inform everyone when dinner was ready.

Maud and Pearl

One day I informed them I wanted them to dress especially nice as I would serve a three-course meal. When they came to the table, I served the first course. It was rubber band soup.

Herb served as class president very well, and I like to say he "grew in stature and in favor with God and man." He was student director of the first play in the new auditorium. Bill and I organized a couple of shows for the elementary school PTA and presented them in the new high school auditorium. Since the street was Broadway, we called them *A Night on Broadway*. One was a *Ziegfeld Follies* variety show. Bill purchased a trick rope and was Will Rogers as MC. About eight men, prominent as doctors, teachers, and business men, dressed in drag and did a chorus line of "Sweet and Lovely." The song leader at church had a great tenor voice and knew a woman who excelled as a soprano. They did a Nelson Eddy and Jeannette McDonald duet. He was also good at imitations so he and I did a W. C. Fields and Mae West conversation. Another friend, who had the local travel service, imitated Marlene Dietrich in a number. Another show we presented was a collection of scenes from *Music Man*.

Herb was also selected in the group of boys going to Boys State. Boys from around the state spent a week in the pines of Flagstaff during the summer, running a government, electing officials, and such. At Tempe High, he had run for Student Body President, but lost that contest to a friend who also ran. It was just as well because he finished senior class mid-year and entered Pepperdine University in January 1960. He had enriched our lives and would continue to do so for many years ahead.

A Look Back at the Family Car

It was a 1956 Dodge, with a push-button automatic transmission. Other than the albatross Ford Edsel, I don't remember another push-button automatic.

To start, there was something askew concerning the lack of air conditioning. To placate Dad, Dodge Brothers installed a Frigidaire-type ultramodern air conditioner. The mechanic then took the car for a test drive—and T-boned an unfortunate bovine, bloody awful. All night, the Dodge was cobbled together to pass off on Dad. It likely did not have enough coils in the radiator to begin with, but the mechanic slapped it together anyway, doing the bare minimum.

All said, that Dodge had Edsel-like qualities. The air conditioner never worked, and Dad never spent enough money for proper antifreeze. Instead, he bought canvas water containers.

I remember that when we were in town, we pretty much had to sweat it out and choke on the collective smells of family time. Driving to church, many of the Ten Commandments were bent. Getting into the car late was roundly condemned. Pushing and shoving often occurred. Tussles under the church orange trees, including orange fastballs and change-ups, were deemed hypocritical behavior on the way home. The road to sainthood dimmed.

Yet the true poetry of the Dodge was its complete domination of the Andree clan during "vacation time." Dad was a controller, but the Dodge turned him into a blubbering idiot.

Maud and Pearl

Kudos to the Dodge and cars of the 1950s for their incredibly strong door handles and bumpers. We'd tie all the containers to them and head out Griswold-style with anticipation.

Today the trip from Tempe to the South Fork Little Colorado River might be five hours. Back then, that would have normally taken several more hours. We could do it in no less than eighteen to twenty hours, of course in harmony with nature and bonding in the bosom of family love. If we left Tempe at 3:00 a.m. and made it all the way to Superior by noon, the clan was on a roll... like a herd of gypsies fleeing a volcano. Thirty-six or forty miles in eight or nine hours was unbelievable, especially if you add in the ambiance of the air conditioning and our chumminess. Then we realized that we had many more hours of pure vacation bliss to go.

I'll extrapolate more about the Dodge. One vivid memory of the poor misfortunate car was firing up some Pikes Peak/Matterhorn-style mountain loaded to the gills with family fun stuff plus three hundred pounds of water suspended from the door handles and bumpers. Probably a wrong turn on the Yosemite trip. This brilliant driving feat once achieved culminated in a substantial hole ripped into the oil pan. The top of the hill harbored a lost tribe yet to be discovered by modern science. The best they offered was sticking a masticated gob of gum in the Dodge's gash. With the park garage's fiberglass fix, we moseyed along. Truly Orwellian.

Herb got the Dodge instead of the cool '52, split rear window, flip out-turn signals VW bug of all time when he left for college. Surely, his driving aversion came from those traumatic family experiences. He's blotted out those memories with worthy intellectual pursuits.

Pat Goggin, Pearl and Jimmy's son, an Allen cousin

Building Polynesia in Tempe

OUR apartment collection had increased. In the summer of '59 we put a swimming pool in on vacant space, built a fence around it, and furnished tenants with keys to the gate. Later we built 14 two-bedroom townhouse type apartments around the pool and called it "Place of the Happy Talk." Bill thought of building a raised tree house at one end of the pool, which we reached via a ladder stair. We named everything with painted signs, so he was thinking about "Tea House of the August Moon" when Janet piped up, "Why don't you name it Tree House of the August Moon?"

We bought more property adjoining to the south and built more apartments, some studio size and some two-bedroom townhouse-style. We named them "The South Seas." Altogether, on that street there were 45 apartments. We bought property a mile away, near the new second high school. We built 11 two-bedroom townhouse-style fourplexes. We called that the "Lotus Flower Apartment Village." That made 89 in total. We decided to stop there so we could still continue personal management of them. We also bought a couple of rental houses, which we eventually sold. Bill also wanted to build houses, which came later.

Louise passed away when Ray was around two. She had been chronically alcoholic and died of cirrhosis of the liver. I went with Bill to help her and the last time I wasn't able to even help lift her. She looked like she was nine months pregnant, and her stomach was hard as rock. Her brother came and took care of final arrangements, but I never met him.

Herb, at Pepperdine, met Bonnie Glenn, the daughter of Joel Glenn, Comptroller at the University. In June of 1962 they were married at the church building on the campus. We had acquired a VW camper van by this time and took the kids to California for the wedding. Joel and his wife Dolores lived in Ventura and it was nice meeting them.

The 1960s: The Blended Andree Family

WE WERE a working family in the early '60s. There were plenty of jobs Dan and Pat could do. They learned to clean swimming pools and, of course, do yard work. Bill began building houses in the new Shalimar Country Club. Danny had been playing Little League baseball for several years at the baseball diamond at the high school. His coach was Ladmo, a local TV children's show personality, part of a duo called Wallace and Ladmo.

When Pat was seven, he started playing too. One early summer morning their teacher at school, Joe Spracale, called me. He said he had been up watching the Little League players and noticed Pat wasn't getting much playing time. He was also the city's swim team coach. He said to me, "If you'll bring him down tomorrow morning to Tempe Beach (the city public pool) at 7:30, I'll get him on the swim team and he will be a better athlete by the time he's 12." I did that and Patrick went on to excel in sports, especially football and swimming.

I had started gaining weight and gone on a diet with Dr. Flynn's oversight when, having lost 14 pounds, I realized I was pregnant! Dr Flynn said, "So, you got so good-looking, you got pregnant?" As a result, I was a few months along at Herb and Bonnie's wedding. The bride was fine—it was the stepmother of the groom who felt it took 18 instead of nine months to complete this cycle.

Despite his flawed parenting, Bill didn't mind laughing along with the children, although his "har, har, har" sounded off-note, and he was all about teachable moments for the kids.

Character

I HAVE to say more about the good character qualities that Bill, who was an extraordinarily complicated person, passed on to each of the children. However, this is hard to qualify without the negatives. To paraphrase, he suffered our older children badly. He parented autocratically, sometimes arbitrarily, even though I intervened when I thought I should. The children have expressed these recalls to me: headstrong, difficult, impatient, strifeful, and short-fused. He was not easy for the teenagers, beginning with Herb, to love, various interactions were not ideal, and at times being around him was not easy. He vented on them and occasionally made unbeneficial decisions that limited their school or athletic participation and that were hurtful to them.

Yet, he had a kindly side to the small children, loving and playful. He was an indelible influencer for good character on each child in a number of ways. When he found himself plopped down in a large family, which he'd not experienced before, he coped by quickly creating rules to live by: chores listed on the refrigerator to be checked off, extra emphasis on consideration in all things, trash to be picked up even if not yours, and sitting in your specified chair at the evening dinner table—on time—where you were expected to be heard from and not just seen during family discussion. Not wanting to learn was not tolerated. And woe unto our child expected to give a report on a far-flung corner of the earth or a newspaper article who showed up unprepared. The latter backfired when Danny reported an article on a 101-year-old Iowa man attributing his longevity to corn whiskey and chasing wild women. Bill was about to fire up at that, but Herb burst

Pearl Allen Andree

out with such a loud laugh that everyone got jolly happy, and the waters got calmed.

Mainly, Bill modeled good character by what he did, rather than what he said. He perpetually had a fountain-of-youth energy, and what he created and designed—beginning with building out a hobby room from the garage at the El Camino Drive house, where he allowed any kid to build whatever on the bench, even using his tools, to the apartments and the custom homes—he built mostly by himself with few subs. And, he had to build it right. If not, he took it apart and rebuilt it. He'd work through the burning Arizona desert. With his powerful mind, he reasoned well and used sound judgment, which the children assimilated. When he had the kids with him, he expected hard work, but he never over-did or exhausted them. And he was able sometimes to pick a kid up, to see the need for moral support and give it.

Our children's benefits: each one of them has a strong work ethic in his or her respective field; a vision of the mind to create a design or a solution to a problem; a perfectionistic style; and an appreciation of art, architecture, and adventure. Later in their adult lives, each of our children had to bridge the gap between life with Bill and achieving individual emotional and mental equilibrium. But they also gained a penchant for working with challenging individuals throughout the years and become self-aware of when they themselves are being difficult.

The Outcasts of Tempe Flat

Janet once reminded me of a hilarious incident involving herself, Pat, and Bill. This reflected how sometimes Bill's fervor and zeal for teachable moments went awry.

Janet: Do you remember a camping trip in the snow when we were young? It was in the Volkswagen camper. Were Danny and Ray along, too? I don't remember Mom. But Mom packed dinner, hamburger balls with potatoes and carrots in foil, that was cooked on a fire. They were delicious. I think Danny was there because the two of you dug a hole in the snow, lined it with tarps, and piled snow on top to make an igloo, but Dad in the camper was so cold that he said we were going to freeze to death and made us all get up and go home in the middle of the night. Pat, can you remember this?

Pat: Weirdly, it was only you and me, no Dan or Ray. I can't remember Mom making the dinner, but that dish was a Boy Scout staple. Of course, if you screwed up cooking that dinner, the camping trip would have been termed a failure. I doubt that I would have taken a chance on letting Mom put that meal together.

Janet: My puzzlement was what possessed Dad to take us camping in the snow for one night? Mom said that because he grew up where there was snow, he thought it was important to go north at least once a year and see snow. Perhaps it was 1962 when Lilly was a baby, so Mom didn't come for that reason. Does that sound right? I would have been 10 and you would have been 12.

Pat: Maybe it was the winter of 1962-1963. My personal worry is that he feebly hoped we'd die. I never once thought of him as an instructive moralist. I figured he was freezing his bottom

Pearl Allen Andree

off waiting for us to expire. Can you imagine his surprise when he came and found us alive? My biggest surprise was that he didn't drive off to get coffee and leave us there.

Middle Child Syndrome

OF THE seven children, it was a stretch to call Janet the middle child. Shielded above by her older brothers, she was understatedly sly. She had an unusual knack for bending Bill's ear yet staying out of trouble. She had several unknown accomplishments.

Dean Todd was a high school math teacher and a church leader as well as a youth group Bible teacher, a good and religious man. Danny and Pat chose mischief in church class to get Dean's face very red and themselves in the classroom doghouse and in hot water at home. Not so Janet. "I got along famously with Dean Todd. He was one of the best teachers that I ever had. He intuitively realized that I was a lot smarter than most people thought I was, and I appreciated that. So, I never got in trouble for not doing my homework as long as I could go to the blackboard and work the problem correctly."

Janet also caused the red spider plague of 1967 or 1968, which she didn't confess for decades. One day she borrowed Pat's car before she had learned to drive. She took it for a little spin around the Bala Drive circular driveway. Although she knew how to drive a stick shift, she had not driven an automatic yet. While trying to navigate the drive, she rammed the arborvitae tree at the end and busted the fence behind it. Fortunately for her, a young man from the neighborhood happened by and helped her get the car back in the drive. The two of them fixed the fence and managed to push the tree upright, so it wasn't noticeable. When Pat came home, Janet was giving his car a nice wash, and he wondered what he had done to deserve such kindness. The Good Samaritan neighbor was sworn to secrecy, and no one ever suspected a thing—never even noticing the patched fence. After a few weeks the arborvitae tree turned brown, but Bill was sure the red spider had gotten to it. However, no amount of toxic insecticide was able to remedy the problem. Janet's neighbor rescuer remained an enigma to her. He was tall, dark-haired, and handsome, as well as quiet and polite, and he did not drive a fast and flashy car as others did in the neighborhood.

More 1960s, More Blending, More Growing Up

AFTER Herb's wedding we took the kids to the San Diego Zoo then back to Arizona. Pat started that summer going each year to visit his Aunt Alma and Uncle Lee in the Texas Panhandle, where he helped with the horses and later learned to drive early on a tractor. He loved every minute of it. He also played Monopoly with his cousin Dick.

During these years I saw Mama at least once a week. We brought her to the house for dinner often. Mama was able to get along with everyone, and she and Bill developed an accepting relationship.

Dan was always asking, "Why don't we take a family vacation?" So we decided to do so; after all, we had a camper van. We took the kids (sans Pat) to the Seattle World's Fair. The daytime temperature in the Phoenix area was 117 and I felt every degree. The first night we camped along a creek, still desert, and it was still 117! Bill and I had a large sleeping bag in the back of the camper, Ray was in the front seat, and Danny and Janet were in a pup tent. I was looking forward to the Grand Canyon but they were having a heat wave! Finally, at Bryce Canyon I became comfortable at a lovely 51. When we looked at Danny while we were driving he was always sleeping. We took a dip in the Great Salt Lake and floated. We camped overnight in Glacier National Park and wondered at the beauty of Coeur d'Alene, Idaho. Near Spokane we visited a friend I had known in Laredo whose husband was still in the military, and we stayed overnight.

Pearl Allen Andree

In Seattle we found a space in a camping ground and managed to see a lot of things. The Space Needle was so swamped with people we opted out of dinner in the revolving restaurant at the top. We did take the ferry over to Vashon Island, which I wanted to see after reading about it in Betty McDonald's books. Our visit came to an end and we got back onto the road. As navigator, I asked Bill if he wanted to take the coast highway through Oregon. I had heard it was very beautiful. His response was, "The only scenery I want to see is a white line down the middle of the road." I reckon he was rather tired of camping. Ah, but our vacation wasn't over yet.

I washed my support hose before we left, so my varicose veins were free to expand. We decided that first night on the road to stay in a motel, have a dinner in a nice restaurant, and get a good night's sleep. We chose Medford and arrived there about 5:00 p.m. We could not find a room in the whole town. We saw on the map there was a town about ten miles down the road and we thought we would find something there. The first town we came to was Ashland and a big banner across the highway said, SHAKESPEARE FESTIVAL. So there were no rooms there either. We kept driving. About 10:00 p.m. we pulled over and fixed cereal and milk for all then kept driving. About 10:00 a.m. we found a park near Shasta Dam. We put sleeping bags on top of picnic tables and slept. My legs were hurting but we finally got home. A few years later my brother Ornan moved to Ashland, but that's another part of the story.

In November, my baby was born. We sent out over 200 Christmas cards at this time of our working life. I printed up inserts with the pertinent information for the world: name, Lillian Stella; date, November 29; weight, eight pounds, twelve ounces. I found out what my Mama had been talking about. She had described me as the child of her old age. A nurse in the hospital nursery came to my room to meet me because in her six years there it was the first time anyone had named a baby girl Lillian, which was her name. Mama had several grandchildren named Maud or Maudina, but no one had named one Stella after her. Bill's mother was a Lillian, so she was named for both grandmothers. Our Lilly was our frosting

Maud and Pearl

on the cake. She only had a small amount of hair, but Janet and I would scotch-tape a pink ribbon bow on her head. She already looked like a swimmer, with muscles in her arms! When she was six weeks old, I made her a "teeny-weeny yellow polka dot bikini" and took her into the pool for the first time.

In 1963 Bill began building houses, one at a time, to sell. Herb and Bonnie lived in the Los Angeles area and their baby boy, Christopher Timothy, was born on April 19. In the latter part of the year, Bill started on a house for us to move into. There was a 40' x 20' pool with diving board and an outdoor kitchen. He had built three already in the Shalimar Country Club area, and ours was in that group, too. After ours, he built another next door to ours. About the time Lilly turned one, he began digging the space for the pool. There were always tragic drownings of children and our first pool, with a fenced enclosure, had already caught the attention of city leaders and set a precedent for future building codes. When we saw that hole, we both started having nightmares. I have always been buoyant in the water, not able to get to the bottom. I dreamed my baby was drowning and I couldn't get to her to save her.

An Olympic diving coach, Dick Smith, had built a gym in Phoenix, so in January 1964 I started taking Lilly there three mornings a week for swim lessons. "Uncle Mac" was the teacher for the children. He spent 15 minutes with her each class time, concentrating on dog paddling and climbing out of the pool. By the time we moved into the house on St. Patrick's Day, she was doing that quite well. Often tragedies happen when there are many people around but no one is paying attention to the pool. We had a family dinner on Mother's Day when Mom and my brother Leo's family were there. We were eating around a picnic table in the outdoor kitchen and Lilly was running around in just her diaper, it was so hot. At one point we looked up and she was walking away from the pool, dripping wet! We had a "Mae West" life vest for her but she wouldn't go near the water with that on. She hated it, so it served two purposes. We had a couple of fund-raising luaus around the pool. One was for the Republican Party, probably when Senator Barry Goldwater was running for President. The

Pearl Allen Andree

other was a luau for Associated Women for Pepperdine, of which I was a member. At the luaus we had plastic lotus flowers floating in the pool. We set up low tables all around and hired ukulele players to walk about and serenade us. And I had some of the kids wear sarongs or muumuus to greet guests. At a certain time our Lilly, in her muumuu, walked out onto the diving board and jumped into the pool. I was serious about this!

Dull times remained unlikely at Bala Drive. What soured Bill and me a lot within months of moving in was that some college kids came, probably from the "Sin City" part of the ASU campus (rowdy, loud, late-partying apartment area), and burglarized us. They stole all the Tiki gods and the fishnet off the roof and the monkey faces off the wall and the doors. We did not hear them, despite the fact that they obviously tripped over the croquet wickets and fell in the mud right outside my and Bill's sliding glass doors. Riled, Bill bought three shotguns and took the boys to the shooting range.

Shalimar Country Club began to have events and celebrations like Fourth of July and one part was having the swimming kids dive for pennies and win prizes. Ray was on their swim team, and he excelled both in events and diving for knickknacks.

A swim meet was scheduled at the new city pool and the Shalimar coach considered it a good time for his team to enter the six-and-under group. He rightly thought the length might intimidate them so suggested they swim the width instead of the length. Lilly, age five, didn't care for the width, so he said not to insist. The following week we psyched her up to prepare for the following Saturday when the meet would be at a pool at a high school in Scottsdale. She was ready. Unfortunately, she was the only one in her group on either team! The coaches thought they ought to have her swim anyway. Even the opposite team stood poolside, yelling, "Go Lilly!" She won her first blue ribbon.

Patrick was a freshman when McClintock High School first opened in 1964. The city built an Olympic-sized pool at the new school and Pat was on the school team. He was elected class president two years, and was a popular athlete on the football team. The hippie long hair was prevalent but I told him that his birth

Maud and Pearl

father and the other pilots got a buzz cut to keep their heads from getting too hot and sweaty in their helmets. He went out and got one, and some of his teammates did too. Twenty years later I heard how McClintock was highly rated in state for their great football team. The coach was the same man and, in an interview, he mentioned that the whole team shaved their heads for the season!

An incident took place involving Pat that was reminiscent of "The Ol' Fire and Wasp Story" when he was about fifteen years old. We had some palm trees and it fell on his work duty to climb a ladder to trim off the dead fronds. He was wearing shorts only, and at the top of the ladder he disturbed a wasps' nest. He kept his cool descending from the ladder, but his torso was covered with stings. I dowsed him with vinegar (Mom's old remedy) and called the doctor. He had a tetanus shot.

Pat also made himself a surfboard. It was round and he surfed on the irrigation when the water covered the golf course. That caught on, too. His room had an outside entrance, which was passed on the way to the front door. He bought a welcome mat that had Go Away on it. And, oh, the girls liked him too.

One person who locked horns with him was Bill. One summer Bill told him he didn't want him working for him. Pat went out and found a job at Taco Bell, and met some not-so-good friends. Added to that, one night Pat had gone to a party and Bill started drinking. It turned into one of those nights. Danny kept the phone in his room all night, in case he had to call the police. After ranting and raving for about three hours, Bill finally went to bed and we went to sleep.

Like Herb, Danny had really enjoyed being around his classmates, many of whom he'd been together with since grade school. They became the largest and last class that stayed together in the high school district, because part of the class below went over to McClintock High. I had gotten to know a number of them too, by having hosted them at the house either for girls socials or as a Cub Scout den mother. They were happy kids, and unusual in that everybody liked nearly everybody else. They even had a class motto: "We have fun, we have kicks, we're the Class of '66!"

Pearl Allen Andree

Danny started his senior year the fall of '65. He took driver's ed and got his driver's license so he could drive himself to school, football practice, or wherever. This freed me up somewhat as I was going to the office at the apartments every day. Danny had some trouble with his eyes and the doctor at the Air Force Base that monitored his eye condition told him, "When you decide to go out on the road driving, I want you to call me so I won't be out there at the same time." Danny injured his hip when playing football scrimmage his sophomore year and he didn't make varsity team his junior year. His senior year, the team was not doing well, but the coach put him in at the homecoming game long enough to get his long-awaited letter. I had knitted him a letter sweater, but he refused to wear it till he actually won it for football. To him, the letter for concert band his junior year didn't count.

When Mom was 80, I found her pulling up Johnson grass to clean out her irrigation ditch, so we asked her if she would like to live in one of our apartments. After living in the house I bought in Tempe for about eight years, she was glad to move to the apartment. She moved into one of the original ones at Vali-Hi. The church building was only a half-block away, so the walk would be easy for her.

In October '65, she was expecting Zeke and Ellen to come visit from Oklahoma City. There was a small fenced-in area outside her bedroom door where we had a picnic table and bench set. She went looking for someone to help move it outside her kitchen door. When she asked a man to help, he told her to get the manager. The manager wasn't home so she did it herself.

I did not find this out until I visited her the next day. When she walked in her bedroom and very gingerly sat in a chair, I said, "Mom, are you all right? Are you hurting?"

She replied, "Oh, I was hoping I wouldn't have to tell you." I took her to Dr. Flynn and he gave her some pain meds. When Zeke and Ellen came, he was sitting at the kitchen table talking to Mom and I was standing behind her. She said something and her words were garbled. Zeke and I had eye contact, but it didn't happen again so we didn't say anything.

Maud and Pearl

In January '66 Lilly and I were at South Seas talking to the manager's wife one morning, and Lilly needed to go to the bathroom. I told her to go to Grandma's apartment and knock on her door. She came back saying her door was locked. I went with her and used my key to open her door. Mama was lying on the kitchen floor by a leg of the table. She'd had a stroke and was taken to the hospital. She was in a coma for a few days and my siblings came to see her. The nurses couldn't handle her hair (it was below her waist) so Babe cut it. He had to cut it short on one side but long on the other because of how she was lying in bed.

After about two weeks Dr. Flynn told us, "We don't know how long this will be, and since she is entitled to the County Nursing Home, we should move her there until we know how it will go." My brothers, sisters, and I talked about where she should go if able to leave the nursing home. I could take off work a few days in an emergency, but I could not take care of her full time. We all agreed that if she was released, I would fly with her to Albuquerque and Alma and Lee would take her to Texas. Alma was a Practical Nurse and although she was busy, she was at home daily. As soon as I found out that Mama was sitting up in a wheelchair, I took a beautician friend over and she cut her hair evenly, about three or four inches, and gave her a dry shampoo. We already had enough of her natural colored hair to make a braid to keep, and now her hair was completely the most beautiful white, luminous hair and since it was naturally curly, it was beautiful.

Two weeks later I received a call one Saturday telling me I could come and pick Mama up—they needed her bed! I called Alma and made reservations to fly to Albuquerque the following Wednesday. Lee, Alma, and Babe would meet us there and put Mama in the back seat of their Cadillac and take her to Texas.

On Tuesday, the day before that Wednesday, Bill received word that his dad in Chicago was not expected to live through the night. He flew there that evening. It was the first time he'd been told his dad was ill. His dad died that night. Bill stayed a few days.

I stayed home the few days Mom was with us before I flew with her to Albuquerque. It was February and the weather was already warming up (Bill called it our "million-dollar weather"). I wheeled Mom onto the patio, and she enjoyed the sunshine.

Grandma's Quilts:
My Soul Is Fed by Needle and Thread

MAMA loved to make quilts, but they have been given to other people, so very few are still around.

The first thing Mama did in her the house I bought her at 919 Wilson in Tempe after Jimmy died was to walk three blocks to the lumberyard and buy 1" x 2" strips of lumber for a quilt frame! She had someone hang it from the ceiling over her bed so she could let it down and sit while quilting. Many grandchildren who slept beside her, including my kids, fell asleep at night saying "Goodnight, Moon" to that quilt frame.

Mama taught me at the early age of five how to sew and how to embroider. When I was in high school, a fad occurred with patchwork quilting—for clothes. I sewed together some pieces like a crazy quilt, and I had a square big enough to cut out the pieces for a jacket. I never finished it, but Mom kept the pieces. A few years later, when Grandma Hall passed away, Mom received in the mail her mother's white slip. She laid my jacket pieces on top of the slip and made a quilt out of it.

Mama was a generational quilt-maker, too. Margaret (Totsy) Scott recalled her own quilting education:

> It was lots of fun to have Grandma Allen come for a long visit from Arizona. In the house that Daddy built, there was a porch-like area with a wooden floor between the garage and the kitchen door, which was where we set up camp for quilt making. Mama and Daddy had a quilting frame that hung from the garage

Maud and Pearl

open rafters, made from four boards (I think they were old broomcorn shed slats).

It was a new experience for me to make a quilt. Exciting! First, we gathered fabric scraps from Mom's stash of scraps from making clothes for Tanny and me. We cut 12½-inch blocks of newspaper and hand-sewed strips of fabric, right sides together, on the diagonal to the squares. We trimmed the fabric to the paper square, pressed it, then carefully tore the newspaper off. Then we sewed the squares together, making a quilt top that was about seven feet by eight feet. This took about a week, but it was fun talking and telling family stories in the cool breeze while we worked.

Grandma had a design she used to make the quilting. It was in the shape of half a rainbow, starting in the corner of a square, then another bow would attach to that. As the hand quilting progressed, we rolled the sides of the quilt and it got smaller on the sides until we finally finished it. It was such a good feeling to finish a big job! Of course, Mom and Grandma did the biggest part of the quilting, as Sister and I had sometimes gotten sidetracked making dresses for our dolls. Those were the days… Little girls, you miss out if you don't have a grandma that quilts.

I still make quilts, but not like the ones that Grandma made. Mine go to the County Fair and are works of art and win blue ribbons. I still get great satisfaction from making a quilt, and my sister and I cherish those days spent with our sweet Grandma Allen.

Tanny added, "I still have the quilt that Grandma made for me. I remember that Grandma said, 'I like woolen scraps; they will keep you warm with cotton inside.' Grandma used little pieces of clothing that had been worn out."

When Janet was later remarried to Anthony Thompson, on one occasion in the mid-1990s he took his three piece band to New York City for an appearance in a restaurant/bar. Janet

Pearl Allen Andree

wrote to Ray, who lived near the performance location, about the event. Ray went over early to meet Anthony and see the show. His band members thought Ray was from the restaurant and wouldn't believe him. He persisted, saw Anthony in the van napping, and commented, "That's my Grandma's quilt he has on him."

Anthony replied, "This is my quilt; I got it from my wife." Ray convinced him it was Grandma's quilt, and he realized Ray was his brother-in-law! About that specific quilt, "still waters ran deep."

My daughter Janet recalls, "That was the only dual quilt ever made by my two grandmothers. Grandmother Goggin sewed the one-inch squares together in a pattern as part of her physical therapy after she had her disabling stroke in the late 1950s. Then Grandma Allen received it and hand-quilted it onto the backing." It brought the extended family together four decades later, on the streets of New York.

Mama learned to quilt probably as a child, and quilted all of her life until her first stroke in her early 80s. For survival from those Oklahoma frontier days through the Depression and past World War II, she had to make quilts for those she protected and loved out of scraps and, well, hardly anything. Within the family, everyone knew that her quilting accomplishments were amazing.

Forks in the Road: Finishing High School

Danny graduated that semester. He was one of six valedictorians—four boys and two girls—all of whom finished four years with 4.0 grades; that is, each had made straight As. He tried to get a job in a hospital but couldn't because he didn't have experience. So, he went to Yuma to stay with Leo, who got him a job picking cantaloupe! We had rented an apartment to a man who had a personnel position in St. Luke's Hospital in Phoenix, and he arranged for Danny to be hired for the summer the next year, 1967, as a hospital orderly. It was a summer of unrest with potential riots and such, termed "a long hot summer." Sometimes he stayed overnight at the hospital for safety reasons.

Patrick was beginning to assert himself against Bill's—and the high school's—authority and I thought maybe he would like to go to a private Air Academy high school in Fort Lauderdale, Florida. They taught flying and I thought he would like that. Arrangements were made for him to go there though he protested. Unfortunately, two weeks after entering, he and another boy went AWOL and hitchhiked back to Arizona. It turned out that the academy charged extra for the flight training, and instead of taking the boys to their church of choice, they bused them to the same church so there wasn't a choice. We sent him back anyway as I had already paid for a semester. After that, he came home to stay and got back into McClintock High.

Danny entered Abilene Christian College and Janet moved into his room. He had received scholarship offers from Arizona

Pearl Allen Andree

State, University of Arizona, Pepperdine University, and Abilene. We found out academic scholarships were not as forthcoming as athletic ones. He chose Abilene Christian because the Director of Admissions took the time to write him a personal note about the quality of the science departments and the pre-med curriculum.

I never realized my son Danny had a sense of humor until he went to college and wrote home. He wrote some pretty funny things in those letters.

Also in the fall of '66, Bill's mother came to stay awhile. We didn't know how long she would stay so we let Pat stay in the office apartment so she could have the guest room. She had been diagnosed with diabetes in her 20s, and was experiencing the side effects. Her right foot was not in good shape so she used a cane. She idolized Lilly but picked on Ray. She stayed about two months, going back to Chicago before Christmas. She heard us saying that my mother might come to visit, and I think she thought she would end up as a caretaker for Mama.

Janet had already exhibited much creative ability and she expressed it in transforming her new room. She wanted a round bed so we purchased two foam rubber cot mattresses from Yellow Front, glued them together and cut the four corners to make a circle. Bill made a wooden platform a few inches off the floor. He made it square so the corners served as places to use as a night stand. She talked Bill into getting her a barrel rattan chair swing and hanging it from a beam in the ceiling. All her friends were jealous. Pat's room was large enough to accommodate Danny's twin bed and we used his room as a guest room when needed.

During the summer of '68, Ray brought home a goldfish. I didn't have a fish bowl, so we put it in the punch bowl, which of course flared out. That was the summer Danny took classes at ASU while studying for his medical exams for applying to medical schools. He studied late and one early morning he decided to go into the kitchen and fix himself a milk shake. As he passed the island counter where the punch bowl was, the goldfish jumped out and landed on the kitchen floor in front of him. He just picked it up, put it back into the bowl, and continued on his mission.

Maud and Pearl

Pat had an incomplete course or two in 1968 when his class graduated, but in the fall, he signed up to finish his degree and take classes at Mesa Community College. He made good grades in his classes, especially English and philosophy. It proved what I already knew in my heart—he had a sweet heart, in spite of inner turmoil. He had lots of girlfriends, and one in particular reminded us all of Goldie Hawn, since we watched *Laugh-In* on TV. That senior year he had noticed celebrities wearing tuxedos with plaid Bermuda shorts and knee socks. When he rented a tuxedo for the prom, he bought a pair of "formal" shorts. The word got out and one of the girls asked the principal if that was all right. Principal Bill "Bull Dog" Boyle said, "No, of course not."

Pat was going to cancel out of the prom, but the girlfriend was on the phone, crying, and her mother was on the phone crying, so he relented and wore the pants he had rented. Janet had attracted the attention of a senior boy at Tempe High, and he invited her to be his date to his prom. She told him if he would wear Pat's formal Bermuda shorts she would go with him, and he did. Nothing negative was ever said about it. He had been accepted to MIT.

Later in 1968 and in early 1969, there was a recession going on in the real estate market. Bill had seven houses for sale, including the one we lived in. We had seven pools to care for. Having the apartments helped to borrow from Peter to pay Paul. If it hadn't been for the apartments, we wouldn't have gotten the bank loans for each of the houses Bill had built. Two of the houses were in the desert community of Carefree, so when we sold our house, we moved into one of them, selling the other about the same time.

Desert living in Carefree meant desert creatures as well. Near the house, there was a covey of quail that adopted Lilly, age six, as their mother, which was quite hilarious to watch. In the house garage, a rattlesnake tried to go inside with Janet, and Bill tried to kill it with bug spray, which only made it quite angry. Once in the summer of 1969, Danny and Janet drove out to the house together and Danny chopped off the head of a snake, which I recall was a coral snake. Later, home briefly from medical school in the summer of 1970, Danny grabbed Lilly and put her in a corner,

Pearl Allen Andree

took a shovel, and killed a Gila monster, not caring whether or not it was a protected species at that time. I'm sure Danny decided living in Carefree wasn't so carefree.

Janet had finished high school in three years and wanted to go to Northern Arizona University in Flagstaff in the fall of 1969. She stayed with friends in town that summer so she could work. In June we took Ray and Lilly to Santa Barbara to visit Herb.

Eventually, selling some of the houses got us to a better place financially. I had handled the extra stress in a way that I had found successful throughout my entire life. Once in bed at night, I decided to not let the worry and the stress linger.

In Santa Barbara, Herb and Bonnie's marriage had disintegrated, and they divorced. He was working on his Master's degree there. We also visited with Charlotte and Dick Cosby and their three little girls. One of them had a birthday while we were there. Herb and his girlfriend, Jennifer Onstott, were getting married in Los Alamos, New Mexico, in September and we were attending. Janet could not attend as she would already be in classes. At that time of his life Pat was a sharp dresser, but I had never bought him a suit. Before the rest of us left, I gave him my Penney's charge card and told him to get himself a suit. At the wedding, the groom didn't wear an actual suit; Danny, the best man, didn't wear an actual suit (although they both looked very handsome). Pat and his girlfriend flew in a day or so early, dressed to the nines. His girlfriend was in a beautiful brown pantsuit, looking like a Powers New York model.

Danny had begun medical school classes in Galveston, Texas that fall. Bill was beginning to get the travel bug so we took a trip to Minneapolis where he had lived at one time, then to Winnipeg, Canada, where we took the Canadian Pacific train across Canada to Vancouver. We stayed three days in Banff, and in Vancouver we took the ferry over to Vancouver Island, where we stayed in the city of Victoria. We stayed at the Empress Hotel and had high tea with the required scones with strawberry jam and whipped cream. The Butchart Gardens were especially beautiful, having been created in a rock quarry. Janet had planned on learning to ski in Flagstaff but found they wouldn't have ski classes available till

Maud and Pearl

second semester. I had told her take classes she wanted to take, so she signed up for pottery, survey of western civilization, and other subjects, totaling 17 hours. Second semester she came back to the valley and took classes at Mesa Community College.

There would be more difficult times in my marriage to Bill, but what he had accomplished and what he would accomplish cannot be understated. He had both a boundless architectural creativity and a boundless energy to build, build, build.

The Steel-Drivin' Man

BILL hardly ever told me about what he had accomplished in life before our lives began together. At the *Tempe Daily News* before leaving to start his own building company, he was an effective advertising manager and well known in town. From the beginning, I knew that he'd long admired the architectural style of Frank Lloyd Wright, who had relocated to Arizona and built Taliesin West in northwest Scottsdale. He may have even studied the renowned designer in college courses. Certainly he was overjoyed by his proximity to the acclaimed architect, and often on a Sunday afternoon after church and lunch, he drove the whole family out to Paradise Valley, a north Scottsdale suburb, and walked through open houses of Frank Lloyd Wright planned homes, or those by Taliesin West students.

He had his own creative mind and brilliance. As we built and expanded the apartments we owned, he kept their Polynesian theme skillfully and consistently and carried some of those themes over into his custom homes, including our own Bala Drive home in Tempe. He was a physical force in appearance, 6'1" and 185 lbs., hammer and nail in hand, perspiration and blazing sun ignored. He had chameleon creativity: homes designed aside golf courses, Spanish adobe/pueblo styled homes in Monument Valley, and dessert living homes in Carefree. In our upcoming Australian adventure, he would build several homes, an apartment fourplex, and an apartment building that he built out into condos in southeastern Australia, adapted to the land and nearby sea.

He had received Phoenix metropolitan recognition for his excellence in design and construction, The Arizona Republic's

Maud and Pearl

Medallionaire award in February 1965. At age 75 he built a cabin by himself on a rustic mountainside close to an abandoned mineshaft near Prescott, innovating methods of water and electricity supply by rainwater runoff storage and solar panel use. No award, but seeing was believing, and anyone who did could instantly admire what he had done.

The Andree family
L to R: Ray, Janet (Goggin),
Lilly, Bill, and Pearl
about 1967

Leo, Vergin, Ronnie, and (front)
Marsha
probably Yuma, Arizona
circa 1960-1961

Maud and Zeke Jr.
Oklahoma City, Oklahoma, between early 1950s and early 1960s

Together with Grandma at Christmastime
the Devine children; Back, Mike Jr.
Front, L-R: Judy, Denise, Dorothy holding Kelly, Mark
Margrave Ct. house, Walnut Creek, CA, December 1961

Four Allen generations
Back, L to R: Dick Cosby holding Kirsten, Charlotte, Dorothy, Pete
Front, L to R: Jo Ellen, Lisa, Maud
Brentwood, California, August 1965

Herb and Bonnie
at their wedding
Ventura, California
1962

Danny Goggin
Eagle Scout uniform
Tempe, Arizona, 1964

Andree Development Co.
Bill Andree, architect and builder
Arizona Republic
Medallionaire Award
Tempe, Arizona
February 1965

Allen Great-Grandchildren Collage

Robin Toche

Lori Allen

Monica Barnes

Susan Canning

Ricky Canning

Michelle Toche

Danny Toche

Denise Devine

Mike Devine, Jr.

Judy Devine

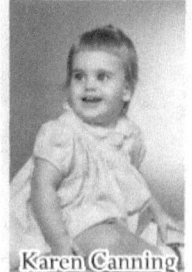
Karen Canning

Allen great grandchildren, 1950s, 1960s, and later

Maud Allen post-stroke with granddaughter Lillian Stella at left, 1967

"How Ya Gonna Keep 'em Down on the Farm (After They've Seen Paree)?"
Rear view of the six Devine children (photo by their mother Dawn)
L-R: Denise, Kelly, Marty, Mike Jr., Judy, Mark
Vernal Falls bridge in Yosemite National Park, California, 1967 or 1968

Lee Curtis's winning horse, Lee's Toy
L to R: Alma, Sabrina in front, Lee, Mary, Dick, Marvin
and friend in front, groomer, horse, jockey, and trainer
Ruidoso, New Mexico, 1972

Ellen and Zeke with their grandchildren
Back, L to R: Karen, Jo Ellen, Susan
Middle: Esther, Zeke, Heidi, Allen, Matthew
Front: Ellen, Rick
Christmas at the Spencers' place, "The Pink House"
Rush Springs, Oklahoma, 1972

Together with Grandpa
Christa and Earl's daughters
L to R: Esther, Zeke holding Heidi
Oklahoma City, Oklahoma
1970-1971
Sketch by Louis Daniel

Confident, resolute
Lanier and his three daughters
L-R: Dominique, Lanier,
Michelle with head turned, Lori
at Dick and Charlotte's house
Belmar St., Sacramento, California
early-mid 1971

Three Cosby sisters and a cousin
L to R: Lisa Marie, Kirsten Joan, and Jo Ellen with
cousin Lisa Diane Wills sitting in her lap
Carmichael, California, 1973

Rita Jo and Bill Grieb
and family
L to R: Allen, Jo
Ellen, and Matthew
Oklahoma City,
Oklahoma
1973

Marvin (20), Shanda (1), and
Sabrina (18) Curtis
Amarillo, Texas, 1981

Janet Goggin
Age 15
Tempe, Arizona, 1967

Ray Andree
4th-5th grade
Tempe, Arizona
1967-1969

Bill and Pearl
Tempe, Arizona
1977

Australia immigrants
L to R: Pearl, Lilly holding koala, Bill, Ray
1970

Tanny D'Orville and children
L to R: Shawn, Robin, Danny, Jane, Michelle, Tanny, Mike
Robertson place, Bray, Oklahoma, November 1984

Sabrina and Rocky Gafford wedding
Back: Rocky Gafford; Middle, L to R: Marvin and Delia Curtis,
Athel Hickam (maternal grandmother), Susie Davis (maternal
great-grandmother), Sabrina Curtis Gafford, Norma Jo, Dick Curtis
Front: Shanda Curtis. Amarillo, Texas, July 22, 1984

Allen children
L-R, Back: Martha, Pearl
Front: Leo, Ornan, Pete, Zeke
Bray, Oklahoma
August 1977

Father and Son
Dick and Marvin Curtis
probably Amarillo, Texas
circa mid-1990s

Pearl and Bill Andree
Mountaintop cabin
near Prescott, Arizona
late 1980s

Pearl Andree
on her and Bill's 40th anniversary
Sun Lakes, Arizona
January 23, 1997

Bill Allen and Dan Goggin
Allen cousins
Fort Worth, Texas
early 2000s

"Once upon a time..."
Burns Community School
Left: remnants of storm cellar with door,
Right: merry-go-round pole
Comanche County, Oklahoma, 1901/2023

Australia

IN THE spring of 1970 we took Ray and Lilly and went on a tour to Australia and New Zealand. Bill was researching countries and towns and was fairly certain he wanted to live in another country so the kids could go to school elsewhere. Later when people asked why we lived in Australia for a few years, I said, "I was married to the happy wanderer." I joked that he planned our trips, and I simply got on the plane and asked, "Where are we going this time?" It was a great trip.

The Bonamys came to Sydney to visit us at the Menzies Hotel and when Bill asked about tipping, they coached him not to tip overly much with the remark, "Don't spoil it for the rest of us!" We had met the Bonamys, Stan and Anne, while he was a visiting physicist at ASU teaching in thermodynamics and they had rented a Lotus Flower apartment from us.

We visited the fjords in the Southern Alps in New Zealand and the hot springs on the northern island. We were in a small biplane going up to the high country and Lilly turned to me and said, "I think I'm going to be seasick." I convinced her to relax, and she closed her eyes and went to sleep. We landed in a sheep meadow.

I had refused to give permission to Pat to ride a motorcycle before age 18. After that he was on his own, so of course he bought himself one. When we came home from our tour, Janet met us at the airplane with the news that Pat had been in an accident. He was going around a curve on the highway in Tempe when a milk truck hit him. He was wearing a helmet and slid across the highway on his head and broke his leg as well.

Pearl Allen Andree

We hadn't been informed because we were already on the way home. He was in the hospital and would recover. The incident didn't stop him from riding motorcycles.

We decided to immigrate, mainly so we wouldn't have to buy round trip tickets. Bill really wanted Ray and Lilly to go to school in another country for a few years. We had to get applications and other paperwork from the Australian Embassy as a part of the process. Pat was managing a property we had bought from Ed and May Adams. Ed had been born there, and it was grown up with all kinds of plants and trees. He had rented shacks and spaces to some hippies, and Pat had weeded them out and had in their place moved his friends in.

The accommodations were not exactly modern. Even inside the house, although there was indoor plumbing, a construction error had been made so that no water was piped to the kitchen sink. Pat and all his friends had been raised in good homes, but this was their rebellion, I guess. One of the girls was supposed to be the housekeeper.

About the time summer started, Pat got hepatitis. I went to check on him and was not pleased with the lack of cleanness. It may not have been the answer, but I wanted my boy to have some healthy and clean food, so I went to the grocery store and bought about $50 worth of groceries.

When I got back to our Carefree home and told Bill, he became very angry with me. In his mind I was exposing us to the illness. He started drinking, and it became one of those nights. It evolved into his threatening that he was going to shoot me and bury me in the arroyo that bordered our property. I knew he kept a loaded gun on the upper shelf of the closet, so I decided on action.

I made sure Lilly was in her bed and asleep, then Ray, whose room was on the other end of the house. Then I called the sheriff's deputy, who was the local law enforcer, and told him the situation. Bill knew what I was doing, so he promptly went into the bedroom and went to bed, immediately going to sleep—or passing out. When two deputies came, they went into the bedroom and observed he was sound asleep, stayed a little longer, then left.

Maud and Pearl

The one immigration document we didn't have was a statement from the local police department about our good character. Obviously, we could not get one in that town, so Bill went to Tempe and his buddies at the police department gave him one

Danny came home for the summer and went to the doctor, got a gamma globulin shot, went to Pat's, and helped him to recover. I never told them about that night as I was afraid that they would confront Bill, and if things got out of hand, there might be consequences for them.

Janet turned 18 in August. We asked her if she wanted to go to Australia with us, and she said yes.

We arrived in Sydney on December 17, 1970 and the Bonamys met us. We stayed with them in Wollongong for four days and took possession of the car Stan had purchased for us, a Ford. Bill had researched various towns and had decided on a small town in Queensland on the Sunshine Coast called Buderim. Of course, we drove on the left side of the road, with the steering wheel on the right side of the car. I decided to sit in the back behind Bill to get the feel of that. Ray was in the navigator's seat as we went through the Christmas traffic north through Sydney. Ray was good at his job, and we only had to correct one mistake, which we noticed right away. We worried we might burn out the brakes on the new car, but we crossed the North Harbor bridge around 1:00 p.m..

We had prepared the kids for not having a real Christmas, but on the night before Christmas Eve we rented a motel room in Grafton, New South Wales. We were driving up the coast road and when we drove into town, the street was lined on both sides with blooming Jacaranda trees, all in those beautiful purple flowers. They were having the Annual Jacaranda Festival. The next morning the kids wanted to shop for small presents for each other to exchange wherever we would spend Christmas Eve. At one stop along the road, we stopped to watch dolphins playing in the surf.

We stayed in a nice motel near the ocean owned by a German who had immigrated there after the war. He had just had

Pearl Allen Andree

new carpet installed in the dining room, and he insisted on giving us a small tree to have the room more festive.

During the night I had to get up and found myself walking on water! It had rained a gully washer. Not only was our carpet wet, but the owner's new carpet was soaked. Also, we had left luggage on the car's luggage rack and Janet's suitcase had water soaked through the zipper.

The Australian Years

WE WERE planning to live in the small town called Buderim (pronounced "bud-rum"). It was on the top of a small mountain not far from the beach of the Sunshine Coast of Queensland. The Aborigines call the creation time the Dreamtime and they have a story about Buderim. It is written on the wall of the local utility company.

Buderim was the chief of his tribe back in the Dreamtime and had a beautiful daughter named Maroochy. She fell in love with a young warrior named Coolum. Her father favored another warrior who wanted her. The father's favorite cut off Coolum's head and it landed east, in the Pacific Ocean. You can stand on the north side of Buderim Mountain, look north, and see a huge monolithic rock with a very flat top, then look to the northeast and see a rock jutting out of the ocean about fifty yards from the beach. That is Coolum's head. At the bottom of the mountain a river flows out to the ocean. The river contains the tears that Maroochy shed grieving for her love. A small town called Maroochydore is there, and the high school there was where Ray enrolled.

One of the first things we did was get Ray and Lilly into a swim club. I drove them ten miles each day to Nambour to the club and coach. The first day I was sitting on the bleachers, as the other mothers were doing, watching and listening to the mothers talk. One mother said, "Rainey isn't doing so well today. She's all knocked up!" I was shocked, but found out later it was like our saying, "She has a bug." And we thought we had come to a place where we understood the language.

Pearl Allen Andree

Lilly entered the fourth grade at Buderim Elementary. About three weeks after school started, I picked her up after school one day and while we were walking, she said, "Mama, they say this prayer in the morning, like, "Our Father which is in Heaven..." and I thought, Oh, my child has never learned the Lord's Prayer! (Prayer had already been cut out of school in the US.) So, I thought, it's a good time to do so. A couple of weeks later when I picked her up, she said, "Mama, I found out why they say that prayer. This morning Mr. Kelly forgot to say it and everything went wrong!" The school had a 30-minute period a week for religion instruction and parents could choose which church for their kids. I thought she could learn about other religions, so I chose the Anglican. Their priest didn't come till Ash Wednesday. When she came home, Lilly announced, "I got blessed today!"

I talked to the headmaster about my coming to the school for that 30 minutes and spend it with her in Bible study. He suggested I make up a brochure and he would send it home with students and some parents might like their kids to join us. I did so and ended up with a dozen kids in two grades. To do my weekly volunteering, I had to get permission from the State Board of Education and additionally get a letter from the minister at the church we attended. Our church was in Gympie, 60 miles away, which meant driving that twice every Sunday. I obtained the letter from our minister there, who was a missionary from Arlington, Texas. I did those classes for the three years we lived in Queensland.

The Church Potluck Legend: Grandma's Buns and Antiquitas

GRANDMA Allen was famous for her yeast rolls. I began to search for the origin of her famous rolls. It seems when the family was living northwest of Marlow, Grandma used the lid to a drum to put the rolls on to cook them. The drum was probably like a water barrel used to catch rainwater off the house. It would have been about two feet across. Another bit of information was that she used potato water in the recipe.

Having been a Home Economics teacher, I know a little bit about yeast breads and the ingredients needed to make them. Flour is needed for structure. Yeast is needed to make the bread rise and sugar is needed for the yeast to feed on. Salt is needed to give flavor. Most recipes have milk in them, but Grandma's recipe had potato water in it that had the sugar that fed the yeast that made the dough rise. Most recipes have an egg to give strength to the dough and make the dough rich in flavor. Fat of some kind is needed to make the bread tender.

The method of preparation is important when making yeast breads because it requires kneading and time to rise. The following is a recipe much like the one Grandma made. However, Pearl said Grandma didn't have measuring utensils, so much of her preparations were from memory and not exact measures.

Pearl Allen Andree

GRANDMA'S YEAST ROLLS, IMAGINATION AND ESTIMATION
(Recipe Can Be Doubled)

1 package dry yeast
1 cup warm potato water
3 tablespoons sugar
1 teaspoon salt
3 tablespoons melted Crisco
3 cups flour

Stir yeast, salt, and sugar into very warm potato water and let it set and dissolve, then add melted Crisco and stir.

Place flour in large bowl. Make a hole in flour with fist.

Pour liquid mixture in hole in flour. Use a wooden spoon and stir flour and liquid together till flour is mixed in.

Turn dough out onto floured surface and knead about 5 to 10 minutes, till dough is elastic.

Place dough in a greased bowl and let rise till doubled in bulk.
Punch dough down, deflating air. Make into rolls and place on greased baking pan, or barrel lid, and let rise again.
When rolls are doubled in size, bake in oven at 350 degrees.
Remove from oven and brush tops with butter.
Get out of the way, because hungry family and churchgoers are waiting to devour the buns.

Margaret (Totsy) Scott, Martha and Babe's daughter
an Allen cousin

Letting Jesus In: Wedding in Buderim

JANET decided to go to James Cook University in Townsville, about 1,000 miles north of Brisbane and 300 miles south of the Great Barrier Reef. She found a room in a boarding house with other students. A nearby family was American, and their son drove her to classes. His name was Cohn Barnes, and his parents were Dottie and Gene. We went on coach tours during the two-week school holidays Ray and Lilly were between the terms. That first year, one we took was to the Barrier Reef and we had a chance to visit Janet.

Later that year Dottie and Gene came to visit us. Cohn came with Janet and spent Christmas with us. A few nights before they came the doorbell rang and I went downstairs to see who it was. We had moved into the house Bill built for us. A young man was there, with hippie-like appearance and rain soaking him completely. He had a bedroll and asked if Cohn and Janet were there. His name was Jason Gathercole. He said he was to meet them there. He obviously needed shelter, so I invited him in. He was actually a Canadian young man with long hair. Ray had two beds in his downstairs space, and there was a shower, too.

When I went back upstairs, Bill was livid. We were all going to be murdered in our bed, and so on. The next morning at the breakfast table Bill asked Jason, "Where are you going now?" He took him outside of town so he could hitchhike to Brisbane, where he got work to finance college after the holidays.

On Christmas Eve, at 2:00 a.m. the next morning, the phone rang. It was Cohn's mother Dottie. She had been in line for four

Pearl Allen Andree

hours to call Cohn. They were having a cyclone in Townsville, and they had decided to return to the States in January.

At Christmastime, Cohn and Janet told us they had decided to get married and planned to do that January 22. They explained that Jason had a room in the boarding house where Janet lived, and he would work and suspend classes until he had enough money to go back. She said one morning he came home so early he tripped over the milk delivery outside and broke four bottles of milk. He would be best man. He wore a mauve suit and handled the job superbly.

Bill got a bee in his bonnet and refused to give Janet away. Bill was a brilliant, multi-talented, persuasively conversational person who nevertheless had trouble relating to children, certainly his own, at times even mistreating them, and sometimes other young people as well, more so when drinking. Prior to marrying Janet, Cohn was staying in one of the fourplexes that Bill had built in the area. On one occasion, Bill made an off-handed remark to him, and Cohn called him a name in response. Janet talked back to him as well. That's when he refused to participate. I made a powder-blue suit for Ray and he stepped up to give his sister away, at age 13. Louise Bonamy and her fiancé came up from Wollongong and she was maid of honor. Lilly was junior bridesmaid. Janet made her wedding dress and I made Lilly's dress. Thurman Self came down from Gympie to perform the ceremony in the local Anglican church building. Thurman was quite zealous on his part, baptizing Cohn in our swimming pool before the nuptial. Despite the turmoil, Janet and Cohn got married.

After the wedding, Dottie and Gene returned to their home state of Florida. Janet and Cohn went with them, where they raised two beautiful daughters.

There were many important experiences for my family and me in the Australian years, 1970-1977. I told the following story about one of them to my friend Dorothy Anderson. Later, Dorothy wrote it down in narrative form and gave it back to me as a gift. I'm copying Dorothy's version here. I am grateful to Dorothy, who gave me permission to include her recounting of my emotionally gripping encounter with my Australian friend, Anne Waldron, and her family.

Pearl's Christmas Story

PEOPLE have seasons and times in their lives just like our wonderful planet has seasons and times. And depending on where you are, the earth's seasons may be quite different from what we have here in the American Southwest. Pearl and her husband lived for several years in Australia and in some ways, she looks back on those days as a special time in her life to have had the experience of living in a different country with its own traditions and customs.

But in the southern hemisphere, such as in Australia, winter comes in July and August and summer is in full force in December. So, Christmas in Australia is often very hot.

Pearl's husband was doing development work in a small retirement town called Buderim (Bud-rum) that attracted many retirees from the large stations. These were the huge, two-hundred-square-mile ranches and farms that are particular to Australia. Through a neighbor, they met many of these couples.

And one couple, Tony and Anne Waldron, became their good, good friends. They were somewhat younger than the usual retirees, having youngsters still finishing up school, so they came from their station for periodic visits and had an apartment where they stayed.

Tony had suffered a heart attack previously but had adjusted his lifestyle accordingly and was in good, stable health. Because of this, he and Anne had put their station under a manager. But it was their hope that their son, who was just about to graduate, would be ready to take over and then they could retire.

They were particularly anxious for this son to take on their station because many couples eventually had to sell their land because they didn't have children, or the children did not wish to take on the station. But Peter, their son, wanted nothing more than to take over that huge parcel of land from his father.

There is a custom in Australia among many of the families to allow their children to travel around the world by working their way with a little help from their parents right after graduation. Because Australia is isolated the way it is, once a person gets started in their career, opportunities for extensive travel are few and far between. So after graduation Peter went to the United States to start his journey and was going to motorbike across the county, getting odd jobs to pay his way. A daughter, Annette, was already doing this and was currently working on a cruise vessel in the Mediterranean.

Whenever Tony and Anne were in town, they gave Pearl and her husband updates on the two traveling children. It was amusing to listen to the letters and particularly to Peter's reactions to the United States from an Aussie viewpoint. He thought Las Vegas was fantastic. "Mom, our Gold Coast is nothing but a mugawampa mud flat in comparison to Las Vegas."

Each time another letter arrived and was shared, Pearl and her husband chuckled with Anne and Tony over Peter's descriptions and enthusiasm—although perhaps their amusement was directed at diffcrent things.

Then the tragic time came. Crossing a street in Florida, Peter was unexpectedly killed by a car driven by an off-duty policeman. The cause of the accident was never fully ascertained, except it was thought that Peter might have forgotten to look in the correct direction for traffic. You see, Americans drive on the right side of the road, in the opposite direction from Australians. The word that they received via letter and phone was that he simply stepped out in front of the car. It was unable to stop in time to save him.

It became a season of great pain for Tony and Anne. All their hopes for the future in one brief moment were shattered. They had to put the station under the control of a manager. Managers are a fickle lot and between losing a manager and the hassles of finding a new one, they had to go back to the station in spite of Tony's heart condition. They couldn't sell the station; they still needed

Maud and Pearl

the income for their own lives and the one younger child they had who was still in school.

Pearl and her husband tried to help in any way they could, particularly in the early days with contacting people in the United States, in getting information and making arrangements. There didn't seem to be a great deal they could do to help them live through this season of sadness.

The daughter, Annette, was supposed to have met Peter in Florida and they were going to come back to Australia together. Now she was to arrive back home on Christmas Day alone.

That Christmas Day was the hottest in people's memory. There was not a breeze to relieve the unrelenting heat. Pearl decided to have Christmas dinner as a pork barbie (barbeque) by the pool. It was too hot to contemplate anything else.

About three that afternoon, Anne drove up to the house. She looked like a wilted limp rag. Concerned for her, Pearl invited her in.

"Can I have a half hour in your pool to cool off," Anne said, "before my husband and Annette get back from the airport?"

"Of course, I'll join you," said Pearl. "This weather would fry a lizard's tongue."

For a while they splashed in the pool in silence and then Anne began to talk.

"I want our daughter to have a traditional Christmas dinner with all the trimmings for her first meal back home," she said.

"Good grief," Pearl replied, "not roast turkey."

Anne nodded with a certain weary determination in her face.

"But you don't have air conditioning in that mobile of yours," Pearl said as she began to realize the cause of her friend's limp exhaustion.

Anne shook her head. "I cooked in my underwear and when I couldn't bear it a moment longer, I'd jump into the shower and not even towel off and then stark naked continue. But everything's ready for when they get back from that long trip from the airport. Everything is just the way it should be for Christmas, just the way it should be."

Pearl Allen Andree

Anne's face registered a series of emotions as she spoke. That is when Pearl began to realize that the healing season was beginning for her on that day, that day that is remembered as the time of our Lord's birth.

Quilts, Faith, and the Tie that Binds

OLD memories trickle back. Ornan and Dorothy's children grew up using Mama's ever-present quilts. Gradually, many cousins received quilts as gifts. In this way, the next Allen generation became interlaced like pieces of her quilts.

The cousins treasured their beautiful quilts. But behind the things that Mama made was the person that Mama was. She labored in poverty many hours over many years quilting together tops, insulation, and backing in a near-magical way, transforming them into mysteries of beauty and usefulness, one after another. In a sense, Mama sewed all of the Allens into a seamless tapestry with part of herself.

Over time our big tent family faced a broad range of adversities. In addition to the daunting nemeses of tragedy and poverty, Mama's were the trials and tribulations of her own life, her marriage, and those that came to the generations of her family. It's a universality of life that any form of abuse can occur. It did, whether emotional, verbal, physical, or sexual, some of which I have described and have not chosen to candy-coat or hide. There were vices that some succumbed to, and some decisions that were mistakes, however costly. I'm sure that Mama was informed of much that went wrong in the lives of the family along the way, although she was more protected from such after she reached her eighties. One of her religious tenets was "now we see through a glass darkly; but then face to face: now I know in part; but then I shall know fully..."(I Corinthians 13:12 KJV). However my son Danny recalled reading a letter sent to his grandmother aloud to her, sometime after her stroke, that referred to a relative having

Pearl Allen Andree

married at a young age. She burst out crying, verbally lamenting her loved one's vulnerability of age.

The granddaughter of a Civil War chaplain, raised in a strongly religious environment in Parker County, Texas and Oklahoma Territory, Mama's character was steeled by her birth-order caretaker role and her unquenchable thirst for education. As the psalmist wrote, "Your word is a lamp unto my feet, and a light unto my path," (Psalms 119:105 KJV) and off she went.

Really, how did Mama survive when she had just turned twenty and was pregnant when her daughter Effie Bernice died? Along with grief and despondency, how much guilt plagued her? Nearly a quarter century later, she lost her beloved son Ira, ironically while again pregnant. For the next year, did she battle melancholia and struggle to want to live? It is known that she was physically sickly during that time. She survived the loss of her husband to divorce by 35 years. At her core, she was religiously faithful and had a developed spirituality. Her surviving children became and remained religious throughout their lives. What she believed, she lived, as in the Scripture that says, "The Lord will keep you from all harm—he will watch over your life; the Lord will watch over your coming and going both now and forevermore." (Psalms 121:7-8 NIV)

Mama meant and lived what she said. She believed that she should "train up a child in the way he should go, and when he is old, he will not depart from it." (Proverbs 22:6 KJV) Her nature was to be sweet, "but the one who loves their children is careful to discipline them." (Proverbs 13:24b NIV)

The change of destiny when Allendale defaulted to the bank changed her always. She was forever frugal. My niece, Charlotte Cosby, reminded me that her son Pete and his Dorothy always bought things with cash, sometimes having had to save up for a long while to do so. That vestige of Pete's early childhood trauma, of poverty to riches to poverty, Mama may have linked to such verses as "...if you have put up security to your neighbor...if you have shaken hands in pledge to a stranger...you could have been trapped by what you said...so do this, my son, to free yourself...

Maud and Pearl

Go—to the point of exhaustion... allow no sleep to your eyes...free yourself, like a gazelle from the hand of the hunter..." (Proverbs 6:1-5 NIV) This was succinctly summarized by Shakespeare in *Hamlet*: "Neither a borrower nor a lender be." (Act. 1, Scene 3)

Decades before either I or her grandchildren came along, on the plains of the western Oklahoma territory even while area maps were being remade, Mama charted her journey of Christian faith. By horse or wagon, she took her children and found religion in schoolhouses, church buildings, or tent revivals. While devoutly Church of Christ, a restoration faith, she loved worshipping where she could among evangelical and protestant churches. A Methodist church remains in Catesby. Eventually of course, religious change came to the Allen family.

Mama herself faced changes of religious choice among friends and family, and was happy and accepting of those who had made them. Her faith was molded by her love and tolerance, and the Allens adapted similarly. Mama was always forthright about the good works enacted by those of other faiths and gladly discussed religion with others. In these ways, she exemplified her spiritual self. "Rather, your beauty should be that of your inner self, the unfading beauty of a gentle and quiet spirit, which is of great worth in God's sight." (I Peter 3:4b NIV) It's hard to imagine who wouldn't have enjoyed sitting down and talking to Mama. "Blessed are the meek, for they will inherit the earth." (Matthew 5:5 NIV) "The fruit of the spirit is... forbearance, kindness, goodness, faithfulness, gentleness..." (Galatians 5:22-23 NIV).

In the last ten years of Mama's life after she began living with Ornan and Dorothy, many Allen family trips were made to see her. Sometimes, relatives had to stay upstairs in rooms to which the heat was not well vented. It became so cold that Mama's incredible old quilts had to be brought out, seemingly transported in time, to be used again.

Against the cold and transported in time? Over two centuries ago, the English Baptist minister John Fawcett wrote in one of his hymns: "When we are called to part, it gives us inward pain; but we shall still be joined in heart, and hope to meet again." That sounds like what Mama would say.

Perth

IN 1972 there were tours to go on, swim meets to attend, books to read, and more to get acquainted with in the country. In 1973 we went on a European tour during a school holiday and finished it in the U.S. We visited Zeke and Ellen in Oklahoma City and Alma and Lee came over from the Texas Panhandle to see us. It was the last time I saw my sister. About six months later she suffered a cerebral hemorrhage and lived only three weeks more. She was only 57. Her favorite hymn was *Where We'll Never Grow Old.* .

We attended Dan's graduation from the University of Texas Medical Branch at Galveston and met the girl he had written us about, Lyn Hunt, who was finishing her first year of medical school. Lyn had asked him to change his nickname from Danny to Dan. He decided to become a psychiatrist shortly before graduating, but he still did a family practice-style rotating internship before his residency began.

Back in Australia at the end of 1973, we decided to move from Buderim across the continent to the city of Perth on the southwestern coast. Bill and I continued to buy and sell properties occasionally. But after the move Bill did not build much, except to build a rather large gazebo in the front yard of the house we bought there. He'd ordered the materials in a kit, and Lilly, at age 11, read him the instructions and directed the project. Our Aussie neighbors teased us about the gazebo, asking us how to get out of the forest. We enjoyed the lifestyle we adapted to in Perth. We had a boat built in Sydney, which we kept at a yacht club on the Swan River. We took it out into the ocean. We played golf, and we made friends. We liked the drier county because it reminded us of Arizona. We liked the church congregation there as well, and we wanted to live in a city a while. We also were attracted to the good schools there. My lifestyle had changed dramatically from my humble beginnings, and I was grateful.

Bill had applied for Ray to be in Scotch College and Lilly in Methodist Ladies College. She would be a day student, but Ray was 15 and we wanted him to be around others more. Since he had become an accomplished swimmer, Scotch College boarding school was attractive because it had an Olympic-size pool and he would potentially train for Olympic swimming.

Ray's Choice

Ray had been asking us to let him go back to the U.S. for school, but Bill and I felt he needed experience living and socializing with other people, and time to mature. The school chosen for him, as noted, would have had excellent aquatic facilities that we thought Ray would benefit from. He had in fact become an excellent swimmer, and we hoped that his abilities would improve.

We had driven our two cars to Perth: Lilly with her dad in the large Datsun and Ray with me in the Mazda rotary engine. The boat that Bill had built in Sydney was a 36' fiberglass with flying bridge and Caterpillar engine. Stan Bonamy called it a "bloody yacht." We had that shipped on a container ship. Bill had found a house we rented for a year before buying one. Lilly educated her dad on the geography of Australia and Ray helped me drive. He couldn't get a learner's permit, but we had allowed him to practice in back of our house. When a dirt road became the highway he said, "This is my kind of road, Mama." If I thought it was safe I let him take the helm.

Our plans blew up in our faces when Ray refused to board at Scotch College. He was only 15—teen rebellion time. Bill gave him three choices: 1) go to work as most Aussie boys did at his age; 2) go to school as a boarder; 3) go back to the U.S. on his own. Big mistake. We should have never given him that third option, which of course he took. It was the worst decision we ever made. Before he boarded the plane, he felt rejected.

We sent him to Dan, who was living in Fresno, thinking he could batch and help in the apartment, since he was good in the kitchen, and could clean and take care of himself while going to

Maud and Pearl

school. Dan, the future psychiatrist, became alarmed, saying, "He needs to be in a family situation." Of course, he was right, so Dan took him to Oklahoma to stay with my niece Rita Jo Grieb and her husband Bill and their family, because Rita Jo graciously agreed to help in this crisis. However, the Griebs' two older teenagers understandably reacted to Ray's sudden, if not imposed, presence. As their father said, "It was like mixing oil and water."

In May, Bill and I went back to the States to get him settled in Arizona. Lilly sort of liked the idea of boarding, so she did that while we were gone. In Arizona we were able to get Ray in a men's dorm at Arizona State, and he took a course to complete high school. One of our friends mentored him for future real estate work, for which he proved to be a natural. He was welcomed back at the home church congregation, and the minster was especially good to him.

We had brought the piano to Australia, but I told Lilly she wouldn't be required to take lessons there. For three years she hadn't touched it. Only a few days after school had started, she asked Bill to get her a specific work from the local music store. Her new friend Ruth, the headmaster's daughter, was planning on becoming a concert pianist. She had asked Lilly if she played, and Lilly said yes. Then, Ruth asked her to play a duo in an upcoming festival, and Lilly agreed! Her dad had to show her where middle C was. By the time we returned from the states, they had won second place at the festival. Years later I told her husband, "Don't ever tell her she can't do something." She excelled in her studies, as well as swimming, and had many friends.

Mama's Moonlit Years

AFTER Mama's stroke in 1966, she had residual aphasia and a mildly halting gait, but retained her good mind. In seven of her last 11 years, I was living in Australia. She was always on my mind. Alma took care of her the first year after her stroke but had much to do, including co-managing her storefront ceramics shop in Sunray. So Dorothy and Ornan took Mama to stay with them in Oregon. They were earth-pillar caregivers. Every year before we went to Australia, and during four trips back from Australia, we stayed with her for lengthy visits while Ornan and Dorothy took time off.

Mama had a way of saying things. If she was surprised or impressed by something, she might say, "Well, I declare," or "Lord of Mercy!" or "Well, I do say." Convalescing at our Bala Drive home before going to Alma's, she watched Lilly, only three but a good swimmer, in the pool, and exclaimed, "Well, I do say to my time!"

One summer, in either 1969 or 1970, when Danny was visiting in Ashland, Bill and I were there, too. Mama was watching Danny eat his breakfast, and I asked her if she would have trouble drinking some orange juice.

She said clearly, "I can swallow, but I can't talk!" It was strange that with her difficulty speaking, sometimes she said something straight out and clearly.

Occasionally, more of the family got together. One time at dinner, Leo asked her, "Mama, which piece of the chicken do you like?"

She exclaimed, "The back!"

Maud and Pearl

In the Oregon years, my siblings visited her when possible. I wrote to her regularly, and she wrote back, but less often as time went by. After a bout of illness in 1973, Dorothy encouraged everyone to visit her, yet she did recover. By early 1976, it had become too difficult for Dorothy to care for her at home, as she had become increasingly weak, and with Ornan's support, she agreed that Mama go into a nearby nursing home. My last two visits with her in 1976 and 1977 were there.

Mama was never wealthy and was poor virtually all of her life. She wasn't able to give us, her children, some things, but what she had given each of us was quite something—her love, kindness, her deep joyous laugh, and things of value morally and spiritually.

Not glamorous by any measure, she was worn down from having borne nine children. Yet she had an inner beauty that showed in the loving care she gave others.

She had lightened my path through life with wisdom such as pretty is as pretty does, pride goes before a fall and a haughty spirit before destruction, and lay aside the sin which doth so easily beset you. She sometimes got on her knees and prayed, whether at home or at church. I was not allowed to use four-letter words such as hate or kill, even in jest, because she believed God taught that we should love even our enemies. Many times while I was growing up, Mama walked three miles to church with me, carrying me if I got tired, and having the faith that someone would take us home.

Mama raised each of her children to be religious individuals, which we have remained. So was Ira. He was well-rounded, well-liked, and had his life before him when he died. His last gifts to Mama before he died were a keepsake boudoir vanity set and that set of Blue Willow dinnerware. The last piece of that gift to remain unbroken was the sugar bowl.

After I returned to the States and Mama was gone, I did purchase a Blue Willow set. Once I had it, I thought back to the years I was associated with the Air Force with Jimmy. In England, Mr. Oakley, who would have been our landlord, gave me a Blue Willow platter and I thought I would hang it. However, when I received my household goods later, he had not put it in as promised.

Pearl Allen Andree

Its meaning had an added level to me. Just as Ira had gifted Mama, and Mama had gifted everyone, eventually I, too, gave away the Blue Willow. I gave it to my daughter-in-law, Lyn, because she appreciates a story with deeply woven threads.

I found the story version of the picture on that platter that I remembered, and I have used it occasionally in storytelling.

Bicentennial

DURING the summer of 1975, we had Ray come and visit us in Perth for a few weeks. The minister in Tempe had suggested he would do well to attend Freed-Hardeman, a Christian university in Tennessee, as a choice for college. Ray wanted to do that and we agreed. It was a good idea at this juncture in his life. Ray, though, had always been hyperkinetic, and his one year at Freed-Hardeman was no different. He was funny, though, when he confided, "You have to be careful about having *Playboy* magazines on this campus!"

The following April we had a letter from Ray with a form for us to sign to allow him to get married. He'd met a nice and attractive young lady, Dana, at Freed-Hardeman. I knew he could get married when he turned 18 in June, but no way would I sign that. I wrote Dana a letter to try and get her to delay marriage for a while. She responded with a very sweet letter, and I knew this girl had no idea what was ahead for her. One of my friends said, "I can't believe he would marry someone you don't know." I said, "I don't have any worries about her, it's him I know is not mature enough."

Since 1976 was the Bicentennial year for the States, we decided to take Lilly out of school during her school holiday and take a trip back. We went to Oregon first, and while there we bought a Winnebago RV. It was 23' long and had a bed above the driver and passenger seats where Lilly could sleep and a bath with shower. We could be mobile for traveling around the country. Ray was out of school for the summer so we hoped we could delay him getting married at least until the end of summer. Our friend,

Pearl Allen Andree

Ralph Hogan, hired him in the real estate office; he turned out to be a natural for that.

While in Arizona I tripped and seriously sprained my ankle. Bill teased me that I did it on purpose so I wouldn't have to drive. He was half right. I was much happier as navigator. We journeyed to Oklahoma, visiting in Texas on the way. While at Dick and Norma Jo's, Mary came over and brought Lynette, age seven, with her. Alma was gone and the Allen family would mourn her loss for years to come. In a bittersweet moment, little Lynette wrapped her arms around my knees, looked up into my eyes, and exclaimed, "You look just like my Grandma!"

We went on and saw Zeke and Martha's families. Someone told us about Silver Dollar City in Missouri, so we enjoyed that a few days. Then we traveled on to Chicago to see Bill's sister Em and Aunt Hazel, and the Upper Peninsula of Michigan, Minnesota, and into Canada. We camped one night in a park, surprised that the mosquitoes were prevalent. We bypassed the Olympics in Montreal and found out later that a boy Ray had beaten in swim meet sprints in Brisbane had taken third place in men's freestyle.

We reentered the U.S. in the Green Mountains of Vermont where we had a delightful few days visit with Janet's longtime friend Trudy and her family. Trudy took us to the Von Trapp family's restaurant for lunch. Lilly was on cloud nine when she sighted Maria Von Trapp.

We traveled down the east coast to Florida where Cohn and Janet and Monica lived. On August 5, Janet's birthday, we girls planned to go out to lunch and Janet would accompany me to the bank to get a check cashed. Bill had taken the RV to get maintenanced as we were leaving the next day for Mississippi for the wedding, because Ray and Dana had decided not to delay longer.

Unfortunately, Janet couldn't find her car keys. I walked a mile to the bank in 85 degree heat (and 85% humidity), where they wouldn't cash my check. They finally changed their mind and I decided to call a taxi to return. While I was waiting, a hippie on a motorcycle offered me a ride, but I refused. When I returned, I went into the room where the ironing board was set up. Lilly's

Maud and Pearl

dress that she was to wear as a bridesmaid at the wedding was lying on the ironing board. I picked it up and there were Janet's keys. We had looked all over for them.

On the road again we visited old church friends Jerry and Betty Gorum in Opp, Alabama, then traveled on to Ripley, Mississippi. Dana was a beautiful bride, and in the later years I characterized her as a virtuous woman I could put on the pedestal beside my mother.

Back in Arizona, we rented an apartment for the rest of the year and Lilly entered the high school Pat and Janet had attended. We found out Dan's friend from high school, Craig Joyce, had an apartment near us, and one evening he came over when we had our friends the Szalays for dinner. Steve Szalay was familiar with the law firm Craig had joined and they discussed a certain woman judge who was the wife of John O'Connor, one of the partners in Craig's firm. Later, Sandra Day and John introduced Craig to her young cousin, Molly Armstrong, whom he would marry. In 1981, of course, Sandra became Supreme Court Justice Sandra Day O'Connor, the first woman to achieve that distinction.

Dan was in Fresno, so when we were returning to Australia in December, he came up to San Francisco to see us off. About five minutes before we entered the plane he said, "I think I ought to tell you that I am about ready to make a commitment." Of course, it meant he would ask Lyn to marry. In mid-January, he wrote us in Australia, "Well, the deed was done. Lyn would tell you it took forever, but I of course consider it a whirlwind romance." It had taken four and a half years. He did have a unique way of stating things. Earlier in his residency, he had purchased a Buick Skylark and given his VW bug to Ray. He wrote us, "I like my new car, but it has a drinking problem."

Odysseus: Voyage Home

Back in Perth in January 1977, Lilly was back in school. I noticed after a couple of months Bill's mind was turning to an obsession with the new sexual revolution. The university offered a course to the community senior citizens for their sexual awareness. I figured if seniors hadn't discovered it by that age, it was too late. Bill wanted to go to the course, so we went. We met new people, of course, and Bill wanted to get acquainted. One couple we liked were Hungarian immigrants from the war years. If they were swingers, they didn't blow their cover. I became aware that this unhealthy sexual thinking had begun to fascinate Bill. How much of this preoccupation had built up in his mind, I didn't really know. We had them over for dinner, and they invited us to their place. The night we were there Bill started drinking heavily and I was thoroughly embarrassed. He began inappropriate suggestive talk and I couldn't tell whether the other couple was for or against. One thing they comprehended was that I was not for this behavior. They helped get him into the car, with me in the driver's seat and the keys in my hand. He rambled on and on all the way home, acting like I wouldn't let him have any fun. He was still like this when we arrived home, waking up Lilly.

I finally saw that he was asleep, and I saw that this was going to become another night of what am I going to do tomorrow? I began thinking and planning for the next day—and the rest of my life. As I had done at previous similar junctures, I thought through things, then made decisions, and then went off to sleep. One thing I was sure of was that I was through with these behaviors by Bill. The innuendos of considering unacceptable practices had been

Maud and Pearl

increasing over time, and I was going to stop them. In my mind, at age fifty, I was going to make a life of my own, and if he didn't like that, it would be too bad. Furthermore, if I was going to be on my own, I was going to need to return to the States. However, the great irony was that, just like Mama so many years ago when I was only 12, I didn't think of it as the marriage ending. At this time, Lilly was 14.

The next morning, I informed Bill that I was taking Lilly to downtown Perth and booking our return for two weeks later, when she finished the school term. Of course, he was very apologetic, as in the past, but I had had it.

Why Am I a Member of the Church of Christ?

LIKE many others who answer that from time to time, I was raised in the church. But why have I stayed there?

When I was a child there was much rigidity in the brotherhood, and I occasionally heard grown-ups discussing pros and cons; but what did I see?

I saw a father who only showed up occasionally at services but read the Bible at home as men today read James Bond. I saw a mother who struggled to go to services as much as possible, sometimes frying chicken on Sunday morning so she could take me and walk the three miles into town, even carrying me when I was tired. I saw a grandmother who had become a Christian at 16 and talked of the church as though it had been a living, breathing force in her and her husband's life. I saw families who invited us to their homes for Sunday dinner and helped each other in times of death.

A word about Mama. She had so much loss, hardship, and rejection in her life, yet she was so devout religiously and such a good example by her daily living, that all of her children became active Christians themselves, married religious spouses, and had religious homes.

At the same time, I learned principles: obedience to God was necessary; the steps to salvation; the church was not a fraternal club, but a kingdom whose monarch is Christ and was established on the Day of Pentecost; that we are to "love even our enemies" and "pray for those who despitefully use us."

Maud and Pearl

The latter principle was pressed home often by a mother who taught me the finer point of Christianity: love. She prayed aloud at night so I could hear and know how a woman should pray.

As a teenager I had an older brother who filled in as a father substitute. He did so out of duty at the time, but he was a learned scholar of the scriptures. He enjoyed the intellectual discussion. To him it was the (not a) word or the scriptures, the (not a) church.

From him I learned that you can't convince an atheist there's a God by using the Bible. True science does not contradict the Bible, and vice versa. I have to decide there must be a Creator, then I learn about the Creator from the Scriptures. If I accept His Book, I must accept all of it. Leo strengthened and increased my knowledge of church history through the centuries, the universal church then and now. Ever since man was banished from the Garden it's God's eternal purpose to bring us back to Him, and the ray of hope for that is Christ.

I wish all teenagers could have someone like Leo to spark their thought processes and encourage discussion about things eternal.

One friend I had, when asked what had attracted her to the church, said, "The social life." It seemed funny to me because I thought the Church of Christ was the least social of all churches. But she was a faithful and spiritual Christian, so we never know what might start a ball rolling.

The church is many things: bride, the prototype of a happily married woman; a kingdom of congregations with governance; individuals with many different functions; universal; a fellowship of hospitality; eternally it will be faith and hope realized.

It isn't so much why are we members, as, why don't we use our blessings to open more doors of opportunity for ourselves and others?

Why am I a member? Because I have a clear and simple religious faith that others share.

The Summer of 1977

LILLY and I returned to Tempe the latter part of May 1977. We rented a partially furnished apartment and I enrolled in a summer school course on Shakespeare at ASU. Bill and I had decided that I would buy a new VW at Steve Szalay's dealership, but his son was managing there and didn't have any VWs. He sold us a lovely silver four-door Fiat Sedan and it proved to be a great car. Lilly eventually took it to college. We called it the Silver Streak. I restarted our earlier effort to buy the house in Sun Lakes and managed to buy that in June. Our lawyer had accomplished completing the foreclosure on the Lotus Flower apartments (the original buyers had reneged on payment) and sold them to another client. Since Lilly was still in high school, we needed a house in town, so Bill would sell the house in Perth, but I didn't really care how long it took him.

Someone reading the darker episodes in these pages may wonder why I continued my marriage and relationship with Bill Andree. There were the obvious taboos of the era we were living in, as well as my religious convictions about divorce. However, I always believed and still do today, that I needed a man in my life who would stick with me through thick and thin, and that He had sent Bill into my life for that purpose. We had a lot in common and enjoyed many adventures together. More importantly, the struggles of our relationship challenged me spiritually. At this point, overcoming these difficulties enriched my walk with God. I had reflected and gotten to the point that I could consider the mending, if not the redemption, of the previous closeness with Bill.

Maud and Pearl

I found a nice house in Tempe across the street from a pretty park with a golf course. It was our house in town until Lilly graduated. Then we turned it over to Ray and Dana, who had returned to the area after they married because of Ray's real estate job.

It turned out that Bill sold the house in Perth right away and returned for us to take up residence in Sun Lakes. I finished the summer course and stayed in Tempe overnight with Lilly, going out to Sun Lakes in the daytime. I took up tap dancing and golf, and life resumed.

In the meantime, while Lilly and I were still in the apartment, Dan and Lyn were getting married on July 16 at the Golf Course Road Church of Christ in Midland, Texas. They drove through on their way and stopped on the 9th where Lilly and I were. Since it was summer in Arizona, I think Lyn thought she had gone to hell. She wanted to get back on the road as quickly as they could.

Bill, Lilly, and I went to the wedding, as did Pat and Shelly, who had been married the previous February. We expected to provide the rehearsal dinner, but Macie and Don's church friends wanted to do it, so all they wanted us to do was furnish the ham.

The next week we started on a trip to Oregon to see Mama. We stopped in Santa Barbara for a few days to see Herb, who was just back from his sojourn for two years in Europe. He had brought back Anne, and they were married the weekend of the 30th. Bill asked if they wanted us to stay for it, but Herb said, "No." They just wanted to have a simple civil ceremony, so we continued on to Ashland to see Mama.

August Sunset

MAMA was as sweet as ever, and it was good to see Ornan and Dorothy. After visiting her at the nursing home, we said good-bye to Mama on the 9th. A week later, she passed away.

Ornan and Dorothy found it would be less expensive to send Mama back to Oklahoma to be buried in the Allen family plot than to buy a plot in Ashland. So, that is where we had her funeral. As she had requested, Pete led congregational singing. She was buried beside Ezekiel, her husband of 37 years, despite her statement years before that she didn't want to go back "even in a box." I like to think she had changed her mind about that. I know she loved that man till her dying day.

A large group of us were eating in Martha's living room after the service. Mama's younger sister, Eula, and her daughter, Fern, were there. We took pictures of all the siblings (the only missing one was Alma), and it was a happy gathering. I looked around and thought how Mama would have loved being there, and I felt her presence.

ALLEN CHILDREN AND SPOUSES
L to R: Ornan, Dorothy, Zeke, Ellen, Pete, Dorothy,
Babe, Martha, Lee, Pearl, Leo, Vergin
BRAY, OKLAHOMA
AUGUST, 1977

ALLEN FAMILY REUNION
LAKE MURRAY STATE PARK
OKLAHOMA
1980

ALLEN FAMILY REUNION
PINETOP, ARIZONA
1988

ALLEN FAMILY REUNION
JUNE 22ND ON EZEKIEL AND MAUD'S 94TH ANNIVERSARY
GRAZIE RESTAURANT, LAKE TAHOE, CALIFORNIA
1996

ALLEN FAMILY REUNION
WALNUT CREEK AND SEBASTOPOL, CALIFORNIA
2004

ALLEN FAMILY REUNION
CHICKASHA, OKLAHOMA
2007

Allen Family Tree

Amanda Augusta Campbell married Isaac Heaton Hall, 1877
    Effie
    Gertie (d. in infancy)
    Stella Maud, b. 1883
    Ernest
    Emma
    Dona
    John
    Eula
    Herman

Martha Bowling and George McIntyre C.
    Ezekiel "EZ" or "Zeke", b. 1880
    Mary Angeline
    Bernice
  married Robert Allen
    Emory
    Norris Jerry "Neri"
    Bertha

Stella Maud Hall married Ezekiel Allen in 1902. They had nine children.

· Effie Bernice, b. 1903, d. 1904 (in infancy)

Pearl Allen Andree

- Isaac Leo, name changed to Wilfred Leo "Leo," b. 1904, d. 1983
    - married Vergin Murdock, 1951
    - ·· Wilda Vernell "Vernell" Broadway (stepdaughter)
        - married Edward Dowdy
            - ··· Edward, Judy, Douglass, Jerry, and Kevin
    - ·· Vedis Marie Broadway (stepdaughter)
        - married William Mullner
            - ··· Stanley, Rhonda, Jolene, and Mark
    - ·· Everett Jacob Broadway (stepson)
        - married Carol McClennen
            - ··· Robin, Dawn, and Patrick
        - married Sandy LaFrance
            - ··· Laurie Michelle LaFrance (stepdaughter)
    - ·· Ronald Edward "Ronn" Broadway (stepson)
        - married Karen Hall
            - ··· Danelle and Courtney
    - ·· Marsha Maudine, b. 1953
        - married Richard Rogers
            - ··· Janessa Cynthia
            - ··· Shannon Michelle
        - married Stephen "Steve" Ford
            - ··· Donna Lee Ford (stepdaughter)
            - ··· Erin Kendall
            - ··· Matthew Stephen "Matt"

- Ira Eugene, b. 1905, d. 1927 (in accident)

- Ornan Robert "Monk," b. 1907, d. 2004
    - married Dorothy Brown, July 13, 1935
    - ·· Bobbie Carlene, b. 1937, d. 1938 (in infancy)
    - ·· Terrell Wayne, b. 1939
        - married Gloria Perez
            - ··· Cherry Lynn
            - ··· Wayne Ralph
        - married Nola Bergman

Maud and Pearl

··· Wanda Lei Bergman (stepdaughter)
··· Lynn Lokelani Bergman (stepdaughter)
··· Shelley Moani Bergman (stepdaughter)
·· Jimmie Robert "Jim," b. 1941
married Darlene Armstrong
··· Terry Robert
··· Jimmy Edward
··· Karen
··· Mark William
·· William Harley "Bill," b. 1946
married MaryEllon Johnson
··· Michal Karrie
··· William Joseph "Joe"
··· Rebecca Erin "Becky"
··· Sarah Elizabeth
·· Phillip Ray "Phill," b. 1950
married Shari Cotton
··· Heather Ann
··· Edward Ornan
·· Wanda Lorraine "Lorraine," b. 1959
married Brian Nichols
··· Yudaska Samuel "Sam"

· Ezekiel Jr. "Zeke", b. 1909, d. 1987
married Ellen Spencer, 1933
·· Rita Jo, b. 1934
married William Grieb
··· William Allen "Allen"
··· Jo Ellen
··· Matthew Kyle
·· Carol Lou, b. 1936
married Harry Canning
··· Susan Gayle
··· Richard Glen "Rick"
··· Karen Jo

Pearl Allen Andree

·· Ezekiel Earl "Earl," b. 1942
   married Christa Swinarski
   ··· Esther Sylvia (stepdaughter)
   ··· Heidi Leann
   married Beki Powell
   married Belinda Anzaldua "Bea"
   ··· Alexis Cano (stepson)

· Martha Amanda, b. 1911, d. 1981
   married Henry Earnest Robertson, "Babe," 1929
   ·· Charles Walter "Charley," b. 1930
      married Betty Ruth Smith
      ··· Betty Charlene "Charlene"
      ··· Glenda Kay "GK"
      ··· Earnest Allen "Allen"
      ··· Patricia Dean "Patti"
   ·· Margaret Louise "Totsy," b. 1932
      married Melford Scott
      ··· Ronald Lee "Ronnie"
      ··· Janet Ann "Jan"
      ··· Donald Brent "Donnie"
      ··· James Dale "Jimmy"
   ·· Martha Anne "Tanny," b. 1935
      married Henry Toche
      ··· Michael Kris
      ··· Michelle Denise
      ··· Daniel Bruce
      ··· Robin Monet
      ··· Jane Lyn
      ··· Joseph Shawn "Shawn"
      married Glen D'Orville
      ··· Glen David D'Orville (stepson)
      ··· Sharon Leigh D'Orville (stepdaughter)

· Huber Ernest "Pete," b. 1913, d. 2006
   married Dorothy Cook, July 13, 1935

Maud and Pearl

·· Dawn Marie, b. 1936
    married Mike Devine
    ··· Michael Edward Jr.
    ··· Juliet Margaret "Judy"
    ··· Denise Diane
    ··· Mark Eric
    ··· Kelly Kathleen
    ··· Martin John "Marty"
·· Charlotte Ruth, b. 1939
    married Richard "Dick" Cosby
    ··· Jo Ellen
    ··· Lisa Marie
    ··· Kirsten Joan
·· Edwin Lanier "Lanier," b. 1940
    married Alice Jenkins
    ··· Lori
    ··· Dominique
    ··· Michelle
    married Cynthia Thompson
    ··· Lee Lanier "Lee"
·· Gerald Lynn "Jerry," b. 1950
    married Pamela Gilchrist
    ··· Megan Gilchrist Allen
    married Emily Flouton
    ··· Gordon MacGillivray "Gordon"

· Alma Mae, b. 1916, d. 1973
  married Lelon L. "Lee" Curtis, 1934
  ·· Virginia Lee "Jenny Lee," b. 1935
    married Doug Evans
    ··· Gloria Lee
    married Don Ague
  ·· Richard Leland "Dickie," b. 1936
    married Norma Jo Hickam
    ··· Marvin Wade
    ··· Sabrina Ann

Pearl Allen Andree

　··· Shanda Nicole
　·· Mary Maudina, b. 1939
　　married Dale Jackson
　　　··· Gary Dale Jackson (stepson)
　　　··· Curtis Dee
　　　··· Alma Lynette "Lynette"
　　　··· Debbie Diane

· **Iralene Pearl "Pearl,"** b. 1927
　married James Daniel "Jimmy" Goggin, 1945
　　·· Daniel Anthony "Danny," b. 1948
　　　married Lyn Hunt
　　　　··· Kathryn Pearl "Katy"
　　　　··· Margaret Lois "Meg"
　　　　··· James Donald "Jim"

　　·· Patrick Leo "Pat," b. 1950
　　　married Shelly Chadwick
　　　married Beverly Ruth Follett
　　　　··· Rachel Erin Drossman (stepdaughter)
　　　　··· Emily Ruth Drossman (stepdaughter)

　　·· Janet Iralene, b. 1952
　　　married Colin Barnes
　　　　··· Monica Danielle
　　　　··· Audrey Lyn
　　　married Anthony Thompson
　　　married Donald Eugene "Don" Adkins

　married William H. "Bill" Andree, 1957
　　·· Kathleen Page "Kathi" Andree (stepdaughter)
　　　married Murray Bullis
　　　　··· Keith, Bruce, and Claire
　　·· Herbert William "Herb" Andree (stepson)
　　　married Bonnie Glenn
　　　　··· Christopher Timothy

Maud and Pearl

    married Jennifer Onstott
    name changed to Tandree
    married Anne Tondowski
       ··· Simon and Lucy

·· Raymond Allen "Ray," b. 1958
    married Dana Carter
       ··· Brigitte Rochelle
       ··· William Norman
       ··· Lindsay Lorraine
    married Carol Pieper
       ··· Gisele Alette "Gigi"

·· Lillian Stella "Lilly," b. 1962
    married Glen Turney
       ··· Myles Andree
       ··· Natasha Laure "Tasha"
       ··· Lane Brellac
    married Chet Clark
       ··· Natalie Michelle Clark (stepdaughter)
       ··· Megan Ruth Clark (stepdaughter)

Acknowledgments

I THINK of so many to whom I'm grateful.

To begin with, I am lucky to be alive, several years after an intravascular heart valve replacement (the TAVR procedure) saved my failing heart. My cardiologist, Dr. Ted Takata, and cardiovascular surgeons Drs. Brendan Reagan and Richard Vigness, provided outstanding care. My extended lifespan has enabled me to complete this work.

Beyond that, this book would never have come to fruition had it not been for the hard work and assistance of my son, Dr. Dan Goggin, and his office manager and assistant par excellence, Beth Gonzalez. Beth ably typed several drafts and additions to the manuscript, some from my rough-handed writing when my computer/printer connection broke down. Dan's wife, Lyn, has been patient with all the "do-overs" that had to happen.

Of course, the taped and written out conversations with my beloved late older siblings, which were begun in the 1980s and continued for years, were precious and indelible and became the backbone of this story.

As Dan pursued proofing and editing the narrative, I became aware that more of my nieces and nephews and their children, who are the "Allen cousins" and the "first cousins once removed," some of them who began to help me as far back as the 1990s, were continuing the family's united effort to contribute, for which I am deeply indebted and grateful.

For two years, Dan worked with older cousins: Margaret (Totsy) Robertson Scott, who recorded reunion historical stories; Charlotte Cosby and her husband, Dr. Dick Cosby; their daughter,

Maud and Pearl

Lisa; and Totsy's sister, Martha (Tanny) D'Orville. From this, significant assistance with history and literary input as well as proofing and editorial review has occurred.

Marsha Ford, Jerry Allen, Jimmie Allen, and Carol Lou Canning have stepped forward and provided significant historic, photographic, and musical chronicling of the family. My dear niece Jenny Lee Ague, who has since passed away, provided some unique stories from her early childhood.

I would also like to thank the following nieces and nephews and their children: Ronn Broadway; Jim and Darlene Allen; Karen Durant; Mark and Kim Allen; Bill and Dr. MaryEllon Allen; Phill Allen; Rita Jo Grieb; Jo Ellen Pierce; Carol Lou Canning; Susan Hemphill; Earl Allen; Heidi Allen; Dawn and Mike Devine; Kelly Janssen; Denise Populis; Mark and Kim Devine; Lanier Allen; Lee Allen; Dick Curtis; Sabrina Gafford; Curtis Jackson; and all of my other children: Pat Goggin, Janet Goggin, Ray Andree, Lillian Andree, Herb Tandree, and Kathi and Murray Bullis.

I also want to thank my storyteller colleague, Dorothy Anderson, who composed and gifted me the real-life story of an experience that I had had in Australia. Along with her, in the sense of career I have benefited from the insights and guidance given to me by many professional storyteller friends and acquaintances.

My family is grateful to staff members of the County Clerk's office in Arnett, Ellis County, Oklahoma for their help with documentation of the Allen homestead, 1904-1913.

Additionally, gratitude is expressed to the Texas Railroad Commission for documentation of Allendale Oil Co and the Ezekiel Allen wildcat wells.

Dan is also appreciative of his esteemed colleague, Dr. Debra Atkisson, and her editorial suggestions.

Additionally, Dan credits the invaluable insights and guidance of his accomplished lifelong friend from childhood, law professor, editor, and legal historian Craig Joyce.

I want to especially thank professional photographer Amanda Coleman. Amanda began "capturing moments and telling stories through pictures" as a teenager, even before digital photography. For two decades she has photographed families and created graphic content for small businesses. She has graciously and ably

Pearl Allen Andree

lent her creative eye, crafted two pictorial collages, and given her consultative advice to organize the photo sections of the book.

Dan has informed me that Erin Donlon, who assisted Amanda through her Etsy business, EditsByErin, is also to be thanked. Erin has commented about the Allen family pictures, some over 100 years old, "[I've] thoroughly enjoyed this project, because the pictures were such high quality photographs from the start... so satisfying to work on!"

For some time, Dan has made me aware of the remarkable efforts of fellow nonagenerian, Louis Daniel, who has provided eleven commissioned artworks for the book. Louis was a charter member of the Texas Association of Magicians for seventy-five years, is a past vice president and art director of Witherspoon Ad Agency in Ft. Worth, and is a recipient of the American Advertising Federation Silver Medal. His portraits and photographs include Helen Hayes, David Copperfield, Van Cliburn, and Bobbie Wygant. A native Texan, Mr. Daniel is also well known for his sketches of Texas county courthouses.

I express my deepest thankfulness to editor Teresa Lynn of Tranquility Press, an IBPA-member partnership publishing company. Tranquility Press is dedicated to empowering every person to share their story in their own way, and assists authors through each aspect of publishing with personalized service to produce high-quality literary works.

There will always be a special place in my heart and in the hearts of each of us for my stalwart nephew, Lanier. He pioneered the genealogy search of the Allen family, and by doing so lifted the hearts and the sense of identity of each of us and encouraged others of us to join him in that effort. He readily responded with his family's history and wrote it quite well. In his life he suffered so much, he accomplished so much, and he left us with so much more.

It all began with Mama. What Mama said often was quoted from the Bible, and she lived by what she spoke. While she suffered, she endured, and she remained kind. Her legacy was leaving behind the family that she grew, that kept growing, that kept close, and that kept loving. Our story won't be finished for a while.

Red River Valley

THIS was one of Pete Allen's favorite songs, especially the first and third verses with chorus, printed below. Its origins are unknown, though it dates from at least late-19th century Canada, and it has been called by various titles but is known most commonly in the US as "Red River Valley."

From this valley they say you are going,
I will miss your bright eyes and sweet smile,
For they say you are taking the sunshine,
That has brightened our pathways awhile.

Do you think of the valley you're leaving?
Oh, how lonely and sad it will be!
Do you think of the kind hearts you're breaking,
And the pain you are causing to me?

[Chorus]
Come and sit by my side if you love me,
Do not hasten to bid me adieu,
But remember the Red River Valley,
And the cowboy who loved you so true.

www.ingramcontent.com/pod-product-compliance
Lightning Source LLC
Chambersburg PA
CBHW020754230426
43673CB00022B/439/J